Growth and Territorial Policies:

The Italian Model of Social Capitalism

Raffaella Y. Nanetti

Pinter Publishers, London and New York

First published in Great Britain in 1988 by
Pinter Publishers Limited
25 Floral Street, London WC2E 9DS

British Library Cataloguing in Publication Data

Nanetti, Raffaella Y.
Growth and territorial policies : the
Italian model of social capitalism.
1. Italy—Economic conditions—1945–
I. Title
330.945′0927 HC305

ISBN 0-86187-651-2

Library of Congress Cataloging-in-Publication Data

Nanetti, Raffaella.
Growth and territorial policies.

Bibliography: p.
1. Italy—Economic conditions—1945– —Regional disparities. 2. Decentralization in government—Italy. 3. Local government—Italy. I. Title.
HC305.N26 1988 330.945′0928 87-25724

ISBN 0-86187-651-2

Typeset by Florencetype Ltd, Kewstoke, Avon
Printed in Great Britain by Biddles of Guildford Ltd.

Growth and Territorial Policies

To My Parents

Contents

Acknowledgements

A number of people helped me to focus on the ideas presented in this study. I would like especially to thank Vincent Wright for his thought-provoking discussions which first led me to the conceptualization of the interpretative framework that underlies this book and Robert Leonardi and Robert D. Putnam for the many subtle insights into the scope and workings of Italian regional institutions. Many people in the field, from regional to neighbourhood politicians, bureaucrats, interest-group leaders, and ordinary citizens, helped me to understand what was happening at the grass roots and how much the workings of local government have changed during the last two decades. This work would not have been possible without the funding provided by the Fulbright Program through a Senior Research Grant in Western Europe for the 1984–85 academic year.

1 Introduction

1.1. Growth and Territorial Policies

The economic recession that began in 1973 had a devastating impact on most of the industrialized world by fuelling inflation while leading, at the same time, to a downturn in economic production and increased unemployment. In Britain and the United States the crisis gave rise to neo-liberal responses. Most predictions were that Italy, as the weaker link in the European economic chain and already subject to massive socio-economic ferment resulting from the 1968-69 student and workers movement, would succumb to increased political, social and economic polarization. However, the evidence of the last fourteen years clearly demonstrates that the country has succeeded in avoiding many of the dire consequences that were forecast. It will be argued here that Italy's success in responding to the economic crisis was due to its ability to develop a unique response that was characterized at the sub-national level by territorially-specific and differentiated policies that were initiated and managed by sub-national governments.

The line of inquiry that informs this work is that in the period in which Italy witnessed an affirmation of the diffusion of enterprises (*decentramento produttivo*) in its economy the country was going through a process of institutional decentralization (*decentramento istituzionale*). The latter was initially accomplished through the creation of the fifteen ordinary regions and was then followed by a strong surge in the decentralization of other institutions at the sub-regional level. Interestingly enough, up to now, no one has looked into the potential connection between these two forms of decentralization. The connection has not been studied either by economists who have looked into the diffusion of enterprises or by students of administrative law analysing the institutional consequences of political decentralization.

The former have conducted numerous studies on the profound changes that have taken place in the Italian socio-economic context during the last twenty years and their impact on economic activity, but they have not looked at the potential impact of these changes on the decentralization of institutions (Bagnasco & Trigilia, 1984; Fua & Zacchia, 1983; Paci, 1980; Antonelli & Balcet, 1980; Cantelli, 1980; Capecchi, 1978; Del Monte & Raffa, 1977; and Bagnasco, 1977). In fact, these studies completely ignore the role of the region and other levels of local government. The diffusion of entrepreneurship is analysed in a context of social spontaneity that autonomously ignites local resources—such as, the existing forms of entrepreneurship in the specialized artisan shops or the widespread diffusion of sharecropping in agriculture—to fuel a self-sustaining process of economic development and growth. The mechanism for this spontaneous diffusion of enterprises is sought in the demographic and social changes that brought about the drop in agricultural employment and the increase in educational levels and social mobility in the population. The process has been appropriately referred to as 'spontaneous localism' (Unioncamere, 1983 and 1984; CENSIS, 1982 and 1983). Only recently has the analysis assumed a position of promoting this model as an alternative form of development. As a consequence, the model will have to depend less on spontaneity and more on the policy outputs of political institutions, in particular the performance of the regions (Bagnasco & Trigilia, 1985).

Students of the decentralization of production have advanced three explanations to account for this. The first considers small and medium-sized industry as a residual category that comes, in terms of importance, after large private and public industries that are conceived of as the engines of economic growth. Thus, the phenomenon of diffusion is explained as a cyclical—thus unstable—occurrence of attempts to employ resources when the large corporations are in temporary difficulty and the small and medium-sized industries are filling the available gaps. However, when the large enterprises regain their dynamism the importance of the small/medium-sized industries recedes.

The second explanation looks at the growing need for specialized types of production in the world market that cannot be satisfied by mass-produced goods from other countries, especially those in the Third World. This approach attributes the growth multiplication of small and medium-sized enterprises to the ability of the diffused system to develop unique, and thus competitive responses to demands from segments of the market where competitors remain behind.

The final explanation focuses on the opportunism of Italian capitalists whose response to the changes in the economic and social fabric of the country and the trade union mobilization of the late 1960s and early 1970s was tied to the decentralization of their large enterprises in order to throttle the trade union movement. The expectation here is that, once the unions are weakened, there will be a movement back towards re-concentration of production. All three of these approaches focus on an economic explanation for the phenomenon. Even though they admit that there is a linkage between economic diffusion and social change, they keep the former separate from any connection with institutional changes in the country.

Moving on to the second group of students, those concerned with institutional decentralization, one finds a rich array of research on the administrative-juridical aspects of the legislative powers of the region, the inter-governmental relations between the State and the regions, and the administrative aspects of regional activities (Dente, 1985; Cammelli, 1984; Bartole, Mastragostino & Vandelli, 1984; Aniasi, 1982; Gizzi, 1981). In addition, other studies (Giannola *et al.*, 1985; INU, 1981; Confindustria, 1980) in the field have adopted a more empirical-evaluative approach in analysing how the regions have governed since 1970.

One study in particular (Putnam, Leonardi & Nanetti, 1985) arrived at the conclusion that the historical and social/economic contexts in which the regional governments operate are important factors in predicting how well the regions perform from a policy-making as well as administrative point of view. The research, however, did not investigate the link between institutional decentralization and economic decentralization, but it did posit the hypothesis that better performing regional governments had a far greater potential for interacting with their social and economic environment than is the case for less productive regional governments.

Figure 1.1 conceptualizes how the present work places itself in relation to the two lines of research discussed above. Keeping in mind the three dimensions under discussion—the social-historical context, economic decentralization and institutional decentralization— Figure 1.1 illustrates the causal relationships posited by three different models:

- The first model, 'spontaneous localism', traces the origin of economic decentralization, which is its main concern, from the spontaneous stimuli originating from the surrounding social-historial environment, and it posits no relation between economic and institutional decentralization or between the social fabric and local institutions.
- The second 'institutional reform' model is used, instead, to explain different levels of decentralized institutional performance and, like the previous model, traces variations in performance to variations in the social-historical fabric.
- In contrast to the previous two models, the final 'three-dimensional' model is concerned with both economic decentralization and decentralized institutions, and by building on the first two, posits the existence of a third, symbiotic relationship—i.e. a correlation between economic and institutional decentralization—which must be studied over time to measure the level and extent of its interaction. The nature of the three-dimensional model opens up a new line of inquiry in analysing the relationships between institutional and economic factors.[1]

The general hypothesis presented here is that the correlation between economic decentralization and institutional decentralization has a distinct temporal dimension: the strength of the relationship increases over time, the

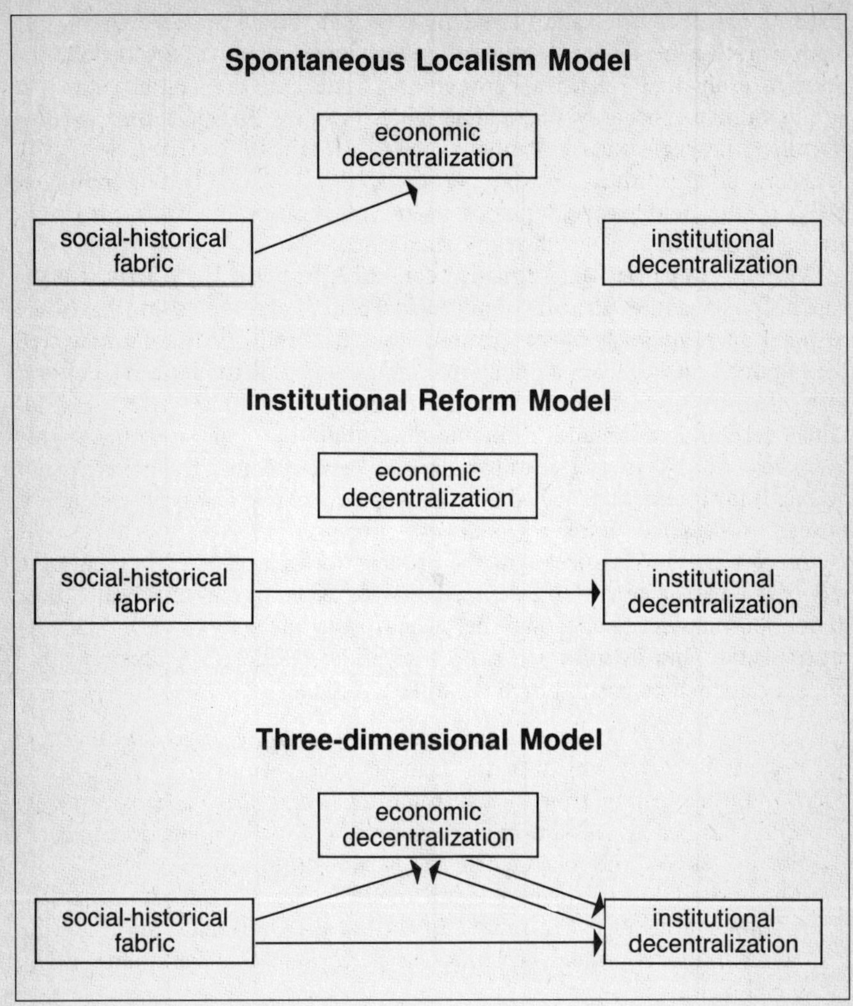

Figure 1.1 Model for the analysis of the dimensions of decentralization

two processes develop together, and they tend to mutually reinforce each other. While one cannot exclude the fact that the decentralization of production could have taken place under the conditions of centralized institutions, historically speaking, in the Italian case this did not take place. In addition, recent research has underlined how the difficulty encountered in developing the model of economy decentralization in the South can also be attributed to the economic choices made by the State in maintaining an 'assisted' form of economy—i.e. an economy dependent on transfer payments and investment decisions made by the national government rather than endogenous economic forces—and, therefore, discouraging the development of endogenous initiatives (Giannola, 1985).

On these bases, the hypothesis can be further refined by postulating that the increasingly specialized and diversified system of production exists within a decentralized system of institutions and that the success of the former is based on the presence of the latter as a precondition. In Italy, this line of institutional development became operational in 1970 with the creation of the regions and the initiation of a restructuring of all other forms of local government—from a conceptual as well as an experimental point of view—such as with the area-wide planning districts and neighbourhood government. More recently, the relationship was strengthened through the reformulation of the province's role in support of economic activities and those of the commune and neighbourhood government as promoters and organizers of urban and personal services.

The subsequent development of regional powers and the various experiments with decentralization—with all their limitations—place into question the view that sub-national institutions must be homogenous throughout the national territory. For example, the area-wide planning districts differed in both conceptual as well as operational terms from one region to another. These institutions affirmed the principle of the specialization and diversification of their activities on the basis of the region's legislative autonomy. In other words, the fifteen ordinary regions were very much similar at their birth in 1970; they are much less so in 1987, given the choices that they had made with regard to their legislative and planning priorities. Just as the decentralization of the economy has highlighted distinctions among types of economic centres (Unioncamere, 1983: 21), the decentralization of the institutional structure has had the same result: it has stressed the differences and the specificity of each regional context. As they have developed, however, the two systems of decentralization have sought even more systematic forms of cooperation that go from the expansion of economic decentralization beyond its original boundaries into other geographic areas, to inter-regional agreements among regional governments promoting economic growth.

When institutional decentralization was just getting started, it conformed to the spontaneity typical of economic decentralization, and the impact of the regional institutions was minimal. In time, economic and institutional decentralization have begun to come together and to intersect, creating a web of interrelations that produces a clearer series of demands from one side and the assumption of greater planning and policy responsibilities on the other. Expanding Bagnasco's thesis that 'this society has found its form of economy' (Bagnasco, 1983: 149), the present work adds to the thesis the proposition that this society, which produced economic decentralization, has also found its new institutional form. Institutional decentralization is the congruent response to the reality of an economically vibrant and growing but increasingly differentiated and complex society.

The challenge posed by the future consists in increasingly honing the terms of the correlation between private management and public management. The managers of small private industries have a strong need for their regional counterparts. The expectation is that in the future the success of the partnership will be measured by the capacity of regional and sub-regional institutions to formulate policies to support and promote the new model of decentralized development. The continuous search for fine tuning the endogenous formulae for development which rely on the potentials of existing resources necessarily includes the reality of regional institutions since, as has been pointed out by Cassese (1978: 243), 'the regions have the tendency of becoming the primary vehicle for local representation . . . by exercizing their role in aggregating the political-territorial demand directed toward the political institutions'.

1.2. From Welfare State to Social Capitalism

In the 1960s and early 1970s Italian Welfare State policies were expanding in three directions: larger amounts of financial resources were allocated to cover an increasingly greater number of people, authority was ever more concentrated in the political centre, and the scope of public policies was broadened to cover new areas of need. At the same time, the economic recession of the early 1970s brought to a head a deeper crisis of trust which had been simmering for a long time—that is, the perception of an increasingly wide gap between, on the one hand, the social and economic expectations generated by the broad spectrum of physical development, economic, and social policies of the Welfare State and, on the other, their actual outcomes.

Thus, it is possible to conceptualize the Welfare State credibility crisis in the early 1970s as the cumulative impact of five perceived *gaps* between the demands being posed by society and the key characteristics of Welfare State policies. Two of the gaps called into question the roles of traditional policy-makers and the other three challenged the significance of the outcomes of existing policies.

- Legitimization. The increased de-legitimization of, or dissatisfaction with, nationally elected authority as the makers of social and economic policies was underscored by many factors, from the beginning of a decline in voter turn-out to increased protest votes. Correspondingly, there was also a surge in radical parties, demands for direct democracy, and a call for institutions closer to the people.
- Responsiveness. The perceived lack of accountability of the bureaucracy

in control of policy implementation increased in relation to the growth in the size and power of the bureaucracy. The responsiveness gap was underscored by the introduction of institutional rather than personal responsibility clauses, greater cost of legal recourse, inadequate internal administrative reviews, and interdependence of agencies' tasks, which made it more difficult to determine responsibility. The increase in civil rights cases and calls for ombudsman-type citizen advocacy programmes as well as proposals to decentralize administrative structures were just a few of many attempts to break the hold of the bureaucracy.

- Environmental quality. In time of economic crisis many pointed to what were seen as failures of physical development policies. In addition to the criticism of public policy-makers over the lack of sensitivity toward issues dealing with the conservation of natural resources, there was growing concern over the low levels of quality of life found in urban environments, such as high-density public housing and suburban dormitory communities. Responses to these concerns manifested themselves in the growing appreciation for smaller-scale developments, a rejection of the equation that urban growth equals progress, the back-to-the-city movement, and the placing of environmental concerns higher on the political agenda.
- Economic opportunity. One of the most immediate consequences of the economic crisis was the need to promote individual economic opportunity. State-owned economic enterprises were strongly criticized for their low economic performance, high costs, and burden on the rest of the economy in terms of draining scarce financial resources from the private market. Government policies also came in for criticism in failing to provide adequate incentives to fuel the emergence of new and more competitive enterprises, and in engaging in the over-regulation of industry and commerce. Here, the demands were for the expansion of higher educational opportunities, access to economic incentives and credits, and greater use of merit criteria in hiring and promotion decisions in the public sector.
- Community solidarity. The undermining of community solidarity was seen as a negative by-product of Welfare State policies. Allegedly, public policies were diminishing mutual aid activities in communities, increasing institutional dependency, and leading to a standardization of services. The perceived need was to create personal and more flexible services, and experiment with new concepts in the delivery of services, including the provision of smaller-scale services.

The ensuing economic recession called into question the effectiveness of the Welfare State approach and forced the reassessment of its components in terms of: (1) 'who should decide' (i.e. policy-makers); (2) 'what should be received' (i.e. policy content); and (3) 'who should benefit' (i.e. policy recipients). The redefinition of the Welfare State placed in question a system where public policies were designed and managed from the centre for the creation of basic physical infrastructures and the development of human resources. The combination of the economic, social and political crises of the late 1960s and early 1970s led to the transition to a second phase of evolution in the Welfare State system which is defined in this work as 'social capitalism', the phase in which public policies are formulated for the creation, support and pervasive distribution of private wealth by sub-national governments.

Table 1.1 illustrates the three dimensions of change that have been redefined in the transition between phases one and two. In the second phase of social capitalism, sub-national governments have assumed the primary initiative for the making of policies congruent with the needs of local economic and social interests. The role of the State has receded in importance because basic physical (i.e. roads, aqueducts, dams, power lines, railroads, ports, etc.) and human development (education, health care, pension system, etc.) infrastructures are in place. The local governments' role in the formulation of new policies is to plan for the rationalization of services and to be responsive to new needs with an increased ability to conceptualize, experiment and formulate adequate policies. In this manner, the recipients of policies (and those who interact with the primary policy-makers) are the economic and social groups that are active in the surrounding community. Thus, social capitalism provides a means of conceptualizing and operationalizing the relationship between institutional and economic decentralization discussed in the three-dimensional model presented in Figure 1.1, and social capitalism refers to the policy initiatives taken by the decentralized institutions (i.e. institutional decentralization cell) in the three-dimensional model.

Table 1.1 Evolution of institutional policy-making in the post-war period

Dimensions of change	Phase I Welfare State (1945–1969)	Phase II Social Capitalism (1970–)
Primary policy-maker	State	Regional and local governments
Policy content	Physical infrastructure and human development	Planning and support services
Policy recipients	Local governments and social groups	Economic and social groups

With regard to the economic decentralization cell in the third model, social capitalism suggests the existence of a high degree of congruency or compatibility (which will increase over time) between public policies and the creation and distribution of private wealth. The role of the local government institutions and public policies is not to stifle private growth or designed to limit economic initiative. Rather, it is seen as providing essential support for the continued growth of private initiative and wealth. Social capitalism policies are not conceived or developed as one-shot, piecemeal responses to crises. They constitute a critical mass of public policy to direct the use of public resources to sustain the expansion of private wealth. One of the basic component elements of this phase of development is the existence of a diffusion of private economic initiative; social capitalism is a mass phenomenon. In addition, the society must have the ability to use public resources for promoting broad, socially based rather than narrow, individual private gain (in other words, a policy to stimulate economic production and turnover of wealth rather than a hand-out that only stimulates individual consumption); there must be a sense of the public interest well rooted among politicians and members of the bureaucracy as well as in society at large. Otherwise, public resources will be siphoned off for private non-production, such as in the case of graft and corruption, in which case the nexus between the social-historical fabric and institutional decentralization will be broken.

1.3. Organization of the Study

The objective of the present study is to interpret the economic growth and territorial policies in Italy in the light of the social capitalist model presented above. This requires an analysis of a large number of social and economic policies undertaken by local governments in the 1970s and 1980s. The evolution of these policies will reveal the contours of Italian social capitalism and explain the logic of the course of development pursued during the last two decades in sub-national policy-making. The discussion will provide an explanation for the constant predictions of economic crisis that lace most analyses of Italian society. According to our analysis, the predictions of doom that were repeatedly rejected by reality were reflective of the conceptual as well as policy transition that was taking place from the Welfare State to social capitalism—that has only now begun to surface as a coherent set of policies and congruent institutional forms.

The study takes off from the analysis of the decentralized economy and institutions to develop in nine chapters the thesis on the social capitalist model of Italian policy-making. The book is essentially divided into two parts. In the first, part—consisting of Chapters 2, 3, 4 and 5—attention is focused on the economic and politico-cultural contours of post-1968 Italian society in order to establish the political and institutional bases for the social capitalist line of development characteristic of the last decade of Italian policy-making. The analysis will focus on the expansion of entrepreneurship and the creation of a differentiated labour market; the evolution of the State structure from an extensive form of centralization to a decentralized model based on an institutional framework that runs from the region down to the neighbourhood; and the growth of new needs and ideological outlooks in the 1970s.

The second part of the book—Chapters 6 to 9—concentrates on a range of policies that constitute the essential components of the integrated policy-making structure necessary for the existence and development of social capitalism. For this purpose, analyses are provided of regional strategies for territorial development, the restructure of urban services at the sub-regional level, the control of territorial development at the communal level, and, finally, the provision of personal services at the neighbourhood level.

Note

1. Bagnasco (1977: 208) had intuitively understood the importance of research on aspects of this third relationship. At the end of his ground-breaking analysis that identified the social and economic typologies of the 'three Italies', he called on his colleagues to pursue a research agenda that would concentrate on the activities of the regional government given its important policy-making role. That suggestion went unheeded until now.

2 The impact of socio-economic change: fragmentation and diversity

2.1. The Italian Economy in Comparative Perspective

To contemporary observers of the international economic scene, Italy appears to be in the midst of a sustained period of economic growth, equivalent to a new 'economic miracle' (Turani, 1986; Chase Econometrics, 1986). While this image suggests a throwback to the pattern of economic performance experienced in the 1950s, careful observers have noticed that the recent growth cycle clearly differentiates itself from the previous one in terms of the underlying international features and the domestic sectors that are on the leading edge of growth. On the bases of both characteristics, the Italian case presents a number of anomalies when compared with other Western industrialized societies. In contrast to the sustained growth of the 1950s, the economic conditions of the last decade have been dominated by crisis. In the 1970s the international economy was characterized both by strong recession and high inflation, commonly known as 'stagflation'. The average rate of Western economic growth was half of what it had been in the almost twenty-year period between 1954 and 1972 (Podbielski, 1974: 99): passing from an average of 4.0 to 4.5 per cent to an average of 2.5 to 3.0 per cent (see Table 2.1). An even worse situation characterized the first part of the 1980s when the majority of these countries were, in fact, experiencing *negative* growth rates.

In this international context, the case of Italy is unique because the country experienced a rate of growth in the 1970s that was consistently above the average for the OECD and the EEC. In the 1978-81 period, the growth of GDP in Italy averaged 2.9 per cent, in comparison to the 1.4 per cent average for the EEC. The country dipped into recession in 1982 and 1983, but came out of its downturn in 1984 with a 2.6 per cent increase in GDP (OECD, 1985b). The strong upward trend continued through 1985 and 1986 when Italy's GDP grew respectively by 2.3 and 2.7 per cent. One aspect of the recent economic surge has been the strong increase in Italian exports and the ability of these goods to compete in the world market. The leading elements of Italy's export trade are machinery, textile and fabric goods, chemical products, and automobile parts, a good portion of which come from small

Table 2.1 Economic development indicators in some OECD countries (%)

	Annual growth-rates 1970-1980	Annual growth-rates 1980-1982	Industrial sector: % gross domestic product 1983	% salaried employees 1983	Average family income (in US $) 1983
Italy	3.0	2.4	24.7	70.9	12,009
France	3.5	0.7	24.7	76.8	13,631
West Germany	2.6	–0.7	33.9	86.7	12,062
Great Britain	1.9	–0.5	24.0	85.4	14,520
Japan	5.0	2.1	30.2	71.0	20,108
United States	3.0	–0.9	21.1	90.2	27,885
Canada	3.9	–0.6	15.6	89.6	26,385
Denmark	2.5	1.0	19.1	84.5	18,161
Ireland	3.5	–0.3	20.1	—	—
Netherlands	2.9	–1.1	25.5	80.7	14,500
Belgium	3.0	–0.2	24.0	73.9	—

Source: Britannica World Data, 1985, pp. 622–818.

and medium-sized industries that have made major gains in production during the last fifteen years (Unioncamere, 1985a).

The level of economic performance in the 1980s demonstrates the existence of a heterogeneous economic situation in the country. Surprising gains have been made in some parts of the South, or *Mezzogiorno*,[1] during the first three years of the 1980s. Regions such as Molise, Basilicata, and Abruzzi experienced an increase in their gross domestic products (Unioncamere, 1984: 14, and 1985b: 14-15), while some regions in the more developed North and Centre were undergoing a cycle of economic contraction. Thus, the current economic situation is rapidly developing and, in certain instances, breaking out of the traditional moulds.

Although Italy's economic performance in the 1970s deviates somewhat from that of other countries, its economy did share in the crisis that hit the large, private and public industries that had assumed the leadership role in post-war economic development (Ganapini, 1983). Italian big industry saw a fall in the demand for its goods, an increase in foreign competition, a growing obsolescence of its plants and equipment, and a need to cut production.[2] If Italian big industry shared the fate of its neighbours, what is the reason for its strong performance in the 1970s and 1980s? The answer has to be sought in the contribution made by the small and medium-sized firms that are scattered throughout the country in diverse mixes and concentrations. This chapter will look at the significance of the rise of the small and medium-sized firms and their contribution to economic growth, the pattern of employment, and social aspirations, and it will argue that the social and institutional/political base of the diffusion of small and medium-sized firms are radically different from those that characterized the initial 'economic miracle' of the 1950s, which was based on big industry concentrated within the industrial triangle. The second 'economic miracle' of the 1970s has found support in a wide social strata of entrepreneurs that was totally lacking in the 1950s and finds few parallels in the industrialized world. The chapter will therefore analyse the changing social context in which the diffusion of economic productive capacity has taken place in order to evaluate the prospects for the continued development of this new pattern of economic activity.

The data in Table 2.1 confirm that, in many ways, Italy's recent economic performance diverges somewhat from experiences in other EEC and OECD countries. In 1983 industrial production in Italy contributed to the national domestic product at a level (24.7 per cent) similar to that of other countries in the European Economic Community, with the exception of West Germany (33.9 per cent), and slightly above the level for the United States. Curiously, but very significantly, the Italian work-force has the lowest level of salaried workers (70.9 per cent) of all the countries appearing in Table 2.1. These data emphasize the presence of a large number of self-employed in the country's work-force (see Table 2.2). The overall state of the Italian economy is further illustrated by the steady increase in family income which now places Italy at a level comparable to that of the wealthier members of the

Table 2.2 Reported occupational status, 1951–1985 (%)

Year	Self-employed*	Salaried
1951	42.0	58.0
1961	31.6	68.4
1971	26.3	73.7
1981	28.0	72.0
1985	29.4	70.6

* The ISTAT definition for self-employed is:
'Persons who employ themselves and whose earnings are based on the outcome of that activity (entrepreneur, self-employed worker, self-employed professional, owner of a commercial activity, partner in family economic activity).'

Source: ISTAT, *Statistiche sociali, 1975*, vol. 1, p. 92 and ISTAT, *Le regioni in cifre, 1985*, p. 121, and ISTAT, *Le regioni in cifre, 1986*, p. 84.

EEC, even if it has not reached those of the two North American countries or Japan.

A closer analysis of the composition of the self-employed work-force confirms the view that the changes taking place in the Italian economy, which began in the 1970s, are structural in nature and are not a temporary phenomenon generated exclusively by the social strife of the late 1960s and early 1970s during the 'hot autumn' and extensive mobilization of workers by the trade unions. The existence and success of small firms and artisan enterprises were structural features of the Italian economy long before the 1969-70 crisis changed the perception of the role played in the economy by big industrial enterprises (Paci, 1986; Bagnasco, 1977).

The emergence of a new class of entrepreneur is the major innovation of the 'second' Italian economic miracle. In contrast to the period between 1951 and 1971 when the increase in salaried workers was tied to the creation and expansion of big industrial enterprises (for example, FIAT in Turin, Olivetti in Ivrea, Pirelli in Milan, etc.) and the decline of the agricultural sector, the post-1971 trend is characterized by an increase in self-employment. After 1981, the trend accelerates (see Table 2.3), with a particular accentuation in the areas of services, such as retailing, hotels and restaurants, and transport, and construction firms. In 1982-83 the international recession finally hit Italy, and its impact can be seen in the momentary drop in the number of industrial firms. However, the expansion of firms in the other productive sectors (with the exception of industrial activities tied to the processing of agricultural, forestry and fishing goods) continued at a high rate.

One of the surprising aspects of the entrepreneurial expansion in Italy is that it is taking place at the same time as the number of individually-owned farms is declining. Independent farmers have historically been one of the main reservoirs of a capillary or grassroot-form of entrepreneurship. As is evidenced by the data in Table 2.4, the number of farms has declined substantially in the period between 1970 and 1982 (−327,286, or a drop of 9.1 per cent). This drop follows the 16 per cent decline (a loss of 686,662 farms) registered in the previous decade (ISTAT, 1983: 116). One of the consequences of the restructuring of agricultural production has been the increase in the average size of farms. The increase, however, is more accentuated in the North than in the Centre or South.

The longitudinal trend in the transformation of the Italian economy is summed up well in Table 2.5. Using 1951 as a basis of comparison, the Table shows an overwhelming presence of north-western, followed by north-eastern, regions at the top of the industrialization index. It was in the context of this 1951 ranking that the notion of the 'industrial triangle—linking the regional capitals of Genoa (Liguria), Turin (Piedmont) and Milan (Lombardy)—was developed to refer to the country's major industrial centre. In this period, even the tiny region of Val d'Aosta seemed to partake in the

Table 2.3 Increase in self-employment in the industrial sector and services, 1980–83

(Annual mean in thousands)

	1980	1983	% Variation 1983–1980
Goods and Services			
For Sale:	5,807.0	5,955.0	+2.5
Industry:	1,049.0	1,074.0	+2.4
In restricted sense	762.0	758.8	−0.4
Construction	287.0	315.2	+9.8
Services:	3,073.0	3,347.0	+8.9
Commerce	1,915.5	2,111.9	+10.0
Hotels and restaurants	308.5	329.4	+6.8
Transportation and communication	300.4	311.4	+3.7
Credit and Insurance	3.6	3.6	0.0
Other services	541.0	590.7	+9.2
Agriculture, forestry and fishing:	1,685.0	1,534.0	−9.0

Source: ISTAT, *Annuario statistico italiano, 1984*, p. 280.

Table 2.4 Average size of agricultural farms (hectares, 1961–1982)

Geographic sub-divisions*	1961	1970	1982
North	6.3	7.7	8.5
North-west	5.7	7.3	8.4
North-east	7.0	8.0	8.6
Centre	7.7	8.6	8.3
South	5.6	5.9	5.9
Mainland	5.0	5.2	5.2
Islands	6.6	7.4	7.3
Total	6.2	6.9	7.2

Key: * The regions that make up the five geographic sub-divisions are:
North-west—Piedmont, Val d'Aosta, Lombardy and Liguria.
North-east—Veneto, Trentino–Alto Adige, Friuli–Venezia Giulia, and Emilia–Romagna.
Centre—Tuscany, Umbria, Marche and Lazio.
South—Campania, Abruzzi, Molise, Basilicata, Puglia and Calabria.
Islands—Sicily and Sardinia.

Source: ISTAT, *Compendio statistico italiano, 1983*, p. 116.

Table 2.5 Regional classification according to industrialization index, 1951–1984

(Index = % employed in industry)

1951	1961	1971	1980	1984
Lombardy	Lombardy	Lombardy	Lombardy	Lombardy
Piedmont	Piedmont	Piedmont	E-R	Piedmont
Val d'Aosta	F-VG	Veneto	Piedmont	Marche
Liguria	Tuscany/Veneto	Tuscany	Veneto	Veneto
F-VG	Val d'Aosta	F-VG	Marche	Tuscany
Tuscany	Liguria	Val d'Aosta	Tuscany	E-R
Veneto	E-R	E-R	Umbria	Umbria
T-AA	Umbria	Umbria	Abruzzi	F-VG
Campania	T-AA	Marche	F-VG	Val d'Aosta
Lazio	Campania	Liguria	Val d'Aosta	Abruzzi
Umbria	Lazio	Campania	T-AA	Liguria
E-R	Calabria	Abruzzi	Liguria	T-AA
Sardinia	Sardinia	T-AA	Sardinia	Campania
Sicily	Marche	Calabria	Campania	Sardinia
Puglia	Abruzzi	Sardinia	Puglia	Basilicata
Marche	Sicily	Basilicata	Sicily	Molise/Puglia
Calabria	Puglia	Sicily	Basilicata	Sicily
Abruzzi	Basilicata	Lazio	Lazio	Lazio
Basilicata		Puglia	Calabria	Calabria
		Molise	Molise	

Source: Calculated by the author from data in: ISTAT, *Statistiche sociali, 1975*, vol. 1, p. 91; *Statistiche sociali, 1981*, vol. 2, p. 116; and *Le regioni in cifre, 1985*, p. 101.

industrial pull of the north-west triangle. Turning again to Table 2.5, we see that the regions of the Centre and South are scattered in no particular order in the rest of the ranking. Of note, considering future trends, is the place of the Campania region which, in 1951, was more industrialized than its neighbouring regions in the South and three regions of the Centre: Emilia-Romagna, Umbria and Marche. The latter was fourth from last on the industrialization index, and the other two were in the bottom half of the scale.

Ten years later, the regional ranking had changed substantially, especially with regard to the regions of the Centre. Strong increases in the proportion of population employed in industry had been registered in Tuscany, Emilia-Romagna and Umbria, while the gains in Marche had not altered its position in the ranking. In the South, economic development and industrialization were not keeping up with the transformations taking place in other parts of the country. These data also show that the decisions taken at the beginning of the 1950s in favour of the 'planned industrialization' of the South,[3] did not have their expected effect of closing the gap in economic development between North and South. In fact, it could be argued that the regions that were most favoured by the *Cassa*,[4] such as Puglia, Campania, Sicily and Calabria, have demonstrated the worst levels of economic performance and the regions not favoured by the lavish expenditure of the *Cassa* funds—e.g. Molise, Basilicata, and Abruzzi—are in fact those that have succeeded in developing regional variations of the economic diffusion model that has transformed economic activity in the North (Putnam, Leonardi & Nanetti, 1985; IRPET, 1984).

The 1961 rankings of the regions on the industrialization index show a growing concentration of southern regions at the bottom of the ranking. In the North, Liguria begins its slow exit from the 'industrial triangle' and the gradual absorption by industry of what had been in the past mostly agricultural labour in the regions of Veneto, Tuscany and Emilia-Romagna. The industrialization of these three northeast-centre regions (defined by Bagnasco as 'the Third Italy') was tied to the increased demand for consumer goods—for example, clothing and furniture. By 1971, the vanguard role of Piedmont and Lombardy was still unchallenged, but there was a clear rearrangement in the positions of the other regions. Most noticeable was the fall in rank of Liguria in the North-west, Trentino Alto-Adige in the North-east, and Lazio in the Centre. The most striking change, however, was the general increase in the positions of many of the regions in the Northeast-Centre and the achievement of 'take-off' by one of the southern regions: Abruzzi. With the exception of the latter, all the southern regions continued to occupy the lowest positions in the ranking.

Based on the 1980 and 1984 rankings, it is clear that high levels of industrial employment no longer exclusively characterize the industrial triangle. The latest industrialization indexes show a pattern of diffusion that no longer distinguishes between regions of the North-west and those of the North-east or, even, between North and South. The place of the Abruzzi at the midpoint in the ranking and the rise in position of Molise and Basilicata give credence to the thesis sustained by empirical research (Giannola *et al.*, 1985; Unioncamere, 1984: 96-115, 211-24; Unioncamere, 1983: 172-9, 226-31, 292-335; IBRES, 1983; Pontarollo, 1982: Balloni, 1979) which argues that the diffusion of small and medium-sized industries has also begun to make its appearance in some of the southern areas. Also, the fall of regions such as Lazio and Trentino-Alto Adige on the ranking suggests that industrialization *per se* may no longer be the best measure of economic well-being and social progress. The situation has changed so radically that increased attention must be given to the burgeoning service sector in measuring the overall impact of economic performance.[5]

2.2. The New Entrepreneurs

During the last thirty-five years, Italy has witnessed a change in the model of development. The central role played by the big industry which dominated the first two decades of the post-war period has given way to some extent to a new structure of industrial enterprise dominated by small and medium-sized firms. Who are these new entrepreneurs who since 1970 have radically altered the nature and structure of entrepreneurship in the country? To begin with, many new factors are present in the economic growth cycle. The index of diffusion of enterprises presented in Table 2.6 indicates that between 1971 and 1981 there was a significant increase in the number of enterprises (expressed in the Table as number of enterprises per 100 inhabitants), and the increase in the service sector has been three times the level registered in industry. Therefore, there has been a parallel increase in entrepreneurs in both the industrial as well as the service sector. Table 2.6 uses the standard five geographic sub-divisions of the country to demonstrate that the diffusion of entrepreneurship is particularly marked in the Northeast-Centre in comparison with the North-West and South. The one exception to this generalization is the Lazio region which provides the home for the national bureaucractic apparatus. Industrial diffusion has become particularly intense in the Marche, Emilia-Romagna and Tuscany, whose indexes arrive at almost three enterprises per 100 inhabitants. The fastest growth in the index is registered by the Veneto and, once again, by the Marche.

Of equal importance is the lack of industrial entrepreneurial growth in Liguria, and the fall of the index in the South. The most serious declines appear in Calabria, Sicily and Campania. While the decline in the index could be explained in the southern regions by the substantial population increases —for example, the 8 per cent increase in Campania and in Puglia— Liguria should have been favoured on the diffusion index because during this period it lost 2.5 per cent of its population base. Nevertheless, the crisis of economic restructuring (e.g. finding alternative uses for Genoa's under-utilized port facilities and reorganizing the ANSALDO steel mills) and the lack of a sustained increase in small industrial enterprises have accentuated Liguria's orientation toward a greater tertiarization of its regional economy. Data in Table 2.6 show that the shift to services has increased throughout the region by 24 per cent.

The data on the new entrepreneurs assumes a greater level of significance when placed alongside information on the influx of immigration from abroad (see Table 2.7). According to recent studies (Unioncamere, 1984), Italian workers returning from abroad have made a significant contribution to entrepreneurship, especially in southern regions. Two-thirds of these ex-emigrants were employed, and a significant nucleus of them have had entrepreneurial experience abroad. Considering the decline in the number of

Table 2.6 Classification of regions according to the diffusion of enterprise index, 1971 and 1981

(Index = number of enterprises/100 inhabitants)

	Index of Diffusion					
	Industry			Services		
	1971	1981	Diff. % '81–'71	1971	1981	Diff. % '81–'71
Piedmont	1.7	2.1	+27.5	2.8	3.7	+33.3
Lombardy	1.8	2.3	+25.1	2.6	3.5	+36.7
Liguria	1.4	1.4	0.0	3.4	4.5	+32.9
Val d'Aosta	1.6	2.1	+25.5	3.9	5.0	+29.2
T-AA	1.7	2.0	+20.1	3.0	5.0	+65.1
F-VG	1.6	2.2	+36.5	2.7	4.0	+50.0
Veneto	1.7	2.5	+45.1	2.6	4.1	+55.5
Emilia-Romagna	2.3	2.8	+21.3	3.3	4.8	+44.6
Tuscany	2.3	2.7	+19.8	3.1	4.1	+35.6
Marche	2.1	3.0	+41.8	2.9	4.3	+46.6
Umbria	1.7	2.2	+26.3	2.7	3.6	+34.5
Lazio	1.0	1.0	0.0	2.3	3.1	+35.8
Abruzzi	1.6	1.5	–4.4	2.8	3.7	+32.1
Campania	0.9	0.8	–16.5	2.1	2.7	+26.9
Molise	1.8	1.7	–5.7	2.1	3.3	+24.6
Basilicata	1.5	1.5	0.0	2.3	3.1	+34.6
Sardinia	1.1	1.2	+9.2	2.7	3.3	+24.1
Sicily	1.1	0.9	–20.2	2.1	2.9	+36.3
Puglia	1.4	1.1	–17.9	2.3	3.1	+36.0
Calabria	1.0	0.8	–24.8	2.3	2.9	+27.2
North-west	1.7	2.1	+23.7	2.7	3.7	+34.6
North-east	1.9	2.6	+31.8	2.9	4.4	+50.8
Centre	1.6	1.9	+17.3	2.8	3.6	+27.7
" (– Lazio)	2.2	2.7	+25.5	3.0	4.1	+38.4
South	1.2	1.0	–15.3	2.3	3.0	+30.7
Islands	1.1	1.0	–13.3	2.3	3.0	+33.3
ITALY	1.6	1.8	+13.5	2.6	3.6	+37.3

NB: The calculation of enterprises excludes public administrative and other public services.

Source: Calculated by the author based on data in: ISTAT, *Annuario statistico italiano, 1974 and 1984*, (1974) pp. 10–11 and 224–37; (1984) pp. 11–12 and 154–7.

Table 2.7 Returnees by geographic area and occupational status, 1972–1982

	1972	1982
North-west	15,507	10,957
North-east	27,033	16,976
Centre	10,665	8,436
South	69,655	39,355
Islands	15,386	16,699
ITALY	138,246	92,423
—whose occupational status is:	92,542	54,486
—(self-employed)	(6.6%)	(10.8%)

Source: ISTAT, *Annuario statistico italiano, 1974*, p. 66 and *Annuario statistico italiano, 1984*, p. 34.

industrial firms in the South during the 1970s, the infusion of entrepreneurship from ex-emigrants has not been sufficient to reverse the area's statistics, but field studies have shown that the entrepreneurial spirit displayed by these repatriated workers has been important in fuelling the diffusion of small firms in Abruzzi, Molise and Basilicata.

The entrepreneurs who have fed this economic growth are responsible for enterprises of modest proportions. Indicative is the growth in the number of enterprises that have *no* employees. The owner is the only person employed by the firm. This number more than doubled between 1971 and 1981, increasing from 32,406 to 69,827 enterprises. Numerous examples of the employee-less firm may be found in the large concentration of textile industries located just north of Florence in the Prato area where the break-up of the production process tied to the fashion industry has been extensive. The owner mainly does the work himself and subcontracts out what he cannot manage or hires part-time help. In this manner, the productive unit maintains a maximum of flexibility in meeting the challenge posed by changing tastes, trade patterns and employment requirements. The pattern of one-person firms is even more common in the service sector. However, maintaining the distinction between service and industrial firms, we see in Table 2.8 that there has been a significant decrease in the size of the latter. The implication is that the expansion in the number of employees (+ 672,680) has been far outstripped by the increase in the number of firms (+ 162,861) (ISTAT, 1975: 233, and 1984: 153) and that the diffusion of entrepreneurs is a capillary phenomenon and not restricted to isolated groups or classes in society.

Table 2.8 Number, dimension, and employees of industrial enterprises, 1971 and 1981

	Number of enterprises		Change in number of enterprises	Dimension: employees/ enterprises		Difference in dimension
	1971	1981	'81–'71	1971	1981	'81–'71
Piedmont	74,304	95,578	21,274	12.15	9.06	−3.09
Val d'Aosta	1,830	2,326	496	8.68	6.88	−1.80
Lombardy	155,776	203,994	48,218	11.89	9.09	−2.80
Liguria	26,019	25,400	−619	7.75	7.20	−0.55
T-AA	14,319	17,736	3,417	6.94	6.37	−0.57
F-VG	19,810	26,806	6,996	8.87	6.98	−1.89
Veneto	72,246	110,372	38,126	8.60	6.93	−1.67
E-R	90,504	112,828	22,324	6.66	6.47	−0.19
Tuscany	79,584	97,263	17,679	6.65	6.09	−0.56
Marche	28,824	42,707	13,883	5.93	5.88	−0.05
Umbria	13,197	17,413	4,216	6.90	6.83	−0.07
Lazio	47,243	48,104	861	7.48	8.07	0.59
Abruzzi	17,667	18,436	769	5.09	7.11	2.02
Molise	5,284	5,460	196	2.88	4.76	1.88
Campania	45,305	41,551	−3,754	6.46	8.35	1.89
Puglia	49,055	44,687	−4,368	4.59	6.22	1.63
Basilicata	8,244	8,897	653	3.69	4.83	1.14
Calabria	19,633	16,199	−3,434	3.22	4.75	1.53
Sicily	52,246	44,885	−7,361	3.96	5.06	1.10
Sardinia	15,691	19,000	3,309	5.67	5.68	0.01
North-west	257,929	327,298	69,369	11.52	8.92	−2.60
North-east	196,879	267,742	70,863	7.62	6.70	−0.92
Centre	168,848	205,487	36,639	6.78	6.60	−0.18
South	145,188	135,230	−9,958	4.93	6.67	1.74
Islands	67,937	63,885	−4,052	4.36	5.24	0.88
ITALY	836,781	999,642	162,861	7.92	7.30	−0.62

Number of employees working in industrial enterprises:

	1971	1981	'81–'71
North-west	2,971,712	2,919,000	–52,712
North-east	1,499,255	1,795,000	295,745
Centre	1,144,541	1,350,000	205,459
South	716,848	902,000	185,152
Islands	295,964	335,000	39,036
ITALY	6,628,320	7,301,000	672,680
% '81–'71			10.15

Source: Calculated by the author from data in: ISTAT, *Annuario statistico italiano, 1974 and 1984*, (1974) pp. 10–11, 224–37 and (1984) pp. 11–12 and 154–7.

It is in the industrial sector that noticeable territorial differences arise between North and South. In the South, not only is there a decrease in the number—with the exception of the regions of Basilicata, Abruzzi, Molise and Sardinia—but there is also an increase in the average size of firms, reflecting the process of rationalization or weeding-out of the more uncompetitive. In 1971 the average size of a southern firm was 4.93 employees, while in the North-west it was 11.52, in the North-east 7.62, and in the Centre 6.78. By 1981, the average size of firms in the Centre and North was decreasing and approaching the average size of southern firms.

In social, organizational terms these entrepreneurs are characterized by what, at first glance, may seem conflicting needs. The first need is to be autonomous and assume personal responsibility for the management of the firm. However, at the same time, this diffused entrepreneurship has an increased need for publicly planned and provided economic/social policies and the support of associational groups. The existence of a supportive social and political environment is considered crucial in determining the eventual success of small enterprises. Part of the explanation for the lack of sustained industrial diffusion in large parts of the South is the lack of adequate public services, of stability of the social context, and of effective political institutions. Not surprisingly, entrepreneurial and artisan groups are strong supporters of the increased efficiency of regional (and local) governments in the provision of social and economic services (Putnam, Leonardi & Nanetti, 1985). The reason is that there is 'a decline in the exclusive belief in the automatic self-regulation of the market place' (Bagnasco, 1983; 32). Instead, the entrepreneurs want the regions and other local governments to play an important role in providing the political/social context and economic incentives necessary for the development and continued expansion of the small firm enterprise.

Regional and local governments have used their powers to create an economic environment that provides strong incentives for industry. The areas in which the governments have been most active are: subsidized credit (Fua, 1983: 32), public works projects (Orlando, 1983: 148), technical services, procurement of and equipment of industrial parks, worker training programmes (Zacchia, 1983: 186; Filipucci & Lugli, 1985: 187; Rugiandini, 1985: 127–45), and the provision of expertise and information (Lanzavecchia, 1983: 225). Field studies have revealed that the search for support from vertical or horizontal links that run from subcontracting certain phases of the production process to obtaining accounting and marketing services from their sectorial associations has not dampened the competitiveness of these firms. The result has been the creation of a 'critical mass' that can be described as a form of 'incubator' for small industries (Brusco, 1983: 119). An additional component of this new entrepreneurship is the contribution made by the cooperative movement (Canosa, 1978), which can also be seen as a form of 'associational entrepreneurship' that has been quite successful in Italy. Where these organizational and social factors are missing it has been more difficult for small industries to prosper.

The new entrepreneurs demonstrated their ability to be innovative even in areas of traditional products such as shoes, textiles, furniture, etc. They are characterized by the search for new markets in which to sell their increasingly specialized and diversified products. The 'personalization' of the product has made the goods difficult to substitute in domestic as well as international markets. They need the medium- and high-income consumer who is dissatisfied with standardized products made by large industry or the quality of many goods produced in Third World countries. The prospects for the continued success of this type of marketing strategy seem good for the future.

Another characteristic of the capillary entrepreneurship is the use of non-traditional forms of labour and support that are more common in the agricultural sector. The first is the use of family members in various stages of the production and management process as the need arises. Secondly, there is the willingness to draw upon personal networks and professional and social organizations for support. Thirdly, there is the use of various forms of part-time and piece-work, especially performed by women carrying out this production in the home—referred to in Italian as *lavoro a domicilio*—which is reminiscent of the cottage industries prevalent during the early stages of the industrial revolution. The role of home-based piece-work is an integral part of the diffusion of industry into areas that had previously been dominated by agricultural production.

2.3. The Changing Labour Market

The entrepreneurial initiative that has brought to the forefront the trend of economic decentralization and the aggressive marketing of products on domestic and international markets has, to a great extent, been facilitated by a series of population shifts and by a rise in expectations that were set in motion during the 1960s and 1970s (Salvati, 1982). The shift in population has proceeded in two directions: the movement of people from the country-side to the city and from the South to the North. By the end of the 1950s and early 1960s, the flow of emigrants to northern Italian cities surpassed the number that was leaving the country to find employment. The pace of internal migration fuelled the forces that led to an uncontrolled expansion of urban areas (Campos Venuti, 1967) in both the North and South. In the span of ten years, Italian society saw the bulk of its labour-force move from agricultural to industrial employment. The work-force in agriculture dropped from 43.9 per cent in 1951 to 30.8 per cent in 1961, while that employed in industry rose from 29.5 to 37.9 per cent (SVIMEZ, 1978: 531).

In the 1970s and 1980s the labour market continued to undergo profound changes. The proportion of labour occupied in agriculture dropped consistently, but, as shown in Table 2.9, there was also the rapid rise of the service sector as the country's primary source of employment. Nevertheless, agricultural labour remains an important occupational component in many areas of the South, where it continues to account for a fifth of the labour-force.

Table 2.9 Employment by economic sector, 1971-1984 (%)

	Agriculture			Industry			Services		
	1971	1976	1984	1971	1976	1984	1971	1976	1984
North-west	8.8	6.5	6.4	57.2	55.2	43.7	34.0	38.3	49.9
North-east	18.9	13.7	11.3	44.6	44.4	36.9	36.5	41.9	51.8
Centre	16.4	11.7	8.2	39.4	39.7	31.3	44.2	48.6	60.5
South	33.3	28.7	20.0	31.9	31.7	25.5	34.8	39.6	45.5
Islands	28.4	24.7	18.1	33.3	32.8	23.9	38.3	42.5	58.0
ITALY	19.2	15.3	11.8	43.7	43.0	34.1	37.1	41.7	54.1

NB: Services includes those employed in government.

Source: Calculated by the author from data in: ISTAT, *Le regioni in cifre, 1984*, p. 100 and SVIMEZ, *Un quarto di secolo nelle statistiche nord-sud, 1951-1976*, Milan, Giuffre, 1978, pp. 531 and 547.

The jump in service sector employment has been accentuated in all five geographic areas, with the largest increases coming in the Islands and Centre. Not visible in the data reported in Table 2.9 is the influence that public sector employment has had in different parts of the country. In 1981 the percentage of the non-agricultural work-force employed in public administrative activities finds regions in the North and Centre at a low of 15 per cent in Lombardy to a high of 22 per cent in Umbria. The bulk of service sector employment in the North and Centre is generated by the increased opportunities in both traditional types of services considered to be staples of the tertiary sector—for example, commerce, tourism and banking—as well as new forms of services such as computing, planning, advertising and market research (Filipucci & Lugli, 1985).

The Centre region of Lazio (home of the nation's capital, Rome) is an anomaly since it has 29 per cent of its non-agricultural work-force in the public sector, but it still does not reach the level of public employment registered in a number of southern regions. In the South and Islands the lowest percentage of employment in public administrative work is found in Molise, with 25 per cent, while it climbs to a high of 37 per cent in Calabria (ISTAT, 1984: 155-7). Thus, the number of jobs generated by local government and territorial units of the national bureaucracy in the South is far and away beyond the levels that are normal in other parts of the country. This means that in the South outside agriculture public sector employment is in many cases the primary source for the generation of income. The South is also the area of the country that benefits to a higher degree from public transfer payments tied to the payment of pensions for 'disabled' workers who can retire at the age of 55 rather than waiting until 65, which is the retirement age for able-bodied workers. Thus, the economy of the South is much more dependent on transfer payments and public employment than is the case in the North and Centre where income is generated to a greater extent by locally-based economic activity.

The structure of the Italian work-force has changed dramatically. At the beginning of the 1970s, while small industry began to increase its capacity to create jobs, the official labour statistics did not document any rise in employment. The data in Table 2.10 highlight the paradox that has been signalled by various scholars.[6] While, according to the official statistics, there was a fall in employment (down from 42.5 per cent in 1961 to 35.8 per cent in 1971), there was also a substantial increase in the level of economic development (Podbielski, 1974: 99). The inconsistency between the employment statistics and rates of economic growth gave rise to a discussion of the credibility of the official employment data and, above all, to the discovery of a hidden labour market whose contours and evolution had been overlooked by the official statistics.

The initial reaction to the discovery of the hidden employment was to treat it as part of the 'underground' or 'submerged' economy that had been

Table 2.10 Population employed by geographic area and sex (%)

Employed:	1961		1971		1982		1984	
	42.5		35.8		40.3		40.9	
	1961		1971		1982		1984	
	M	F	M	F	M	F	M	F
North-west	68.0	32.0	70.7	29.3	63.7	36.3	62.8	37.2
North-east	67.3	32.7	70.8	29.2	64.2	35.8	62.4	37.6
Centre	70.0	30.0	73.3	26.7	66.1	33.9	64.4	35.6
South	68.6	31.4	72.6	27.4	67.5	32.5	67.5	32.5
Islands	83.0	17.0	83.4	16.6	73.8	26.2	72.3	27.7
ITALY	69.8	30.2	73.0	27.0	66.1	33.9	65.1	34.9

Source: Calculated by the author from data in: SVIMEZ, *Un quarto di secolo delle statistiche nord-sud, 1951-1976*, Milan, Giuffre, 1978, pp. 533 and 538; ISTAT, *Compendio statistico italiano, 1983*, p. 289; and ISTAT, *Le regioni in cifre, 1984*, pp. 97-9.

generated by the decentralization of production which blossomed after 1970. The underground economy was initially seen as a system of 'illegal' production where employers purposely evaded taxes on their earnings and workers were not protected by government social programmes and union contracts as a way of ensuring acceptable profit margins. Thus, jobs generated by the underground economy were thought to be temporary in nature. Part-time work was prevalent (Frey *et al.*, 1976), and in many cases it was carried out by people who already had one job in the 'official' economy (Gallino, 1985). However. subsequent comparative considerations of the hidden economy have identified its three different aspects. Firstly, it may be composed of 'household' production where the products are designed for self-consumption, such as wine or cheese, and are only rarely sold on the open market. The second form of hidden economy, illegal activities, is associated with criminal elements that produce and distribute goods, such as heroin, that are illegal and punishable by imprisonment. This kind of hidden economy seems to be important in cities such as Palermo and Naples, controlled by criminal organizations (Catanzaro, 1986). However, the type of hidden economy that is of concern here is the third type, which has been defined as an 'informal' economy. 'Informal production is usually carried out quite legally and openly, and neither employers nor employees try to hide what they are doing' (Blades, 1982: 35). What is hidden is the *amount* of goods produced and profit made. In this case, the problem is connected with the nature of the state apparatus—i.e. its inability to keep track of economic activity owing to its antiquated procedures and structures—rather than the nature of what is being produced in the hidden economy.

Studies conducted on the underground economy estimate the existence of a labour-force that ranges from 14 to 25 per cent above that officially declared by the Government, thereby bringing the real level of employment to somewhere between 50 and 60 per cent of the population.[7] In particular, these studies documented the existence of approximately 3,500,000 part-time jobs, a million people holding down two full-time jobs, more than 100,000 children employed in violation of the national labour laws, and half a million foreigners working illegally (Leonardi, 1979). A more recent study on dual occupations has confirmed that the number of individuals with two or more jobs is around 15 to 20 per cent of the employed work-force (Garelli, 1985).

Subsequent legislation forced part of the underground economy to surface, and made owners of small industries and commercial enterprises pay their taxes. There were also provisions designed to alleviate some of the more negative aspects of past labour practices. But it is also true that other empirical studies (Fua, 1976; Allessandrini, 1978) have helped to highlight the more positive aspects of the unofficial employment market which has found in small industries an important point of access and growth. The composition of this labour pool introduced an element of flexibility for the

Table 2.11 Population distribution according to city size, 1936-1981

	1936	1951	1971	1981
NORTH				
Up to 10,000	55.5	50.9	39.9	38.8
10,001-30,000	13.8	15.8	16.3	18.4
30,001-100,000	11.6	10.6	13.6	14.5
100,001-500,000	6.7	10.0	15.3	14.6
Above 500,000	12.4	12.7	14.9	13.7
Total	100.0	100.0	100.0	100.0
CENTRE				
Up to 10,000	38.2	34.5	23.7	22.2
10,001-30,000	25.3	22.3	19.2	20.3
30,001-100,000	15.6	18.2	18.0	19.6
100,001-500,000	5.8	6.0	11.9	11.6
Above 500,000	15.1	19.0	27.2	26.3
Total	100.0	100.0	100.0	100.0
SOUTH				
Up to 10,000	46.9	41.8	35.3	32.2
10,001-30,000	26.1	25.6	22.1	22.4
30,001-100,000	12.2	17.1	20.0	22.5
100,001-500,000	9.1	9.8	12.6	13.3
Above 500,000	5.7	5.7	10.0	9.6
Total	100.0	100.0	100.0	100.0
ITALY				
Up to 10,000	49.2	44.5	35.2	33.3
10,001-30,000	20.4	20.6	18.9	20.1
30,001-100,000	12.6	14.5	16.7	18.4
100,001-500,000	7.4	9.2	13.7	13.6
Above 500,000	10.4	11.2	15.5	14.6
Total	100.0	100.0	100.0	100.0

Source: Calculated by the author from data in ISTAT, *Annuario statistico italiano*, 1944, 1954, 1973, and 1984 editions.

decentralized system of production that hampered growth in sectors where production was saddled with inflexible rules and procedures.

The decentralization of production has also facilitated the decentralization of living—i.e. a move to less congested areas. The big city, with its diseconomies of scale created by congestion and spiralling costs, has declined as a point of reference for those seeking employment. Inter-regional emigration from the South to the North has diminished; intra-regional migration has changed direction and is now orientated toward medium-sized cities; and the intra-metropolitan movements of population have accompanied the exit of industry from the historical centres to the smaller towns in the metropolitan hinterland. Table 2.11 shows that by 1981 the large metropolitan cities—i.e. those with a population of over 500,000—were not keeping up with the natural expansion of the population. The same was also true for the smallest cities with less than 10,000 inhabitants. Instead, the cities that continued to gain population were those in the range above 10,000, and especially those with populations between 30 and 100,000.

Given the wider range of employment opportunities introduced by decentralized production, there has also been a change in the pattern of unemployment. The change particularly affects women, the young, and those who have not completed secondary schooling. The 1970s saw an increased flow of women into the job market, but women continued to have difficulty in finding adequate job opportunities (Seroni, 1977), as well as equal salary scales (Livraghi, 1976). As the data in Table 2.12 demonstrates, while it is true that unemployment has increased in general between 1971 and 1984, women have disproportionally borne the brunt of unemployment. The differences between men and women have increased to the extent that in 1984 there was a difference in unemployment rates that went over ten percentage points. In addition, women are less involved in managing two or more jobs outside the household. The typical individual with a dual occupation is a skilled male worker (Scamuzzi, 1985). Inversely, under-employment is typically a female phenomenon given the accentuated presence of women doing piece-work at home, domestic service, day labouring, and part-

Table 2.12 Unemployment, 1971-1984 (as % of employed population)

	In search of employment (i.s.e.)								
	Unemployed		Search first job		Other i.s.e.		Total i.s.e.		Difference i.s.e.
	M	F	M	F	M	F	M	F	M-F
1971	1.5	1.1	1.5	3.7	0.8	4.7	3.8	9.5	5.7
1974	1.0	0.9	1.7	4.0	1.0	4.7	3.6	9.6	6.0
1977	0.9	1.1	2.3	5.1	1.4	6.3	4.6	12.6	8.0
1980	0.8	1.3	2.8	6.3	1.2	5.6	4.8	13.1	8.3
1983	1.3	2.1	4.1	8.6	1.3	5.5	6.6	16.2	9.6
1984	1.8	2.6	3.7	7.7	1.3	6.9	6.8	17.1	10.3

Source: Calculated by the author from data in: ISTAT, *Le regioni in cifre 1985*, p. 119.

Table 2.13 Unemployed by age, 1977-1984 (%)

Age	1977	1980	1984
14–19	31.5	31.1	27.8
20–24	30.9	31.2	32.7
25–29	16.6	14.0	15.3
30–39	8.9	10.1	12.8
40–49	6.6	6.0	7.0
50–59	4.1	4.1	3.9
60–above	1.3	3.4	0.5
Total	100.0	100.0	100.0

Source: Calculated by the author from data in: Giuseppe DeRita, 'Occupazione e disoccupazione adulta', *Economia, Istruzione e Formazione Professionale 1* (April 1978), pp. 76-7; ISTAT, *Statistiche sociali, 1981*, p. 120; and ISTAT, *Annuario statistico italiano, 1985*, p. 225.

time work on the family farm. In agriculture the estimate is that under-employment affects approximately 750,000 females (Frey, 1976).

Unemployment in the 1970s and 1980s also has a strong age factor. Most of the unemployed are young people (Table 2.13). If we divide the unemployed into age categories and look at those below 30 years of age, we find that in 1984 this age cohort accounted for 84.9 per cent of those without a job, up slightly from the 79 per cent level of 1977. This level of youth unemployment represents another anomaly of the Italian case. In 1977 the level of youth unemployment in other industrialized countries was much lower: from 27.0 per cent in West Germany to 54.4 per cent in the United States (Leonardi, 1979). One of the structural reasons for such a high level of youth unemployment can be traced to the difficulties inherent in the transition from the educational system to the first job in the official job market.

Table 2.14 shows that Italian unemployment is not particularly a problem of 'intellectual unemployment' because the level of unemployment tends to be much worse among those with less than an upper secondary school diploma or university degree. While there is a tendency toward a decline in the pool of unemployed without any formal education owing to the fact that the uneducated are quickly disappearing from society, one finds the bulk of unemployment among youth with only a lower secondary school diploma. The problems of incorporating them into the labour-force have increased owing, in part, to the rigidity introduced into apprenticeship programmes by recent legislation and also to the shortcomings of current vocational education programmes. Vocational education is mainly orientated toward the preparation of lower secondary graduates for the job market, but the current job market requires increasingly diversified and specialized training

Table 2.14 Unemployment by age and level of education, 1977 and 1984 (%)

	Age							
	14–19		20–24		25–29		30–Over	
Educational level	1977	1984	1977	1984	1977	1984	1977	1984
Up to elementary school certificate	27.3	12.9	15.9	10.7	20.1	5.7	76.1	62.8
Lower secondary school certificate	56.4	82.0	30.4	59.7	20.1	46.7	12.4	20.4
Upper secondary school diploma or university degree	16.3	5.4	53.7	29.6	59.8	37.6	11.5	16.8
Total	100.0	100.0	100.0	100.0	100.0	100.0	100.0	100.0

Source: Calculated by the author from data in: Giuseppe DeRita, 'Occupazione e disoccupazione adulta', *Economia, Istruzione e Formazione Professionale*, 1 (April 1978), pp. 76–7 and ISTAT, *Annuario statistico italiano, 1985*, p. 225.

congruent with the exigencies of decentralized production. However, vocational education programmes have had difficulty in responding to these needs where there is a lack of cooperation between the institutions providing the training and the employers. The increased intellectual component in employment is linked to the proliferation of new professional opportunities in the traditional as well as advanced tertiary sectors, the new 'mix' of professional qualifications within industrial enterprises, and the interdependence among economic sectors.

2.4. New Social Needs and Constituencies

Italy has participated in the rapid rise of individual consumption that has characterized the West during the last twenty-five years. In 1958 the vast majority of families did not own a television set, refrigerator or washing machine. However, by 1975 when the Bank of Italy stopped collecting such data, 92 per cent of Italian families owned a television set, 94 per cent a refrigerator, and 74 per cent a washing machine. The increase in private consumption has also been followed by a parallel increase in public consumption. In 1970 Italy's expenditure on Welfare State items such as education, health, pensions and housing accounted for 21.0 per cent of its GDP; eleven years later, that percentage had grown to 29.8. By 1980, Italy had entered the realm of a modern, post-industrial society where its social aspirations and demands on the political system began to break out of the confines of the struggle for strictly material gains into the area of individual freedoms and social rights that had been overlooked in previous political struggles.

The 1970s show a diffusion of new social typologies and groups that were produced by the mobilizations of that time and the increased demand for goods and services. In the Italian case, the crisis of the Welfare State brought with it a new emphasis on individual liberties that had previously been ignored or suppressed, such as those of couples who lived separately, women having abortions, the handicapped and gays. At the beginning of the 1970s, Italian Welfare State policies had not yet achieved the range and consistency found in the more advanced European countries, nor had they succeeded in bridging the wide gaps that continued to exist between North and South.

One of the most serious shortcomings was the lack of adequate hospitals and health care. Thus, in 1971, the infant mortality rate in Italy (28.5 per 1,000 live births) was more than double that of the Netherlands (12.1) and Sweden (11.1) and 50 per cent higher than the rates found in the United States (19.2), France (17.1) and Great Britain (17.9) (ISTAT, 1974: 466). Internally, the differences between the two areas of the country expressed themselves in terms of infant mortality rates around 35 to 40 in the South compared with 20 to 25 in the Centre-North (ISTAT, 194: 63). These figures suggest that the North and Centre were part of the advanced industrialized world while the South continued to maintain characteristics of an underdeveloped country.

Rapid changes, however, did take place during the 1970s. There was a concerted effort to expand social policies in response to the growing demand to fill the existing service gaps. Health expenditure rose by 50 per cent; the restructuring and expansion of hospital services were undertaken in 1974; and the legislation to create a national health system was passed in 1978. The period also saw a rapid growth in the consumption of existing services. There was a considerable increase in upper secondary and university students in systems that had substantially remained untouched by government reform policies—i.e. they were basically the same curricula and structures that existed in the immediate post-war period. The cumulative impact of these two dynamics was to increase the social consumption indicators for the period under consideration. As is evident in Table 2.15, by 1983 Italy had drawn abreast of other OECD countries with regard to social expenditures and individual levels of service consumption.

In addition to being tied to greater governmental expenditure and individual income, the changes in consumption patterns were also connected with four basic changes that characterized the 1970s in Italy. The first was the change in the demographic profile of the country. The change consisted

Table 2.15 Social development indicators for some OECD countries (%)

	1983				
	Infant mortality (1000 live births)	TVs per person	Social security % national budget	Defence % national budget	Level of University attendance* (1980)
Italy	12.3	0.24	27.7	4.1	25.1
France	9.3	0.36	43.9	17.5	25.5
West Germany	11.6	0.36	48.5	9.2	27.6
Great Britain	11.0	0.33	26.2	13.6	20.1
Japan	6.7	0.24	N.A.	5.8	30.2
United States	11.0	0.62	34.1	28.6	57.1
Canada	9.6	0.50	32.8	8.9	37.0
Denmark	8.4	0.37	41.5	7.0	28.6
Ireland	15.6	0.24	N.A.	3.0	21.3
Netherlands	8.3	0.43	36.4	7.8	30.5
Belgium	11.7	0.30	41.6	5.4	25.2

* Calculated as a percentage of students enrolled in universities based on the number of people within the age-group 20–24 (ISTAT, 1984: 360).

Source: Britannica World Data, 1985, pp. 622-818 and ISTAT, *Annuario statistico italiano, 1984*, Rome, ISTAT, p. 36.

mainly of a decrease in the rate of population growth, a reduction in the weight of young cohorts in the population, and a corresponding increase in the number of the elderly (Table 2.16). The fertility rate—which between 1950 and 1970 had remained unchanged at about 70 live births per 1,000 women in the 15 to 49 age-group—suddenly fell to 53 live births in 1978 and again to 46.7 for the period between 1980 and 1982 (ISTAT, 1983: 16), and the percentage of children up to 4 years of age present in the population was reduced from 8.2 in 1971 to 6.0 in 1981 (ISTAT, 1983: 13).

The fertility rate fell in a steady pattern throughout the country—from −18.5 in Sardinia to −20.2 in Veneto— but the fall does not cancel out the initially higher southern birth rates. The regions with the highest fertility rates are Campania, Basilicata, Puglia and Calabria. Those with the lowest fertility rates are to be found in the industrial triangle: Liguria, Piedmont and Val d'Aosta. In Campania the 1978 fertility rate was still twice as high as that in Liguria, and the rates remained uniformally higher in the regions south of Rome. As a consequence, many regions of the North have seen a net decrease in population. In 1983 Italy's net increase in population (number of

Table 2.16 Change in demographic profile of population

	Fertility level* 1978	Diff. fertility levels '78–'72	Natural increase pop.** 1979	Natural increase pop.** '70–'72	Old age index† 1980	Diff. old age index '71–'80
Piedmont	42.5	−16.6	−2.2	2.6	102.4	4.7
Lombardy	44.9	−17.1	0.7	5.8	77.8	8.0
Liguria	34.4	−17.3	−5.8	−0.2	139.7	19.5
V. d'Aosta	46.8	−13.8	−1.4	3.3	90.9	7.6
T-AA	50.5	−21.2	1.7	7.6	70.4	8.8
F-VG	41.7	−16.1	−4.0	1.1	118.8	12.5
Veneto	48.0	−20.2	1.1	7.1	74.1	9.8
E-R	38.5	−16.1	−2.5	2.8	115.5	18.6
Tuscany	41.9	−13.9	−2.0	2.8	117.1	10.9
Marche	48.4	−9.5	1.0	4.6	100.1	18.0
Umbria	46.1	−7.8	−0.2	3.0	108.5	18.3
Lazio	49.0	−17.8	3.4	9.3	67.9	11.3
Abruzzi	54.3	−10.7	2.7	5.7	87.6	12.2
Campania	73.5	−17.1	9.1	13.4	46.9	4.1
Molise	56.1	−9.0	2.5	4.7	90.8	11.5
Puglia	72.5	−14.0	9.2	12.9	50.8	4.3
Basilicata	64.7	−14.5	6.0	10.4	62.8	8.9
Calabria	69.2	−13.7	8.1	11.1	59.0	9.0
Sicily	67.1	−14.8	6.7	10.3	63.1	5.6
Sardinia	65.2	−18.5	6.9	11.7	55.5	5.7
ITALY	53.0	−15.8	2.5	7.2	76.6	8.5

Key:
* Live births from women in 15–49 age-group per 1,000 women in that age-group.
** Quotient of live births minus deaths among resident population.
† Ratio between population 60 years or older and that up to 14 years of age.

Source: Calculated by the author from data in ISTAT, *Statistiche sociali, 1981*, Rome, ISTAT, pp. 18, 21, 40.

births minus the number of deaths) was its lowest in history, 49,129 people, mathematically very close to zero population growth. Studies have shown that there is a close relationship between birth rates and social and economic progress, educational levels, health services, nutrition, employment, income and female emancipation. Italy has improved in all of these categories during the last two decades, and the zero population growth is therefore to be expected.

Parallel to the drop in fertility rates was the increase in life expectancy. In 1931 the percentage of the population above the retirement age of 65 was 7.14, and in 1979 it had reached 13.1 per cent. The estimate is that by 1991 one-seventh of the Italian population will consist of people over 65 years of age. In territorial terms, the aging index consistently finds the regions of the North above and those of the South below the national average. Liguria and Campania are, respectively, the regions with the oldest and youngest populations.

The second important change that was noticeable in the 1970s was the increased conviction that education was important,[8] especially education that provided access to the university and/or professional qualification. During the latter part of the 1960s and 1970s there was a rapid rise in upper secondary enrollments that jumped from 19.2 per cent of the age cohort in 1962 to 42.4 per cent ten years later, and it reached 51.8 per cent in 1981

Table 2.17 Indicators of vocational and general education levels

	Upper secondary graduates		University graduates		Vocational education quotient*
	(% population from 6 years and above)				
	1981	1971	1981	1971	1981-82
Piedmont	11.3	6.5	2.4	1.5	16.7
Lombardy	12.1	6.9	2.8	1.8	13.4
Liguria	13.7	8.6	3.4	2.2	7.0
V. d'Aosta	11.0	6.3	2.0	1.3	40.9
T-AA	9.4	5.7	2.2	1.3	33.3
F-VG	12.0	7.3	2.5	1.6	12.3
Veneto	10.4	5.4	2.3	1.4	13.7
E-R	12.0	6.9	2.9	1.7	20.6
Tuscany	11.4	6.6	2.8	1.7	7.6
Marche	11.4	6.7	2.8	1.6	12.6
Umbria	12.9	6.9	2.9	1.7	14.3
Lazio	15.6	10.3	4.5	3.4	11.5
Abruzzi	11.6	7.1	2.6	1.5	16.8
Campania	10.3	6.6	2.8	1.8	6.3
Molise	10.4	6.4	2.4	1.4	13.9
Puglia	9.5	6.0	2.3	1.5	7.8
Basilicata	10.5	5.4	1.9	1.1	7.1
Calabria	10.7	6.5	2.5	1.4	3.0
Sicily	10.0	6.5	2.8	1.9	9.3
Sardinia	9.5	5.9	2.3	1.4	6.6
ITALY	11.5	6.9	2.8	1.8	12.1

* Calculated as a ratio of students enrolled in vocational education courses per 1,000 employed.

Source: Calculated by the author from data in: *ISTAT, Compendio statistico italiano, 1983*, Rome, ISTAT, p. 72, 288; *Le regioni in cifre, 1985*, p. 22; and *Statistiche sociali, 1975*, p. 69.

(ISTAT, 1981: 86). This trend was reflected in the 1981 census by the general increase in all regions of the population with upper secondary diplomas and university degrees (see Table 2.17). Between 1971 and 1981 the rate almost doubled, from 8.7 to 14.3 per cent of the population above 6 years of age.

On the other hand, there has not been a clear preference at both the upper secondary and university levels for curricula providing access to jobs and careers in new and promising economic activities (Table 2.18). At the upper secondary level, there is a net change in favour of technical and professional types of education. The table shows a clear drop in the percentage of students choosing to do their upper secondary work in classical lyceums,[9] while the scientific and linguistic lyceums have suffered no erosion. And there is also a

Table 2.18 Enrolments in upper secondary schools and universities by type of specialization (%)

	1982-83	1972-73	1970-71
Upper secondary schools:			
Classical lyceum	8.4		12.4
Scientific/linguistic lyceum	15.9		15.3
Arts lyceum	2.5		2.4
Teacher training schools	9.6		13.4
Technical institutes	44.5		40.8
Professional institutes	19.1		15.7
Total	100.0		100.0
University:			
Sciences	12.9	13.9	
Medicine	15.7	15.2	
Engineering	14.5	14.8	
Agriculture	3.8	1.9	
Economics/Business admin.	11.6	8.0	
Pol. Science/Sociology	5.1	6.3	
Law	14.4	10.1	
Literature	19.8	28.7	
Music	2.2	1.1	
Total	100.0	100.0	

Source: Calculated by the author from data in: ISTAT, *Annuario statistico italiano, 1984*, Rome, ISTAT, p.87; *Annuario statistico italiano, 1974*, Rome, ISTAT, p. 122; Richard L. Merritt & Robert Leonardi, 'The Politics of Upper Secondary School Reform in Italy: Immobilism or Accommodation?', *Comparative Education Review*, October 1981, pp. 371-2; CENSIS, *XVII Rapporto, 1983*, p. 205.

clear decline in those opting for teacher training schools *istituti magistrali*).[10] These data show that there is a growing awareness (and preference for) among the young and their parents that a professionally orientated diploma is, in the last analysis, a greater hedge against the future—i.e. more useful in finding a job if one decides not to proceed with education at the university level—than the more classically-orientated studies that had dominated Italian upper secondary education in the 1940s and 1950s.

At the university level, however, the trend has been contradictory. Looking at the percentage in Table 2.18 of student choices of curricula, there is practically no change in the decade under consideration, with the exception of students specializing in the arts. The percentage of arts graduates has declined, but it is still high considering that in 1982–83 it still accounted for one-fifth of all university students, despite the fall in pace in employing school teachers. During the same decade there has been an increase in the percentage of students taking law, which in 1982–83 matched the levels registered by engineering. The same is also true for graduates in economics—which in Italy also includes business administration—and agricultural sciences. More disturbing, however, is the drop in science graduates. Even though it is difficult to draw any definitive conclusions from these data, it is possible to say that the pattern of university education has not responded to the model of diffused entrepreneurial growth. There has been an increased flow of students into economics and agricultural sciences but there has been no great increase in engineering or the hard sciences, which may still be tied more to the conditions of the large rather than small firm in the economy.

The third major change in the 1970s was the structure and legal status of the family. The number of families has grown, and at the same time they have become smaller (Table 2.19). The increase in the age of the population has been accompanied by the growth of single-person families, in particular composed of the elderly, and a general expansion in family typologies. The composition of the family has now significantly changed from the traditional concept to include couples without children, the elderly living alone, the cohabitation of people who are not related, unmarried women, and homosexual couples.

The 1970s witnessed a basic redefinition of individual rights *vis-à-vis* society as well as *vis-à-vis* the family. These were the years in which important changes were made in the country's laws and, when necessary, confirmed through popular referendum. The law on divorce was passed in 1970 and ratified through the nation's first referendum in 1974 (Magister, 1979); the law on abortion was passed in 1977 and, again, overwhelmingly supported by the votes in a referendum—that of 1981. The 1975 re-writing of the family law was not forced to go to a referendum, but it had a profound impact on redefining the rights and duties of family members by breaking down the old hierarchical, paternal family structure and equalizing the role of

Table 2.19 Indicators of family behaviour

	Illegitimate children/ 1,000 born		Marriages/ 1,000 inhabitants		Divorces/ 100,000 inhabitants		Average family size	
	1983	1970	1983	1973	1983	1973	1981	1971
Piedmont	67	26	4.7	6.7	38.0	43.8	2.7	2.9
Lombardy	51	24	4.8	7.2	30.7	34.8	2.9	3.1
Liguria	78	37	4.3	6.7	39.0	72.2	2.5	2.7
V. d'Aosta	100	31	4.7	7.6	54.8	*	2.6	2.8
T-AA	89	50	5.5	8.1	27.1	26.2	3.1	3.5
F-VG	63	31	4.2	7.2	37.8	51.2	2.7	3.0
Veneto	35	20	5.3	8.0	13.0	18.9	3.1	3.6
E-R	71	24	4.3	7.0	27.5	30.8	2.8	3.2
Tuscany	47	19	4.6	7.1	15.7	21.4	2.9	3.2
Marche	25	9	4.7	7.0	10.1	10.8	3.1	3.6
Umbria	29	14	5.2	7.7	15.3	19.8	3.0	3.5
Lazio	56	30	5.2	7.8	33.8	48.5	3.0	3.4
Abruzzi	28	14	5.1	7.5	11.2	12.9	3.1	3.5
Campania	35	21	6.7	8.9	14.1	30.0	3.5	3.9
Molise	18	13	5.5	6.9	10.9	20.6	3.0	3.4
Puglia	45	15	6.2	8.5	12.2	19.2	3.4	3.7
Basilicata	15	8	6.3	7.7	9.1	14.7	3.2	3.6
Calabria	25	18	5.9	7.9	11.1	19.2	3.3	3.7
Sicily	55	18	6.2	8.0	17.9	29.5	3.2	3.5
Sardinia	50	19	5.5	8.1	8.8	14.7	3.4	3.9
ITALY	48	22	5.3	7.6	22.6	31.2	3.0	3.3

* Inserted in count for Piedmont.

Source: Calculated by the author from data in: ISTAT, *Annuario statistico italiano, 1984*, Rome, ISTAT, pp. 25-7, 30; *Annuario statistico italiano, 1974*, Rome, ISTAT, pp. 55-6, 59; *Le regioni in cifre, 1985*, Rome, ISTAT, pp. 23 and 61; *Statistiche sociali, 1975*, Rome, ISTAT, p. 26; and SVIMEZ, *Un quarto di secolo nelle statistiche nord-sud, 1951-1976*, Milan, Giuffre, pp. 48 and 831.

the female spouse. This legislation reflected demands originating from the women's movement to change Italy's antiquated family law and prohibitions against divorce and abortion. But it also served to consolidate changes that had taken place in public opinion. The legislation moved in the direction of providing greater freedom of choice in matters of individual liberty and the protection of the rights of the female spouse to family property and accumulated wealth.

The passage of this legislation has not broken down the Italian family structure to the extent that some of its opponents predicted, but it did significantly change behaviour and perceptions. The number of divorces increased rapidly immediately after 1970 because of the backlog of cases that had been pending. Once this logjam was overcome, the divorce rate stabilized at levels that are quite modest in comparison with those of other industrialized countries. As Table 2.19 indicates, the stabilization of the divorce rate was accompanied by a drop in the marriage rate and an increase in illegitimate children.[11] Abortions also seem to have declined slightly. Given the brief period in which abortions have been officially recorded, it is too early to tell whether this indicates a long-term trend. Between 1982 and 1983 the number of abortions officially performed in Italy fell by 3,000. The decline is proportionally less than the large decrease in the number of live births—17,000—during the same two-year period (ISTAT, 1984: 42).

Finally, the 1970s witnessed a change in the definition of necessary services and the perception of the measure of a high quality of life. The changes in family structure and employment opportunities for women made the provision of infant and child care services more important. The same was true with regard to services for the elderly, who increasingly lived alone. Estimates suggest that in the city of Rome there are over 100,000 elderly persons living alone (Council of Ministers, 1986), whose quality of life is very much dependent on their access to adequate recreation, economic and social services.

Among the working population, there is an increased attention toward problems of health in the workplace. Attempts are under way to experiment with a reduction in the working week and the use of flexible working hours. There is increased motivation for having a second job or engaging in voluntary work. There is the desire to live in more manageable urban surroundings provided by small and medium-sized cities. With regard to consumption, there has been a noticeable increase in the consumption of goods associated with leisure time, such as vacationing, sport and recreational activities, reading of specialized magazines and newspapers, and attending cultural performances (ISTAT, 1985: 46-7, CENSIS, 1983: 173-8), as well as a growing emphasis on living in owner-occupied housing and placing in one's immediate environment structures and activities that one values as signs of an enhanced quality of life (Donati, 1984b; Ministero del Lavoro, 1983).

The cumulative effect of these four social changes has been to significantly alter the Italian social and economic system. It is no longer a rural society, nor is it an industrializing one. Italy during the 1970s and 1980s has shown all the characteristics of an advanced post-industrial society that has gone beyond meeting basic needs, and is now concerned with post-materialist problems of individual freedom, opportunity and maximization of quality of life. The social significance of the current trend toward the decentralization of production and diffusion of entrepreneurship is that it is taking place in a phase of mature rather than primitive capitalism. As a result, the entrepreneurial opportunities are much more widespread across classes in society and potentially more enduring than the first stage of sustained capitalist development that the country experienced in the 1950s, owing in part to the diffused commitment to sustain the development that is found among diverse political, social and economic organizations. In the next chapter we will turn to a consideration of the political context that characterized the immediate post-war period which, in restrospect, was much less conducive to diffused industrialization than was the case in the 1970s.

Notes

1. The Mezzogiorno consists of the regions south of Rome (or Lazio) and the two islands of Sicily and Sardinia and has historically been the country's most economically underdeveloped area.
2. Italy's steel industry shared the crisis that hit other European and world producers. See Meny & Wright (1985).
3. This was tied to the initial activity of the Fund for the South (*Cassa per il Mezzogiorno*).
4. The *Cassa* was created in 1950 to undertake 'extraordinary' investments in the South for the purpose of creating the basis for economic development (Saville, 1967).
5. In 1986 the service sector grew by 3.2 per cent, in comparison with the 2.7 per cent for industry and 1.7 per cent for agriculture.
6. For a review of the literature and discussion of the points in contention, see Bagnasco (1977: 113-20).
7. It was, in fact, the increase from 14 to 15 per cent in the estimate of the impact of the informal economy that in 1986 permitted Italy to surpass the United Kingdom in GDP.
8. Mass access to education was considerably facilitated by the reforms that took place in the 1960s, eliminating the tracking of students in the lower secondary system and opening up university education to all students with five years of upper secondary schooling. See Balbo & Chiaretti, (1973).
9. The lyceums are upper secondary schools which have educational programmes organized around specific areas of study—e.g. classical studies, scientific disciplines, languages and art.
10. The rapid expansion of the school system above the elementary level has required teachers to possess university degrees. Therefore, the upper secondary *magistrali* are no longer seen as providing the final degree for aspiring teachers.
11. In Italy children born out of wedlock are now referred to as 'natural' children, a concept that does not have the negative connotations of 'illegitimate'.

3 The Changing Political Agenda: The Diffusion of Power

3.1. Political Change: An Overview

The changes in the Italian socio-economic structure during the post-war period and, in particular, since the 1960s have had their parallels in the political and institutional spheres. Unlike the gradual but inexorable pattern of socio-economic growth, the changes in the political sphere have come in short bursts, and in many cases as a process of 'catching-up' with, or in response to, changes that had already taken place in society. Some have argued (Coppola, 1985; De Felice, 1979) that the initial institutional changes, represented by the adoption of a Republican form of government in 1948 through the ratification of the Constitution and abolition of the monarchy, did not really have a major impact in changing governmental socio-economic policies or policy-making structures. Although there was a change in the way that political leadership was legitimized (elections and representative institutions), power remained concentrated in one party. In the late 1940s the hegemonic party was Christian Democracy (DC) rather than Mussolini's National Fascist Party, but the entire state apparatus, assigned the task of administering government policies, was the same one that had been recruited and had served under the Corporate State.

A number of analyses of the DC (Chiarante, 1980; Menapace, 1975) have indeed maintained that corporatism continued to characterize government decision-making long after the demise of Fascism: Ragionieri (1976: 2347), for instance, has written that 'On the 25th of July (1943) Fascism fell but not the Fascist state; its basic institutions remained intact.' This alleged continuity between the Corporate State and the Republican regime resulted, in part, in retarding the ability and/or need for the country to come to grips with post-war political changes—i.e. those reflected in the Constitution with regard to the central role of Parliament in decision-making, bringing into government the new social forces that had been created during the Resistance and post-war periods, and responding to the increased expectations of a more democratic and just society. Ingrao maintains that the political conflict that emerged in 1948 was due, in large part, to the divergence of views on how post-war society should be structured and on the changes that had to be made:

In reality, there was a lot of conflict because the defeat of Fascism signalled a definite break with the past and the society was profoundly different in terms of the level of consciousness and organization of the masses and in the relationship between the masses and the State. There was a diffusion of new ideas and models of how society should be organized. It is not by chance that blood ran in the streets. [Ingrao, 1977: 11.]

In analysing the difficulties faced in the implementation of constitutional provisions during the 1950s and 1960s, it is clear that the course and pace of socio-economic growth outstripped the rate at which changes were taking place at the political/institutional level. Thus, while Italy was going through its 'economic miracle' in the 1950s, it was 'politics as usual' with regard to coalition strategies and political programmes. The Constitution was implemented incrementally, always with a view to not upsetting the status quo or eroding the power base of the hegemonic party.

Despite these precautions, change did come in the 1960s and 1970s in response to three basic trends: (1) the shift of the fulcrum of policy-making from party (DC) to institutionally-based settings (Parliament); (2) the multiplication of relevant political actors follows, firstly, the 'opening-to-the left' or Centre-left (PSI) and, later, the 'historic compromise' (PCI); (3) the entry into the political debate of a wide variety of social and economic forces—especially the trade unions—which had in the past been relegated to subordinate political roles; and (4) the diffusion of policy initiatives to sub-national institutions and socio-economic groups. The result was a policy-making process involving multiple institutional as well as political actors which was richer and much more complex than had been the case previously when the DC had its monopoly of policy-making and could unilaterally determine the access of interest groups to public resources. This chapter will focus on the changing nature of the policy-making game in the post-war period in order to show how power has become diffused in the political system with the expansion of decision-making centres and relevant political actors and social forces.

3.2. Executive Government in Post-war Italy

In reading the literature (Hellman, 1987; Spotts & Weiser, 1986; Sassoon, 1986; Allum, 1973; Zariski, 1972; Kogan, 1962) on Italian government or listening to the later debate on institutional reform (Pasquino, 1986; Miglio *et al.*, 1983; Ristuccia, 1977), one has the impression that the Italian system of government is, and always was, characterized by a strong Parliament and a weak executive. This, however, is misleading. According to the Italian Constitution, the executive branch of government—identified as the Prime Minister and his Cabinet[1]—is responsible for three basic functions:

formulation of policy; coordination of ministerial activities; and the implementation of programmes and laws passed by Parliament.

In carrying out these functions, the exact power of the Prime Minister and the Cabinet depends to a great extent on the nature of the relationship that the Government has with other political institutions, such as Parliament, the bureaucracy and judiciary, interest groups, voluntary groups, the media, political parties—in addition to the level of cohesiveness among coalition members in carrying out the Government's programme and leadership. If the coalition members are not of one mind on the priorities or responsibilities for government activities the strength and authority of the Government suffer—i.e. it is unable to formulate clear policies and there is a breakdown in the coordination of ministerial activities and the implementation of policies. The same could also hold, but to a lesser degree, if the Government found strong opposition within the state apparatus or from powerful social, economic and political groups in society.

The thesis to be developed here is that in the immediate post-war period the Italian political system found itself, for organizational and political reasons, with a strong executive government. However, that strength began to slowly dissipate after 1953 as the Government lost its bearings when conflict over personalities, programmes and political direction became increasingly common within the Government and party coalition—i.e. government cohesion was mined from within. In subsequent years this was followed by a growing autonomy among interest groups and other institutions in formulating their own approaches to problems and imposing their agenda. In the 1960s and 1970s there was increased unwillingness on the part of a number of important interest groups to accept Government policies.

After the overthrow of Fascism and the initiation of the war for national liberation from the Nazi occupation, the first official act in the name of the parties of the Committee for National Liberation (CLN) was the issuing of a decree, No. 151/1944, that gave all legislative powers to the Government and restricted the role of the Constituent Assembly, to be elected after the war, to that of drafting a new constitution. The significance of the 1944 decree was that between the formation of the first Bonomi Government[2] in June 1944 and the election of the first Parliament in April 1948 the Government had *de facto* and *de jure* control of both legislative and executive powers—i.e. it was able to rule by executive decree.

There was no power within the political system that could exercise a check or balance over government action. All the CLN parties had agreed from the outset that the post-war situation required emergency measures, and in the immediate post-war period there were very few, if any, countervailing social and economic forces in society that wanted to or could have opposed this arrangement. The Government had the support of all the country's organized economic and social groups, from the unified trade union movement (CGIL) to the reconstituted employers' (Confindustria) and agricultural (Confagricoltura and Coldiretti) organizations, not to mention the Church and the Allied powers (Ellwood, 1985; Gibelli, 1983; Legnani, 1983; Magister, 1979).

The reasons for this broad support for the Government of the country's active interest groups may be found, in part, in the method by which the country peacefully made the transition between the Resistance and the post-war period. The move from the initial Badoglio governments to those of Bonomi, Parri and DeGasperi[3] was carried out without either bitter political struggle or institutional dislocation. Moreover, all these governments were willing to make use of the Fascist Corporate State structure—which allocated to the State primary responsibility in economic and social affairs—to achieve a directive role in society: Fascism was not the only Italian political force wedded to corporatism as an acceptable mode for social and economic interaction.

The 1943 programme of the Christian Democratic Party accorded considerable prominence to corporatism in its description of the Catholic world's conception of post-war society (Fanfani, 1938; Fanfani, 1945; Basso, 1951; Battaglia *et al.*, 1955). And once DC leaders became ministers, they found themselves very comfortable within the existing institutional framework. Giovanni Gronchi, for example, who was one of the founding fathers of the DC and Minister of Labour and Industry in the Bonomi and DeGasperi Cabinets, fought vigorously to maintain the role of the State in the resolution of social and economic conflicts, and he wanted the state apparatus to control the allocation of, initially, UNRRA (United Nations Relief and Recovery Assistance) and, subsequently, European Economic Programme aid to Italy (Salvati, 1982; Vinciguerra, 1968).[4]

The Christian Democrats, as a whole, played a key role in preserving the existing state bureaucratic structure (Orfei, 1976), and the first DeGasperi Government (1945-46) was formed as a result of the dispute among the coalition partners over: the substitution of the CLN 'political' prefects by career bureaucrats (termed 'non-political' prefects) chosen from lists of eligible candidates drawn up by the Fascist Government between 1941 and 1943; the termination of purge trials against former members of the Fascist bureaucratic, military and police personnel; and the guarantee of the 'independence of the judiciary' through the non-interference with existing structures, personnel and procedures.

With the achievement of these objectives, the DC was able to completely rehabilitate under its tutelage the state structure and personnel inherited from Fascism. No change was made in the structure and procedures adopted by the Italian intelligence community, armed forces, national police units (such as the *Carabinieri* and *Pubblica Sicurezza*), judicial machinery or government bureaucracy (DeLutiis, 1984; Flores, 1983; Canosa & Federico, 1974). There was little awareness on the part of the more progressive sections of the Christian Democratic Party (and even among the parties of the left) that the perpetuation of the existing apparatus would become a serious obstacle to implementing the major political and social changes advocated by the DC in the post-war period. Cassese writes that the entire activity of the DeGasperi Government was conducted in the context of continuity:

> Continuity with regard to Fascism and continuity with the goals of Italy's pre-Fascist period. Continuity in the sense of fully integrating fascist institutions and partial continuity in using old State structures to ends that were partially new. When new institutions are introduced, there is an indication of the date when they will begin to substitute the old institutions. When defascistization is desired, the action is limited to individuals and, for this limited goal, new laws are passed which in large part remain on paper. [Cassese, 1976.]

Control over the bureaucracy remained effectively in the hands of the individual ministers who were understandably quite reluctant to compromise the loyalty of their administrative personnel. Marcello Flores (1983: 20) writes that 'the postponement of any decisive restructuring of the state apparatus thus favoured a sector which remained indispensable for the carrying out of everyday administration and which no minister, for fear of paralysis, wanted to alienate but wished instead to coopt'.

The process of restoration was completed in April 1948 when the Christian Democrats won a landslide victory over the combined forces of the left (Rossi, 1985; Orfei, 1976). The formation, on the heels of the 1948 election, of what can be described as DeGasperi's 'iron Government' effectively put an end to all reforms at the national and local level in government, even to the point of obstructing reforms provided for in the newly ratified Constitution. Thus, Piero Calamandrei, one of Italy's foremost constitutional experts, could write that: 'Our revolution has succeeded in reaching only the first stage: that of the Constitution. Everything else still has to be done' (Cited in Flores, 1983: 58). DeGasperi exercized tight control over all his ministers and coalition partners, and the Christian Democratic party recognized him as its undisputed leader (Scoppola, 1977; Carrillo, 1965). As a consequence, all those major interest groups and organizations not aligned with the left willingly accepted the cues coming from the government arena (Basso, 1958).

The DC used its electoral triumph and absolute majority in Parliament to colonize the state apparatus and establish its domination over key ministries —i.e. those parts of the state apparatus that provided control over crucial social policies such as education, agriculture, police and finance that were also of fundamental importance for the organization of its political base. Thus, the Party's control of the Prime Minister and other Cabinet positions provided it with the opportunity of consolidating its ties with vital socio-economic forces—such as the Independent Farmers' Organization (Coldiretti), the Catholic Church, and Confindustria (the businessmen's association) (Baget Bozzo, 1977; Galli, 1978).

LaPalombara (1964) has described the pattern of relations developed by the DC to interact with key interest groups as systems of *clientela*—i.e. ones whereby an interest group becomes, in the eyes of the state bureaucracy, 'the natural expression and representative of a given social sector which, in turn, constitutes the natural target or reference point for the activity of the administrative agency—and *parentela*—i.e. essentially the existence of a 'close and integral relationship' between certain associational interest groups and the DC.

Control over the Ministry of Agriculture gave the DC full discretion in the management of the Federconsorzi[5] that were literally turned over to Paolo Bonomi's Coldiretti rather than the less politically reliable landowners' association (Confagricoltura). As a consequence, the Coldiretti became synonymous with the Christian Democratic Party in the rural areas of the country and became the major channel for policies and services to the agricultural sector (Calise, 1978).

The interests of the Church were served through the reaffirmation of educational policies and principles for the teaching of Catholic religious doctrine in the public schools by religious personnel selected by the Church (Ferrari, 1985; Prandi, 1968; Settembrini, 1964). The DC was more than happy to meet the needs of the Church since its support was crucial in terms of political organization, and since the parish system and Catholic Action (Poggi, 1967; Falconi, 1958) provided the organizational support for DC candidates until the end of the 1950s. And in 1948 the Catholic Workers Association (ACLI) served as the basis for the creation of a separate trade union movement (Confederation of Italian Trade Unions, CISL) under the tutelage of the DC (Candeloro, 1972).

With regard to the business community, DeGasperi had allocated to their political (Luigi Einaudi)[6] and organizational (Confindustria) representatives the responsibility for formulating government economic and fiscal policies. Apart from political motivations, this decision was also due, in part, to technical reasons—i.e. the economic affairs ministries (e.g. Treasury and Finance) did not have the technical expertise or facilities to follow developments in the economy and mould private entrepreneurs' investment and production decisions (Ganapini, 1983; Speroni, 1975). Consequently, the government's economic policies reflected the *laissez-faire* approach to the economy advocated by Confindustria. In the period between 1948 and 1958 'Confindustria was in charge of the governance of the economy, either directly, through its own staff, or, more often, indirectly, through political leaders and government officials who were very responsive to its views' (Martinelli, 1980: 72). In return, Confindustria and the business community threw their organizational weight and considerable influence in society behind the candidates of the Christian Democratic Party.

This system of interlocking relations among the state apparatus, interest groups and the Christian Democratic Party, combined with parliamentary rules that stifled any role by the opposition, allowed the executive branch of government a free reign in the formulation of policies that served the political interests of the dominant party. Thus, the major reforms of the 1950s were those that aided the groups associated with the DC, as follows:

- The 1950 agricultural reform law which distributed land to the peasants was a way of strengthening the Party's penetration of the rural areas, deflating the left's land occupation movement, and eroding the power of large landowners whose loyalty to the Party was suspect (Amato, 1979; Calice, 1979). In fact, in the 1952 and 1953 elections these forces transferred their support to the Monarchists and Neofascists but soon after they were once again re-absorbed by the DC.
- The Fund for the South (*Cassa per il Mezzogiorno*) represented the first massive use of public funds to finance the creation of a Christian Democratic political infrastructure (in addition to the public works infrastructure that was the official objective of the programme) in the South (Caciagli, 1977).
- The creation of ENI (National Hydrocarbon Agency) (Galli, 1976; Frankel, 1966; Votaw, 1964) advanced the interests of Enrico Mattei, AGIP (the national petroleum company), and an important faction within the Christian Democratic Party (the *Base*).
- The creation of the Ministry for State Share Holdings in 1956 found its *raison d'être* in the 1960s when, as part of the opening-to-the-left, the public sector in the economy expanded enormously and provided added organizational support to a wide range of DC Party factions (Scalfari & Turani, 1974).
- The consolidation of the secondary educational system in the early 1960s allowed the Party and Ministry of Education to recruit a large number of teachers, and made the Ministry the country's largest employer.

In addition, the reforms that the Party did not want to implement took a very long time to see the light of day, and when they did they were hardly recognizable. A case in point is the 1953 Scelba law on regional reform. The DeGasperi Government introduced two bills in 1948 in accordance with the transitional clauses of the Constitution on regional elections and the details of the structure of regional government. The first, which was implemented in December 1948, established the date for the regional elections on 30 October 1949. After a year, a new law moved the elections to the end of 1950, a deadline that disappeared without trace from the government's subsequent list of legislative commitments (Putman, Leonardi & Nanetti, 1985; D'Amico, 1982; Bassanini, 1976). The structure of regional government was debated and changed a number of times until January 1953 when it was implemented by a law which subsequently became known as the 'Scelba law', mentioned above, after DeGasperi's Minister of the Interior, Mario Scelba, who did not want to see regional governments created. The Scelba law attempted to ensure that, should the ordinary regions come into existence, they would constitute only a minor nuisance to the central administration—i.e. they would be completely dependent on the national authorities for their powers and resources (Bartole, 1984). However, the DC was not even ready to implement this kind of lukewarm regional reform. Nine years passed before another government undertook to propose any kind of legislative initiative on the matter. Only with the coming of the Centre–Left in 1963 did the problem of regional reform once again appear on the national political agenda.

It was not until the 1960s that the Christian Democratic Party's defence of the *status quo* and its stonewalling of reform were severely weakened (DiLalla, 1982). The reason for this change was that the economic boom of the 1950s had led to a significant differentiation of socio-economic forces. Big industry saw its dominance slowly eroding, and the public economic enterprises had developed their own concept of self-interest, which began to diverge from that expressed by Confindustria, the voice of the private sector. Thus, after the creation of ENI in 1956 and the Ministry for State Share Holdings in 1956, the public enterprises formed their own association, Intersind, in 1957, and broke away from Confindustria.

Significant changes were also discernible within the Catholic Church hierarchy, especially with the papacy of Pope John XXIII who significantly changed the direction of the Church's social doctrine[7] in addition to convening, in 1962, the Vatican Council. The combined impact of these events on the Church was to radically shift the direction of the pressure brought to bear on the DC by the Church on the matter of social change (Prandi, 1968). Added impetus to change was provided by the growth in the second half of the 1960s of evangelical groups of Catholics organized around local communities, referred to as *communità di base*, whose mission was the reinterpretation of the social and religious meaning of the Gospels.

Politically, the climate had also changed. In 1953, the DeGasperi Government had attempted to consolidate the centrist coalition's control of political power through the enactment of an electoral law providing a bonus for the majority party or coalition (labelled the 'swindle law' or *legge truffa* by the opposition), but the law was rejected by the voters (Ghini, 1975).[8] This forced the DC to search for acceptable coalition partners and considerably diminished the cohesiveness of government action. The dispute within the governing coalition lasted for ten years and was finally settled in December 1963 with the formation of the first Centre–left Government and the entry of the Socialists into the ruling coalition. The integration of the Socialist

Party into the Government meant that the DC had lost its prerogative in having the determining voice in the formulation of government policy (Tamburrano, 1971).

Apart from the expansion of the state economic sector and the country's Welfare State system, the Centre-Left also attempted to make headway in the areas of institutional reform—i.e. further implementation of the Constitution—and the management of government policies through the introduction of planning. The 1960s was thus a period of heightened expectation that significant advances would be made in the area of economic justice and social equality. In addition to the reform of the lower secondary education system, the Centre-Left was instrumental in creating a national system of day-care centres (Fadiga, 1974). But other issues of social reform—such as the creation of a national pension plan system and health system, the elimination of regionally and sexually-based differences in pay scales, the expansion of the university system—received sporadic attention and continued to languish in ministerial offices or parliamentary committees. It was only after the 1968-69 student and workers' movements had substantially increased the pressure for government action that these reforms were implemented.

The Centre-left Government ceased to function as a compact coalition by the end of the 1960s, especially after the attempt to create a unified Socialist Party collapsed in the summer of 1969, and the DC swung to the right in response to the pressure for reform from the student and workers' movements of 1968-69. The bombs that exploded in December 1969 in Rome and Milan signalled the beginning of a difficult time for the DC and the country. The struggle was engaged within the country between the forces of reaction and those of reform, but the Government was becoming increasingly paralysed by its clash with institutional and societal forces which no longer respected the traditional norms or procedures.

3.3. Parliament and the Diffusion of Power

For nearly three decades the Italian Parliament was not the crucial centre of power and decision-making in the political system. That role was assumed by the Government and the dominant political party, exploiting the systems of *clientela* and *parentela*. In many ways, policies were formulated by the bureaucracy and the interest groups that were given privileged access to public resources. During this period, Parliament served instead as the national public forum in which the ideological debate and polemics between the Government and the opposition were carried out. Under these conditions, Parliament had to content itself with being the site for the passage of the legislation necessary to authorize the distribution of public goods and services to sustain the systems of *clientela* and *parentela* put in place by the

DC. Thus, much of the legislative output of this period has been characterized as consisting of *leggine*, or specific group-orientated legislation designed to serve the interests of small groups in society rather than broad social needs (DiPalma, 1977).

The parliamentary norms[9] in existence between 1948 and 1971 gave the Presidents of the two Assemblies—the Chamber of Deputies and the Senate—powers to determine the agenda for parliamentary activity, to assign bills to standing committees, and to determine whether a bill could be enacted by the committee or referred to the floor for final passage.[10] Once a bill was in committee, however, it was the responsibility of the committee chairman to decide the scope and nature of the discussion on the bill and whether in fact the bill would ever come out of committee. The pre-1971 rules thus tended to concentrate power in the hands of a few representatives of the dominant party in the majority coalition, and they provided little opportunity for the opposition to exercise any role.

Given the DC's preponderant weight in the Government and majority coalition, the pre-1971 parliamentary rules ensured Party control over the entire political system. Until 1968, all the Presidents of the Chamber were Christian Democrats,[11] the President of the Senate had always been a member of the DC, and throughout the post-war period the DC had had the lion's share of the leadership posts in the standing committees. Thus, it was possible for the DC to pick and choose the arena that it preferred—Parliament, the Government, public agencies, or the political party organization—for the formulation of important decisions: such decisions were made by the Party rather than according to the formal parliamentary process. In other words, the Christian Democrats succeeded after 1948 in transforming their relative majority among the voters into a monopoly over institutional power.

Thus, through their control of both parliamentary and government posts, the Christian Democrats were able to undermine the principle of reciprocity, by negating what DiPalma (1977) has called the Government's right to govern based on an appropriate confrontation between the majority and minority within the parliamentary arena. The DC governed, instead, through its complex system of intersecting relations among the party organizations, state apparatus, interest groups, and social organizations. The DC started to transfer decisions out of the government sphere as a result of the 1953 electoral defeat which took away the party's absolute majority and undermined its dominant position in Parliament (Baget Bozzo, 1977). Important decisions were consequently transferred to arenas that the DC could be certain that it would dominate.

Through this transfer Christian Democratic leaders extracted power and important decisions from the official government institutions. However, the transfer also represented the first stage in the diffusion of power to other arenas—i.e. that *entificazione* ('agencification') of power a term coined by

Ricci (1977) to describe the transfer of decision-making to the newly-created public agencies and traditional bureaucratic structures. The result of the decision was to move power away from the formal political institutions to informal institutions—such as the party organization—and semi-public agencies that initially responded exclusively to DC Party directives—e.g. IRI (Institute for Industrial Reconstruction), ENI (National Hydrocarbon Agency), RAI-TV (Italian Radio and Television Agency), INA (National Insurance Agency), etc. (Nobis, 1955; Rossi, 1955).[12]

There was little that the opposition in Parliament could do to oppose this change in the locus of decisions. Rodotà (1977: 63) maintains that in the Italian political system there is the tendency to 'monopolize (or steal) certain types of information and prevent access to them by individuals and groups who institutionally, or on a *de facto* basis, are not originally privy to the information.' Thus, it has been quite difficult for ordinary Members of Parliament as well as journalists and ordinary citizens to gain access to information concerning government activities that the Government did not want to divulge. Until 1968, the public and the press were not allowed to follow the deliberation of parliamentary committees, and transcripts of the procedures were not readily available.

Prior to 1971, Parliament could only call the Government to account for its actions through the periodic questioning of Government representatives and the initiation of no-confidence resolutions. Parliament did not have the power to subpoena officials of the bureaucracy or public agencies to testify before its standing committees, and Parliament did not have the right to review the nominations of top public officials before they came into effect. All questions of policy and requests for information had to go through the Cabinet or the minister. Thus, if a parliamentarian was dissatisfied with a response, the only other recourse he had would be to initiate a vote of no-confidence against the entire government coalition. This procedure obviously tended to politicize all inquiries concerning information that the government did not want to divulge and made it practically impossible for Parliament to fulfill its function of overseeing and controlling the activities of Government and its handling of administrative matters.[13]

The shortcoming of the existing parliamentary rules had become quite evident by the beginning of the 1960s, and a debate on the reform of the system was one of the issues that received a significant amount of attention inside Parliament (i.e. a special committee to study changes in the parliamentary rules was created in the Chamber) and outside Parliament, in the form of studies (Sartori, 1963) during the first five years of the Centre-Left coalition. Changes in procedures were initiated in 1968. This was also the year in which the Socialist Sandro Pertini was elected President of the Chamber of Deputies.

It should also be remembered that in 1968 and 1969 society at large had achieved a watershed in the transformation of attitudes and expectations *vis-à-vis* the political system. Combined with the self-doubt that had already crept into Parliament, the mounting pressure for more responsive institutions had both a psychological and a political impact in returning Parliament to its central constitutional role in the political system—i.e. providing political direction and controlling the activities of Government. Between 1970 and 1971 significant pieces of legislation were passed that effectively diffused political power in two directions: (1) strengthening of Parliament as a centre for policy-making and control over administration and (2) reinforcement of other levels of government—e.g. regions and communes—and other social forces such as trade unions, interest groups, social rights groups and voluntary groups as agents for social change. The result was mounting pressure for the creation of an increasingly multi-faceted and pluralistic Welfare State in which power was distributed among diverse levels of government and shared by a greater range of political forces.

Based on the new 1971 parliamentary rules, powers formerly enjoyed by the assemblies' Presidents were transferred to the 'conference of parliamentary group leaders' (the *capigruppo*). The heads of the political parties in Parliament now met the President of each assembly and a representative of the Government to decide on a general three-month legislative programme and a precise calendar of activities for two-week periods. Decisions were then taken on a unanimous basis among the parliamentary group leaders. Thus, the 1971 rules promoted the acceptance of the principle of sharing decision-making responsibility and a rejection of one-party domination.

This arrangement for setting the parliamentary agenda brings up the question of the Government's role in setting the country's political agenda. Cassese (Ristuccia, 1977: 209) has maintained that the Government in Parliament does not exist: 'in Italy we have a unique situation, when the Government comes into Parliament it disappears'. Two reasons are given for this phenomenon: firstly, in presenting its budget, the Government does not submit a single budget to Parliament, but each ministry has to present its own budget to the appropriate parliamentary committee; secondly, the Minister Responsible for Relations with Parliament is a minister without portfolio, which means without a budget or staff, and therefore devoid of any support structure or influence in carrying out his duties.

The formulation of the parliamentary agenda, decisions on the referral of bills to standing committees, and the determination of whether a bill would be subject to enactment by the committee or by the whole house, had been taken out of the hands of the Government (and Christian Democratic party) and transferred to Parliament (and the party system as a whole). Already with some difficulties in the 1960s (but even more so in the 1970s) it became impossible for the DC to determine, on a unilateral basis, which issues Parliament could or could not discuss. Manzella (1977) has observed that, with the 1971 changes, Parliament was finally in a position to perform autonomously the important role of establishing the country's political objectives and formulating policies for the achievement of those objectives.

Furthermore, the 1971 regulations gavè Parliament the power to exercize a more effective control over government operations. Standing committees could now initiate 'informative investigations' to bring committee members and Parliament up to date on the status of particular problems. The investigatory process foresaw three stages: the collection of information from public and private sources; the initiation of hearings through which public officials as well as private citizens could be obliged to testify; and the formulation of a final document that could serve as the basis for legislative action by Parliament.

The most significant achievement of the 1971 rules (Manzella, 1977: 459) was the re-establishment of the primacy of the parliamentary system in creating a political consensus for the resolution of society's important problems:

> The final significance of the 1971 reform of the rules is, therefore, one of re-establishing the parliamentary regime as a whole by transferring to the parliamentary mechanism the role of negotiating between interest groups, attempts to elaborate political programs, the inspection of power centres already free from governmental control [and] the tasks of balancing and stabilizing the interests of the nation with political intiatives coming from the trade unions and the regions. In the final analysis [Parliament] is engaged in a difficult attempt to produce consensus for the benefit of the entire political system.

Thus, in the 1970s Parliament became more than an 'arena' for ideological clashes;[14] it emerged as an institution in which political decisions could be produced in response to demands originating in other parts of the political system. As a reaction to this new interpretation of its role as policy-maker, Parliament began to pass legislation that gave it the explicit task of monitoring, on a continuous basis, the implementation of the programmes by the government and bureaucracy—for example, the 1971 legislation creating full-time programmes (*scuola a tempo pieno*) at the elementary school level and the important legislation of 1975 (law 382) to complete the transfer of government powers to the regions.

Why did the Centre-left Government not succeed in passing significant reform policies in the 1960s? After all, the Government was stronger and more compact at that time, and it did not have to worry about opposition in Parliament. However, what was missing during most of the 1960s was a social movement in favour of major reforms. That gap was filled by the student movement of 1968 and the 'hot autumn' of 1969 that mobilized large sections of the working class into a potent pressure group in favour of reforms.

3.4. Changing Strategies of the Trade Unions

The labour unions in Italy have always been highly political in nature. During the Resistance, the unions had assumed a direct role in the fight against Fascism and had acted to prevent the sabotage of the country's industrial infrastructure by the retreating German armies. In June 1944, representatives of the Communists, Socialists and Christian Democrats signed the Pact of Rome creating a unified trade union movement—the Italian General Confederation of Labour (CGIL). But that unity was to succumb to the strains of the Cold War and party competition. The Catholic wing of the union split off in 1948 to form the Italian Confederation of Workers Union (CISL); in 1949, the Social Democratic and Republican components left the CGIL to create the Union of Italian Labour (UIL); and, in 1950, right-wing groups formed the Italian Confederation of National Workers Union (CISNAL). These schisms left the CGIL under the control of the Communist Party, with the Socialists relegated to a subordinate role, but the CGIL remained the country's largest trade union (Turone, 1981).

The splintering of the unified trade union movement, the setting-up of clearly politically aligned trade union organizations, and the politicization of union activities had two major effects. Firstly, the unions became subordinate to the political parties—i.e. the unions assumed the role of 'transmission belt' between the workers and party organizations. Secondly, there was an undermining of the capacity of the internal commissions (*commissioni interne*) to represent all of the workers on the shopfloor in relations with management and in formulating a unified stance on issues. As a consequence, the trade union movement's position in society was substantially weakened, and it was in no condition to hinder the restrictive economic policies advocated by Einaudi and implemented by the DC in 1947. The Einaudi-inspired policies eliminated the role of trade unions in the management of factories, reduced wages, increased unemployment, restricted credit, and revalued the lira as the means of achieving the modernization of the economy and shaking out inefficient firms.

During the 1950s, the unions fought more amongst themselves than against management, and, as a result, wages did not keep pace with increases in productivity: between 1950 and 1960 wage levels increased at rates much lower than the growth registered in the Gross Domestic Product, which was approximately 6 per cent annually (D'Antonio, 1973; Wiskermann, 1971; Hildebrand, 1965). The 1950s also witnessed a concerted effort on the part of business and government to break the back of the Communist CGIL through the firing, intimidation and isolation of union leaders and activists (Gianotti, 1979). As a consequence, the CGIL lost members. But so, too, did other unions. It has been argued (Barkan, 1984) that the coordinated attack on the CGIL weakened unions in general, by limiting their representative as well as bargaining roles on the shopfloor rather than limiting its impact on only one organization. Workers who left the CGIL, in fact, did not join the rival unions; they remained de-unionized.

The union movement started on the road back to social and political prominence as a result of both economic and social pressures. In 1959, the metal and mechanical workers unions (FIOM, FIM and UILM) belonging to the three confederations stuck together in support of the renegotiation of their national contract.[15] The purpose of the unified drive was to regain in wage increases the substantial growth in productivity experienced by the industry during the 1950s. One year later, a similar unity of action was forged among the unions representing the electromechanical workers. The high point of this mobilization was reached in 1962 when workers went out on strike in record numbers to demand higher salaries.

At the same time, events in the political sphere also served to bring the workers together on a commonly accepted political issue: the prevention of the neo-Fascist MSI party from joining the Christian Democrats in a government coalition in June 1960. The demonstrations and civil disorders sparked by the Tambroni Government brought the unions together in support of the Centre–left coalition formula advocated by the Socialists and other reform-orientated parties.

The impact of enhanced cooperation among the unions and the increased use of strikes to back wage demands resulted in a substantial upward movement of wages. Table 3.1 shows that between 1962 and 1964 wage increases were in the two-digit range and significantly above the rise in inflation and productivity. Salaries rose less sharply between 1965 and 1969, owing to the growing recession, but they did keep pace with both inflationary and productivity increases. After 1970, wage levels soared once again. The rise in wages, combined with the 1974 oil price increase, fuelled the inflationary spiral which rose to almost 20 per cent. At this point, however, the Italian working class was shielded from inflation through the national 'escalator clause' (*scala mobile*) which, on a quarterly basis, adjusted wage levels according to inflation (Lange, 1986).

Just as the student movement of 1968 was set in motion by the 1966 reform of the rules for entry into the university system,[16] the workers' movement of 1969 may be seen both as the final push to integrate the working class and its institutions into the political system and as the movement to increase wages and better working conditions. This strategy has been described as an 'attempt to combine the achievement of both trasformative, classist political objectives and of associational, defensive shopfloor objectives by acting simultaneously in the political and market arenas' (Lange, Ross & Vannicelli, 1982: 98).

However, the pursuit of these two goals required the trade unions to modify their internal organizations to eradicate the divisions of the past,

Table 3.1 Rates of inflation and increases in salary, 1961-1983 (%)

Year	Inflation	Salary increase	Difference Inflation – Salary	Increase in productivity*
1961	2.9	8.3	+5.4	8.0
1962	5.1	13.4	+8.3	7.4
1963	7.5	19.7	+12.2	7.3
1964	5.9	11.6	+5.7	2.9
1965	4.3	8.2	+3.9	5.4
1966	2.0	8.0	+6.0	7.7
1967	2.0	8.3	+6.3	5.9
1968	1.3	7.6	+6.3	6.7
1969	2.8	7.6	+4.8	5.6
1970	5.1	15.3	+10.2	5.2
1971	5.0	13.3	+8.3	1.9
1972	5.6	10.8	+5.2	4.2
1973	10.4	19.5	+9.1	6.2
1974	19.4	21.8	+2.4	2.5
1975	17.2	20.8	+3.6	-3.9
1976	16.5	21.0	+4.5	5.1
1977	18.1	21.5	+3.4	1.4
1978	12.4	16.1	+3.7	2.0
1979	15.5	17.9	+2.4	4.0
1980	21.1	22.5	+1.4	3.0
1981	18.7	21.9	+3.2	N.A.
1982	16.3	17.0	+0.7	N.A.
1983	15.0	15.9	+0.9	N.A.
1984	9.9	12.4	+2.5	N.A.

* Defined as increase in Gross Domestic Product per capita of work-force.

Source: Calculated by the author from data in ISTAT, *Le regioni in cifre, 1985*, Rome, ISTAT, 1985, pp. 144–6.

increase their capacity to mobilize large groups of workers, and expand their relations with alternative levels of government—city and provincial governments in addition to the nascent regional structures. There were also the difficulties posed by the decline in rank-and-file loyalty and competition from unofficial radical leaders. At the beginning of the 1970s there was a proliferation and intensification of relations between the trade unions and public institutions and, in particular, the local government institutions (Regalia, 1985).

At the national level the unions moved in four directions, to force their leaders to choose between political party and union activities; to create an overall unified trade union confederation in addition to merging their sectoral unions—e.g. metal or chemical workers into one union organization; to act in unison in all negotiations with individual employers as well as with their representative organization—i.e. Confindustria; and, finally, to develop a common programme of social and economic reforms to lobby Parliament and the Government. This national aspect of the trade union strategy remained strong until the mid-1970s when it was eclipsed by the entry of the Communist Party into the governing coalition.

At the local level, the unions needed to broaden and strengthen their organizational ties on the shopfloor, in the factory, and in relation to local and regional governments. For this purpose, the unions had to increase their membership base, recruit new delegates and leadership cadres, extend worker assemblies and internal commissions to factories where they were absent, and establish ties with local governments for the purpose of increasing their capacity to influence local decisions affecting their members. Such decisions included the establishment of day care centres, free public transportation during rush hours, the extension of local health services to the plant level, and housing programmes for workers.

With these adjustments at the national and local levels the trade union movement was transformed into a major social and political force in Italian affairs, and in the space of a few years it succeeded in changing the nature of labour-management relations in Italy. In addition to salary increases, the unions succeeded after 1969 in reducing the working week,[17] eliminating compulsory overtime,[18] reducing the differences between blue-collar and white-collar job classifications and salary levels (*inquadramento unico*), increasing the number of paid days off (eighteen) and paid holidays (four weeks), obtaining time-off to attend college,[19] increasing the role of the workers' councils in the determination of work schedules and assignments in the workplace, eliminating piece-work, raising unemployment benefits to 80 per cent of the previous wage, giving union activities greater freedom in pursuing their activities, and significantly expanding the provision of social services by local governments.

The institutionalization of the rights of the trade unions in the factory was achieved through the passage in Parliament of the Workers' Statute in 1970.[20] This legislation was long overdue since it was designed to fulfill the obligations of Article 39 of the Constitution which provided workers with the right to join and be represented by unions in the negotiation of salaries and working conditions. As a result, the Workers' Statute provided the unions with the right to take employers to court if they tried to obstruct the union's activity in factories with more than fifteen employees or farms with more than five employees. It also provided union representatives with time for union activities, the right to hold union meetings on company time, and the automatic deduction of union dues from workers' paychecks.

In contrast to the decline in legitimacy of the political parties, the unions represented much of the anti-status quo movement in that they operated on the basis of a pronounced sense of egalitarianism and the use of an assembly form of decision-making. In fact, all the new groups that surfaced during the 1968-69 period—students, dissident Catholics, neighbourhood groups—made use of the popular assembly as the instrument for the discussion of issues and the making of decisions. In the factory, the resurrection of militant workers' councils representing all of the workers was part of the general societal movement toward assembly forms of self-government (or *assemblearismo*).

The assembly represented, in organizational terms, the substitution of direct for representive forms of decision-making and the desire of the workers to minimize the delegation of powers. Regini (1980: 53) argues that the rebuilding of the trade union organization at the shop and plant level 'carried with it a decentralization of control over union activities in general, and of collective bargaining in particular.' This trend continued into the middle of the 1970s with the increase in the number of factory councils and shop delegates interacting with management, and the proliferation of ties with local government institutions, especially with the regions.

The initial contacts between the unions and the regions did not represent a relationship between equal partners. In the early 1970s, the unions were considered to be the most important interest group in society while the regions were being recognized from both an institutional as well as a public opinion point of view, with great difficulty. The regions took the initiative in seeking union support for their demands to devolve greater powers from the central government and in involving the unions in the formulation of regional economic/social policies in addition to participating in regional boards created for the implementation of local policies:

> Much more intense and systematic are the initiatives of the newly created regional governments which attempt to involve local interest groups and, especially, the trade unions in the formulation of initiatives in a number of social and economic policy areas. This gives rise to a more or less formal process of consultations and even to the practice of involving interest groups in mixed management boards created for the administration of services (transportation, education, health services, vocational education) or in supervisory committees (on prices, awarding of commercial licenses, on wholesale markets and fairs, etc.) [Regalia, 1985.]

The transformation of the workers' organizations in the factories and of their institutional role helped make them the symbol of the movement for change and reform that overwhelmed Italian society in the 1968-69 period. From 1970 onwards the trade union movement was in a position to affect all kinds of political decision in the country—i.e. at the national as well as local levels of government (Alberoni, 1979). There was substantial agreement among the unions that the mobilization of the working class had to be channelled beyond immediate collective bargaining objectives to ensure that the gains of the labour movement be distributed on a wider basis and not be used to fuel intra-class or inter-sector conflict or to cancel out the gains made in the 1969-70 period. And the strategy required the unions to press for their programme of reforms at both the national and local levels of government.

The reforms developed by the union movement in support of its political programme highlighted the need to rationalize private investment as well as public economic decision-making through the adoption of planning at the national and regional levels; the modernization of Italian administrative practices; the further decentralization of decision-making and administration of social and economic policies; the development and transformation of agricultural production in the South; the creation of a national health insurance system to cover all sectors of the population; the institution of a tax reform that would ease the tax burden for salaried employees; the construction of new housing; and the completion of educational reform.

A number of observers (Cella, 1979; Regini, 1980; Lange, Ross & Vannicelli, 1982) argue that the unions failed to achieve a full and immediate implementation of their legislative goals and that by 1975 the unions quickly turned back to more strictly economic issues. There are others (Treu *et al.*, 1979; Cammelli, 1982; Putnam, Leonardi & Nanetti, 1985; Regalia, 1985 and 1986), however, who argue that the results of the unions' reformist strategy were not a failure. The main result was, instead, a readjustment in strategy to ally themselves and to interact with new partners other than the Government—i.e. local and regional governments—in pursuit of union goals.

As a result of the 1975 and 1976 advances made by the Communist Party, the union reform programme was formally introduced into Parliament as part of the government programme worked out by the PCI and the other five parties—DC, PSI, PSDI, PRI and PLI—participating in the 'national solidarity coalition'. In the period between 1976 and 1979 a good deal of the original trade union reform programme was implemented. In this period we see the creation of the national health system, the programme of investments for agricultural modernization (*legge quadrifoglio*), the youth employment bill, the housing act (*equo canone*), the industrial reconversion act and other programmes at the national and local level that will be discussed in greater detail below. In addition, the unions had gained a considerable amount of credibility with local governments, especially in the regions where the Communists participated in the ruling coalition. Thus, even when their status as the all-powerful interest group began to fade during the second half of the 1970s, their partnership with local government—forged during the period of trade union ascendancy—provided them with an alternative arena and support for the pursuit of its immediate economic and social interests and political status.

The emergence of the PCI as the main proponent for reform in the period between 1976 and 1979 presented the unions with a dilemma (Lange, Ross & Vannicelli, 1982). On one hand, it made it appear that the trade union movement had become subordinate to the PCI because the Party became the main channel for the transmission of their demands to the national policy-making apparatus, and, on the other, by accepting the PCI leadership on these issues it put into question the political autonomy of the unions. The strains in the relationship of the unions with the PCI and among the various components of the trade union movement began to appear in earnest in 1978 when the unions accepted a policy of 'austerity' and self-restraint, which became popularly known as the 'EUR line' after the neighbourhood in Rome where the meeting to discuss the policy was held. A policy of austerity had been advocated a year earlier by the PCI Secretary, Enrico Berlinguer, and strongly supported by the CGIL, but the other two union federations were less enthusiastic.

The rift in the trade union movement continued to expand after the exit of the Communists from the governing coalition in 1979 and became a total split on the heels of the suspension of wage indexation by the Craxi Government in 1984 and the push for a referendum on the issue by the PCI (Lange, 1986). By 1985, the unions had run out of options in fulfilling their goals at the national level and had lost power *vis-à-vis* the rise in influence of the business community. The labour movement had to turn more and more to local government to find the political and economic support for its demands (Regalia, 1986). For this purpose, the unions have strengthened their regional organizations and placed more emphasis on the negotiation of local contracts; they have emphasized their participation in the formulation of local government policies toward unemployment and economic development; and they have confirmed their support for a greater role on the part of local and regional governments in determining policies and investment strategies for small and medium-sized industries and the artisan trades. This change in orientation by the trade union movement parallels and, in many ways, may be necessary to meet the challenge posed by the decentralization of industry, discussed in Chapter 2, which has accelerated during the last decade.

Thus, by 1985 Italy finds itself with both a diffused industrial structure as well as a trade union strategy and organization within an institutional and political context that is dramatically different from what the country experienced in the immediate post-war period. At that time, policy-making emphasized the element of continuity with past traditions and structures that permitted the bulk of the Italian state structure to smoothly make the transition between Fascism and Republicanism with the same administrators and legal system, even if the Constitution and the political elite had changed.

However, the economic growth of the 1950s and the social change of the 1960s brought about a diffusion of power through the creation of a pluralist society, and it was the dynamics of this pluralist society that were institutionalized in the diffusion of power to sub-national government institutions and social organizations that took place in the 1970s.

Notes

1. Cassese (Ristuccia, 1977: 206–7) maintains that this collective definition of Government that includes the Prime Minister *and* the Cabinet is a post-war development stipulated by the 1948 Constitution. In previous regimes—Fascism and Liberalism under Giolitti—the 'Government' meant the individual Prime Minister with his close advisors, who may or may not have been members of the Cabinet.
2. This was the first government that included representatives of the CLN parties. The previous government, headed by Badoglio (July 1943–June 1944) was composed of non-party 'technicians'.
3. Bonomi was Prime Minister from June 1944 to June 1945. He was replaced by Parri for six months. DeGasperi became head of Government on 10 December 1945 and remained in that post until 17 August 1953.
4. After leaving the Government, Giovanni Gronchi became President of the Christian Democratic Party group in the Constituent Assembly (1946–48), then President of the Chamber of Deputies (1948–55) and, finally, President of the Republic (1955–62).
5. The Federconsorzi are provincial structures set up under Fascism to organize the local agricultural *consorzi* (consortia) and set policies for them. LaPalombara (1964: 236) describes the function of the *consorzi* as field agencies for the Ministry of Agriculture to 'provide gasoline, fertilizer, and other agricultural raw materials at cut-rate prices; they have special arrangements for the sale and distribution of farm machinery; they can facilitate the obtaining of credit; they arrange to have crops stored, and so on.'
6. Einaudi, a Liberal, was elected as the first President of the Republic in 1948 and served until 1955. Prior to becoming President, he was head of the Bank of Italy (1945-48) and Minister of the Budget in DeGasperi's first centrist government (31 May 1947 to 23 May 1948).
7. The two fundamental encyclicals were *Pacem In Terris* and *Mater et Magistra*. For a discussion of this point, see Furlong, 1985; Kogan, 1983; DiLalla, 1982; Magister, 1979.
8. The results of the 1953 elections were taken by DeGasperi as a personal political defeat. He resigned as Prime Minister (he was replaced by Giovanni Pella) to dedicate himself to the task of consolidating the DC Party organization. At the Fifth DC Party Congress in Naples, DeGasperi's proposal to institutionalize the role of interest groups and notables was defeated (Leonardi, 1980).
9. The rules of the Senate were formulated *ex novo* in 1949 while the Chamber of Deputies made use of rules that were operative between 1900 and 1922—i.e. before Mussolini came to power (Longhi, 1978).

10. Italy is the only Western European country where bills can be passed into law in committee without going to the floor for a vote by the full assembly (Lowenberg & Patterson, 1978).
11. In addition to Gronchi, the other two Christian Democrats were Giovanni Leone and Brunetto Bucciarelli Ducci. Sandro Pertini became the first non-Christian Democrat to serve in the office. Since 1976 the President of the Chamber has been a Communist: Pietro Ingrao and Nilde Iotti.
12. One of the main political goals of the Centre-left coalition was to bring back into the sphere of Government (and Parliament) control over the bureaucracy and state economic agencies (Restifo, 1983). The expectation was that this goal could be realized through the institution of a rational form of economic planning (Amato, 1980).
13. Rodota' (1977) writes that this lack of transparency of government activity increased the likelihood of conflict and the overall fragmentation and irrationality of the system of government.
14. This also continued, especially after the entrance of the Radical party members in 1976 which saw Parliament precisely as an arena for the discussion of major issues and not as a legislative body concerned with the distribution of goods and services. See Teodori, Ignazi & Panebianco (1977).
15. From the beginning of the post-war period, both the trade unions and industry continued the pre-war tradition of formulating national contracts for workers. The CISL was the first major confederation to place emphasis on company-level bargaining, which became increasingly important in the 1960s.
16. Prior to 1966, only students graduating from lyceums could enter the university. That rule was changed to permit all students attending five-year upper secondary programs—i.e. permitting to enter the university students who had chosen to attend 'technical' and 'professional' upper secondary programs. See Merritt & Leonardi (1981).
17. The average number of hours worked per week declined from 39.91 in 1973 to 36.39 in 1983. In the metal-working industry, the working week was reduced in the same period from 40.01 to 35.88.
18. The amount of overtime hours worked was cut in half after 1974 to approximately 3 per cent of total hours worked—i.e. about one hour a week per worker.
19. This programme was instituted in 1973. Workers were entitled to take paid leaves of absence for 150 hours of education within the course of three years. The 150 hours could be used at any level of the educational system desired by the worker, and many used the leave to complete their elementary and secondary degrees.
20. On May Day 1970 the three trade union confederations celebrated the labour holiday together for the first time.

4 The Evolving Ideology: The Rationalization of Necessity

4.1. The Battle for Civil Rights

1968 proved to be a watershed in Italy's, as well as other Western countries', social and political history. The year witnessed an explosion of student protest that, during the following year, fuelled the break-out of worker unrest in the country's large industrial centres. Because of the large number of people that were eventually mobilized and the intellectual stimulus of the ideas being proposed, the events of 1968 and 1969 had a major impact on socio-economic relations and political culture in Italy. The student and workers' movements started within the ranks of small groups—for example, students protesting the inadequacy of university curricula and structures or automobile workers employed on the more dangerous parts of the assembly line. They quickly spread to the rest of society and served to mobilize demands and social groups that had remained dormant during the first two decades of the Italian Republic, into a broadly-based challenge to prevailing norms and procedures. Inglehart (1977) ascribes this kind of switch in the mass public's approach to elites and the policy-making process as a move from 'elite-directed'—petitioning the elites to make the change—to 'elite-challenging'—wanting to take the decisions into their own hands—orientations based on system level changes such as economic and technological developments, rising levels of education, expansion of mass communications, etc.

As discussed in Chapter 3, the socio-economic changes that swept over Italian society in the 1950s and 1960s had practically gone unnoticed by either the governing or opposition forces in the Italian political system. The resulting economic conflicts, regional imbalances and social tensions had, therefore, not been processed by the existing institutions into policies and programmes to meet the emerging needs. The list of problems that afflicted Italy in the 1960s was lengthy and included the housing shortage, the inadequacy of public services, the limited educational opportunities, the lack of channels for direct participation in decision-making, the generational gap in socio-economic expectations and needs, the obsolescence of existing traditions and cultural norms, and the growing irrelevance of the major ideologies. All came to a head in 1968-69. The student and workers movements proved to be the catalysts that ignited the society's concern over socio-economic issues that had been ignored for such a long time and also initiated the transition from a fragmented and polarized to a more open and participatory political system.

Of the new demands, the most threatening to social norms of the day proved to be those articulated by groups and social interests that had been awakened by the new cultural climate: women, youth, homosexuals, conscientious objectors, handicapped, homeless, elderly, separated couples, and others who had been relegated to increasingly contradictory traditional roles or who remained 'invisible' in society. The impact that these marginalized groups were to have on the political system was to significantly change the nature of the political agenda. Previous emphasis on bread-and-butter issues in the Italian political debate dealing with concrete economic problems —such as wages and working conditions, unemployment, economic development, distribution of credit, etc.—gave way to human development and quality of life issues that put emphasis on the parity of the sexes before the law as well as in the workplace, the right to divorce, the right of women to make decisions with regard to abortion, birth control, and their own economic future; the right to access public services without physical, political, economic or social impediments; and the right to live in a clean and healthy environment.

In the Italian political lexicon of the 1970s these demands became known as the struggle for civil rights or the implementation of the social agenda identified in the 1947 Constitution that had remained unfulfilled for over twenty years.[1] Thus, the battle for civil rights in Italy was not one involving a change in the Constitution but rather one of removing those legal and cultural barriers that had been built into the system by the previous Fascist and Liberal political regimes which were in clear contrast to the fundamental document of the Italian Republic and the expectations generated by the Resistance movement in the immediate post-war period.

Nevertheless, the struggle for the implementation of this social agenda was not devoid of conflict or controversy since it put in question two fundamental characteristics of Italian society and the growing ideological crisis that was afflicting Italy's two major political groupings: the Catholic and Marxist subcultures (Mannheimer & Sani, 1986: Sani, 1977, 1976 and 1975; Barnes, 1979). In both cases, the dominant elements in these two subcultures—the Vatican for one and the Communist party for the other—were, at the same time, the chief instigators as well as the main targets of criticism by the movements spawned in the 1968-69 period.

This chapter will look at how the ideologies of the two subcultures have changed and what impact the change has had on Italian political culture and social structure. The thesis that will be expounded here is that the two subcultures have adapted to an open, depolarized partisanship that makes the aggregation of interests across social and economic lines and the pursuit of social capitalist policies not just feasible but even a necessary ingredient in the setting of their respective political and economic agendas. The contours of the evolving ideological structure that characterize Italian society undermine the hegemony of the Catholic Church in social matters and the Marxist foundations of the Communist Party.

4.2. Adaptive Changes in the Catholic Subculture

At the end of World War II the Christian Democrats were badly split between the views of the party's elite and mass base. According to an internal party survey in preparation for the party congress and the vote on the issue at the 1946 party congress, a majority of the DC leadership supported the transition to a republican form of government while the Church remained cool to the idea of abolishing the monarchy.[2] Most Christian Democratic voters were more in tune with the Church than the party leadership and in 1946 cast their votes against the Republic. Christian Democratic leaders therefore found themselves in a situation in which their views on the new democratic political system were not fully congruent with those of the Church hierarchy or the mass of their electorate. This served to increase their anxiety over the implications, for the party and the government, of continued Church support and the less than favourable orientation toward the Republic expressed by the bulk of thier voters.

What motivated the Church to want to maintain the monarchy was the fear that the left would have the upper hand in the new Republic. After the institutional referendum, the Church's primary concern was with maintaining the position of privilege in society that it had gained through the Lateran Pacts and making sure that a government friendly to the Church came to power in Italy. The Church perceived the lay-leftist parties (from the Communists to the Republicans) as being inimical to its interests, and it wanted to ensure that Catholic political support would be concentrated in one rather than dispersed to a series of different political parties. It was in this context that the Church issued its edicts pressuring all Catholic politicians to adhere to the Christian Democratic Party, using the parish structure as the main mobilizing force to back the Christian Democrats in the 1946 and 1948 elections, and the excommunication in 1949 of Catholic members and voters of leftist parties.

The conflict generated between Alcide DeGasperi and Pope Pius XII by the 1952 '*Operazione Sturzo*'[3] and the fall in electoral support for the party in the 1953 elections drove home to the DC that it had to undertake a fundamental change in its political strategy. Firstly, it had to create its own autonomous political party structure so that the DC would no longer be subject to pressures from the Church hierarchy. In the early period of the Italian Republic, the Catholic Church had provided the main organizational and social support for the Christian Democratic Party, and the nature of the Church presence created concern among the Catholic trade unionists (e.g. Domenico Ravaioli and Achille Grandi) and other progressive elements in the party. They felt that the views expressed by the Church hierarchy under Pope Pius XII (who died in 1958) were not in line with democratic thinking, the political values of the post-war period, or the Italian Constitution.

Secondly, the DC felt it had to establish stronger ties with its voting base and undertake a campaign of persuasion in support of the existing political system (Leonardi & Wertman, 1988). Yet, the main points of reference for the Catholic subculture through the 1950s remained extra-political in nature. Catholics owed primary allegiance to the Pope, parish priests and Catholic social organizations, and they were still strongly committed to their religious practice. At the beginning of the 1960s, in their study of political culture in five nations, Almond and Verba made the observation that Italy represented an incongruency between political culture and political structure when it came to the lack of a 'civic culture' among the supporters of the Christian Democratic Party:

> Indeed, if we look at the social composition of the various groups of partisans, we find that in Italy the parochial partisans tend to be women, church attenders, and supporters of the Christian Democrats. Supporters of the left parties are more likely to be open partisans. [Almond & Verba, 1963: 116.]

An empirical study of the 1958 elections found that the Italian political culture was characterized by a surprisingly high level of sectarianism and intolerance that transformed every political disagreement into a clash between value systems (LaPalombara & Spreafico, 1963). Yet, as has been mentioned in Chapter 3, 1958 marked the beginning of a radical change within the Catholic Church with the election of Pope John XXIII who initiated the search for new ideals and a critical re-evaluation of past Church teachings and practices.

Looking at public opinion survey data covering the period between 1953 and 1977, it is evident that there was a decline in the parochial partisanship among Catholics. Data in Table 4.1 show that there was a gradual erosion of intolerance among the DC electorate measured by the increase in the percentage of DC voters who agreed with the view that one can, at the same time, be a good Catholic and a good Socialist or Communist. In 1977 up to 72 per cent of the respondents agreed with the statement that one could be a good Catholic and a good Socialist, as opposed to only 15 per cent in 1953. During the same period, views on the compatibility of Catholicism and the Communist Party rose from a mere 5 per cent in 1953 to 44 per cent in 1977. The data clearly demonstrate that Christian Democratic attitudes towards the

Socialist Party substantially increased during the 1960s (after the creation of the Centre-left coalition) and those *vis-à-vis* the Communists were favourably influenced once the PCI and DC started to cooperate in the government of national solidarity headed by Giulio Andreotti (1976-79).

Table 4.1 Views of the DC electorate on the compatibility of Catholicism and Marxism, 1953-1977

Percentage of respondents identifying themselves as Christian Democratic voters in agreement with the statement that one *can*, at the same time, be a good Catholic and a good Socialist or Communist.

	1953	1963	1970	1974	1976	1977
Good Socialist	15	43	68	61	60	72
Good Communist	5	16	27	27	28	44

Source: C. Guidorossi *Gli italiani e la politica*, Milan, Franco Angeli, 1984, pp. 230–41

Table 4.2 Levels of Church attendance among males and females, 1956–1985 (%)

	1956		1961		1976		1982		1985	
Level of Church attendance	M	F	M	F	M	F	M	F	M	F
Almost every Sunday or more	57	80	45	51	28	47	25	42	19	38
Sometimes or never	43	20	55	49	72	53	75	58	81	62

Source: Calculated by the author from data in G. Guidorossi *Gli italiani e la politica*, Milan, Franco Angeli, 1984, p. 243 and Istituto DOXA 1985.

The increase in the level of political tolerance among Christian Democrats paralleled the process of secularization which has significantly cut into the level and intensity of religious practice. As shown in Table 4.2, the level of regular attendance at religious services has declined sharply during the last thirty years, and the trend applied to both men and women. In 1956 an overwhelming majority of women (80 per cent) and more than half the men (57 per cent) attended Church regularly. Thirty years later that intensity of religious practice was only admitted to by a little more than one-third of the women (38 per cent) and 19 per cent of the men.

The dual process of secularization and growth of tolerance was paralleled by an increase in personal interest in and willingness to discuss politics with friends. Table 4.3 shows that between 1958 and 1981 the level of those expressing an interest in politics rose from 37 to 58 per cent and those who regularly discussed politics with friends almost doubled—rising from 32 per cent in 1958 to 62 per cent in 1980. Thus, the data suggest that significant changes took place in Italian political culture in the 1960s and 1970s which permitted society to consider issues on their own merit and not as part of a general socio-political *Weltanshauung* that had so much polarized political discourse and social relations in the 1950s.

Table 4.3 Levels of political interest and discussion among the Italian public, 1958–1981 (%)

	1958	1974	1981
'What is your level of interest in politics?'			
Strongly or somewhat interested	37	49	58
Not at all interested	62	49	42
Don't know	1	2	0
'How often do you discuss politics with your friends?'			
Often	32	37	62
Rarely	66	63	37
Don't know	2	0	1

Source: Calculated by the author from data in M. Weber, *Italia Paese europeo?*, Milan, Franco Angeli, 1986, pp. 147 and 152.

The growth in secularization of Italian society was also reflected in the growing difficulty in the domestic recruitment of priests and nuns into religious orders, the reduction in the willingness of the public to follow Church teachings on issues of personal conscience, and the change in behaviour on the part of practising Catholics and the Church hierarchy. In 1976 a group of well-known Catholic intellectuals was elected to Parliament as independents on Communist party lists and the Church did not excommunicate them. Enrico Berlinguer, the Communist Party Secretary, had a long and fruitful correspondence with members of the Catholic hierarchy in the 1970s on social and moral issues of mutual concern. Religion has declined as an important social cleavage in society, and it has become increasingly difficult for the Church to rally support around its traditional social values. The two most telling examples of the latter were the results of the 1974 divorce and 1981 abortion referenda that took the Church and public opinion, in general, by surprise, In 1974, 59 per cent of the electorate voted in support of the 1970 legislation legalizing divorce in Italy. Seven years later, 68 per cent expressed themselves in favour of maintaining the 1978 legislation on abortion. The growing difficulty faced by the Church in rallying a large following behind its positions was a clear signal that times had changed.

Thus, by the 1970s, the Church had lost its hegemonic position in being able to strongly influence, if not determine, Italian social policy. The Church's hegemony on social issues had been institutionalized by the Fascist regime through the signing of the Concordat with the Holy See in 1929 and the wholesale transfer of the provisions of the Concordat into the Italian Constitution in the post-war period (Ferrari, 1985). The Church's hegemonic role in post-war society was extended even further by DC-dominated governments that recognized on a *de facto* and even *de jure* basis the role played by Catholic social organizations in a wide variety of social and cultural areas—e.g. hospitals, day-care centres, care of the elderly and indigent, etc.—and the role of Catholic values in informing government social welfare policies.

Prior to the 1970s, the existing Italian legislation basically defined the roles of women as mothers, spouses and housewives (Birnbaum, 1986). The legal implications of these roles were that women did not have legal or economic parity with men in the workplace, nor were they protected from sexual harassment or dismissal from their job for maternity reasons. Married women were relegated to a state of economic dependency on their husbands in that they did not have equal rights to claim or own the economic resources or property produced by the marriage. Earnings and property belonged to the male head of the household. Worse still, a wife was legally responsible for debts incurred by her husband, but she did not have the right to make partial claim to earnings or property in case of abandonment. Dowries became the husband's property. Finally, according to the Fascist penal law (*Codice Rocco*), which had been retained in the post-war period, only the female was culpable of committing adultery, an act that was defined as a crime against the husband, but a male could not be tried for rape if the victim subsequently agreed to marry him or if the rape took place in wedlock.

The Constitution had established the parity of the sexes in articles 3 and 34,[4] but the dictates of the Constitution went ignored until the 1970s when a series of laws were passed to protect the woman's place in the family and in the workplace. The legislation concerning the woman's role in the workplace provided paid leave for maternity, ensured adequate wages and benefits for women employed in cottage industries, and mandated equal pay for women employed in the same jobs as men. The protection of the married woman's rights in the family was addressed by the 1975 family law (*diritto di famiglia*). The 1975 law established the full parity of the sexes in marriage in terms of claims to earnings and property accumulated during the marriage and gave the married woman the right to open a bank account and obtain credit without requiring the permission of her husband. The protection of the woman's civil rights and freedom was addressed by other laws guaranteeing access to family planning clinics and provision of birth control information and the legalization of abortion in addition to the repeal of the law against unfaithful wives and legislation permitting divorce. At the beginning of the 1980s, women's groups also began the struggle—referred to as 'the struggle against sexual violence'—to change the law on rape and adultery.

In the 1970s the Church did not object to the equalization of the economic status of women, but it did object to two issues emphasized by the feminist movement: divorce and abortion. According to the Church's view, these were issues for individual conscience and morality rather than issues of constitutional or individual right. The legal basis for this view had been established in the 1929 Concordat where the Italian State recognized that the Church had the right to decide matters concerning morality and the dissolution of marriages. In fact, when the Italian Parliament passed the divorce legislation in 1970 the Vatican attacked the law as a violation of the Concordat, the Constitution and long-established relations between the Holy See and the Italian State. The fundamental characteristics of the relation between Church and State were established in Article 7 of the Constitution which states that: 'The State and the Catholic Church are, each in its own realm, independent and sovereign. Their relationships are regulated by the Lateran Pacts. Modifications of the Pacts, which have been accepted by the two parties, do not require the procedure of constitutional amendment.' The position of the State was that divorce was a matter of civil law affecting the individual rights and liberties of citizens. These rights could not be abridged by the State nor could they be nullified as part of a bilateral agreement with a foreign power. Ferrari (1986: 135) states that in making its case protecting the divorce legislation, the State even used one of the basic documents that emerged from Vatican II, which argued that the individual should be 'immune from any restrictions' and that the Church could not impose its standards of religious morality and behaviour on members of other religions or non-believers. Therefore, the issue at hand in terms of the Church's traditional hegemony on social issues was—as it was phrased in the 1974 referendum on divorce by the pro-divorce forces and in 1981 by the pro-abortion forces—the need to recognize the existence of and tolerate different beliefs and needs in society.

4.3. Integrating the Communist Party

The events of 1968 also served to bring to head changes in the Marxist view of the socio-economic system. In the immediate post-war period, Italian Marxist intellectuals believed that the economic system of the country was about to enter a stage of 'maturation' that would lead to an increased concentration of capital in the hands of private oligopolies and the continued domination of agriculture by large holdings. Expectations were that the concentration of ownership would bring about economic stagnation, the lowering of wages, and increased unemployment; small and medium-sized industrial firms would experience severe strains, and social and economic development of the country—and of the southern regions in particular—would be severely hampered. Under these economic conditions the South would remain under the domination of the large agrarian interests (Bedeschi, 1983).

Marxists believed that these economic trends would inevitably lead to a polarization of society between the forces for progress and those seeking to maintain the status quo. Despite these pessimistic views of the economy, the Communist Party leaders believed that the advent of the Republic and ratification of the Constitution had represented a major watershed in the growth of democracy based on the role played by the masses in the Resistance and immediate post-war period. To them the defeat of Fascism and the creation of the Republic signified the destruction of the oppressive, centralized State structure and the end of the positions of privilege enjoyed by traditional socio-economic elites.

In this struggle for socio-economic change the Communists felt that the working class could count on the support of large strata of the 'productive' middle classes,[5] which had similar economic and social interests in limiting the power of the oligopolies and broadening opportunities. Palmiro Togliatti, Secretary of the PCI until 1964, observed in 1956 that: 'These shared interests present new opportunities to expand the working class system of alliances and expand the mass base in the pursuit of the democratic and socialist renewal of society.' (Partito Comunista Italiano, 1957: 904).

To promote the renewal of the society, the Communist Party advocated on the economic front the implementation of two structural reforms of the economy. The first was the reform in the ownership of large industrial firms through a policy of nationalization—i.e. expropriation of the oligopolies. The second was the distribution of land to the peasants through a policy of agrarian reform. Several years passed before the Christian Democratic Party became interested in a nationalization policy, but it had to respond quickly to the land-hunger that had reached crisis proportions in the rural areas by the end of 1949 (Renda, 1979; Calice, 1986). But, according to the Communists, the responses devised by the DC in 1950 with regard to land reform were not extensive enough. The extent of the 1950 land reform was considered unsatisfactory and designed more to meet the immediate political needs of the Christian Democratic Party rather than the overall needs of the economy. The PCI assumed the same position with regard to the nationalization of the electric power industry (ENEL) in 1963.

On the political front, the Communists felt that the working class had inherited the legacy of democracy abandoned by the bourgoisie in its headlong rush to join Fascism in the 1920s. This new definition of democracy was incarnated in the Constitution that for the first time recognized the role of the masses and the working class in assuming the leadership of society and the State. Consequently, the Communist Party declared that its support for the Constitution was not tactical in nature and not designed to give it short-term benefits, but was a strategic decision that had meaning over the long term:

> Therefore, the Communist party has declared from the beginning that it does not conceive the Republican Constitution as an expedient of bourgeois democracy to be used only until the armed insurrection to achieve the Socialist State has taken place, but instead it conceives of the Constitution as a unitary pact, freely adopted by a large majority of the Italian people as the basis for an organic development of national life over a long period of time [Partito Comunista Italiano, 1957: 912.]

The most common notion that has been used by observers of Italian affairs to evaluate the PCI is the model based on the Eastern European experience that equates Marxism with an 'anti-system' or 'anti-democratic' stance. Given that the government in Italy after the 1948 election was dominated by the Christian Democratic Party, the automatic equation was made between the DC and the government and between the government and the political system. Therefore, since the Communist and Socialist Parties took a strong stand against the DC and the policies formulated by the government (once they were thrown out of the government in 1947), the conclusion was that these parties were against the entire political system—i.e. Constitution, elections, multi-party system. etc.

This line of argument was historically belied by the left's overall political activity between the fall of Fascism in 1943 and the ratification of the Constitution in 1947. The left, in contrast to the Centre and Right, followed a strategy at both the elite and mass levels in support of the Republic and the Constitution. Examples are provided by the left's vote on the 1946 referendum,[6] and its strong opposition to subsequent attempts to change the nature of the Italian Constitution and political system, all the way from the *legge truffa* in 1953 to the *Grande Riforma* of 1985 (Pasquino, 1986).[7]

In the two decades after the war the party had significantly changed its nature and strategy with the creation of a mass party structure, the formulation of a broad social alliance strategy, and the support for republicanism, parliamentarianism, proportional representation, and a multi-party political system.[8] This broad strategy was put into question in 1947 with the ousting of the party from the government arena and the initiation of the cold war. But the ramifications of Khrushchev's secret speech and the outbreak of the Polish and Hungarian revolts in 1956 demonstrated the wisdom of Togliatti's '*svolta di Salerno*'. Changes that took place in the 1960s —i.e. the creation of the Centre-left and the structural reforms instituted by the new coalition—only served to reconfirm the need for the party to pursue its democratic, reformist goals and the depolarization of the political system.

By 1968, the PCI had made significant progress in distancing itself from the sectarian and anti-democratic notions held by some Marxists on the nature of the political system and the need for violent revolution. As a consequence, the party became one of the main targets for the 1968-69 protest movement—which accused the PCI of becoming a reformist party and abandoning the revolution—and of the 1974-78 terrorist campaign for cooperating with the Christian Democratic Party in government and pushing austerity among the working class in response to the stagflation of the 1970s. The impact of the post-1968 events and the increased demand from society for concrete policies to resolve pressing socio-economic problems served to accelerate the PCI's basically reformist approach to policies and its disengagement from traditional ideological positions with regard to the Soviet Union and Eastern bloc countries and Marxist–Leninist concepts such as democratic centralism and dictatorship of the proletariat.

On the ideological front, the PCI's rationalization of the political necessity to change its theoretical views took the form of Enrico Berlinguer's 1974 'historic compromise' proposal. Berlinguer stated that only through a return to the initial post-war strategy of creating a system of political alliances among popular forces could the left extend its influence beyond its immediate political sphere and begin to penetrate the diverse socio-economic groups essential to the survival of the democratic system. Stability could only be guaranteed through the pursuit of a strategy of broad social alliances capable of involving larger sectors of the public across class lines for the pursuit of common goals. Fifty-one per cent of the vote, therefore, was not a sufficient guarantee that the rules of the democratic game would be respected by the opposition. The struggle for the reform of the State had to be carried out in such a manner that it would not drive center and right together:

> the unity of the workers' parties and leftist forces is not a sufficient condition in guaranteeing the defense and progress of democracy where this unity is opposed by a bloc of parties that goes from the centre to the extreme right. The central political problem in Italy is, and remains more than ever, precisely that of avoiding a stable and organic fusion between centre and right, a large clerical-fascist type of front, and being able instead to shift the political and social forces that are located in the centre toward coherently democratic positions [Valenza, 1975: 26-7.]

One way of ensuring that the Christian Democrats and the small, lay centrist parties would move towards the left rather than to the right was to re-establish the post-war tripartite agreement that had united Communists, Socialists and Christian Democrats in the struggle against Fascism, the creation of the Republic, and the ratification of the Constitution. Such a movement would have both the mass support and the political muscle to push through the reforms of the socio-economic and administrative system demanded by the public. For this approach to be successful, the PCI and the rest of the left had to reinforce and consolidate the broad system of alliances with the Catholic world, business and the middle classes, and work together through political institutions to bring about change. The ramifications of this collaboration were immediately evident in the passage of watershed legislation on, for example, regional decentralization, the family, neighbourhood government, the national health system, etc. and the allocation to Communists of important positions in Parliament.

These events and trends had a significant impact on public perceptions of the Communist Party. After 1970 there was a considerable decrease in the number of people who conceived of an eventual PCI role in government as a negative development. In an analysis of the change in public attitudes towards the Communist Party, Guidorossi (1983: 111) concludes that:

> With the transition from 1967 to 1974—and then in an accelerated manner—the Communists benefited from an increasing belief that they had a number of good proposals, to the point that by 1976 they represented the party that scored the highest on all three of these indicators.

Changes along the same lines towards greater legitimacy of the PCI as an integral part of the democratic political system were also evident in the decline in partisan antagonisms towards the PCI as reported by DC voters. In the 1970s the level of sympathy generated by the PCI among DC voters doubled and the same took place among identifiers with other centrist and right-wing parties. In addition to the party's growing moderation on issues and greater attention towards its public image, there has been a significant depolarization of the Italian political system with regard to previous stands taken by the Communist and Socialist Parties. Table 4.4. shows that the average scores attributed by voters to the position of the PCI and PSI have significantly decreased in the period between 1968 and 1983. While the two major parties of the Centre (DC) and Right (MSI-DN) have remained stable, the mass perceptions of the Communist and Socialist Parties have moved towards the centre, respectively, by 13.2 and 10.2 points on the scale.

A longitudinal study of regional councillors between 1970 and 1981 showed that a parallel shift in views concerning the ideological positioning of the PCI has also taken place at the elite level, both in terms of positioning on the left-right scale as well as attitudes towards specific socio-economic issues,

Table 4.4 Mean scores on left–right spectrum* for the four major parties, 1968–1983

	PCI	PSI	DC	MSI-DN
1968	15.8	31.1**	55.0	76.7
1972	20	33	56	83
1973	18	32	56	87
1975	25	37	59	87
1982	24.4	36.8	57.6	84.7
1983	29.0	41.3	59.2	82.3

* The scores go from 0 on the extreme left to 100 on the extreme right.
** In 1968 the PSI and PSDI were united in the PSU. The score in the table refers to this latter party (that is, it represents a combination of the PSI with the more moderate PDSI).

Source: G. Guidorossi, *Gli italiani e la politica*, Milan, Franco Angeli, 1984, p. 107 and DOXA *Sole-24 Ore* 1983 survey.

such as views on capitalism and nationalization (Putnam, Leonardi & Nanetti, 1985). In 1970 there was complete agreement among the Communists that capitalism represented a threat to Italy. Eleven years later the level of agreement decreased to 20 per cent. Among the Socialists the level of agreement between 1970 and 1981 dropped from 75 to 5 per cent. With regard to nationalization, the views among the two leftist parties went from complete agreement in 1970 that the country's large industrial enterprises should be nationalized to that position being supported eleven years later by only 39 per cent of the Communists and 24 per cent of the Socialists (Putnam, 1986). These changes in attitude on key economic issues show that the Communist Party has come a long way since the end of World War II, but in the process it has not changed its support for the political system that emerged in the aftermath of the 1946 institutional referendum and the 1947 passage of the Constitution. During the course of these last forty years, the PCI has assumed an increasingly important role as an indispensable participant in the resolution of the society's problems and in keeping the political system responsive to the evolution of social and economic needs.

Notes

1. The social agenda outlined in the Constitution consisted of: equality of the sexes before the law and the participation of workers in the determination of the political, economic and social policies of the country (Art. 3); the decentralization of the administrative apparatus (Art. 5); free and obligatory elementary and lower secondary education (Art. 34); parity of the sexes in the workplace (Art.

37); the right of the handicapped to a livelihood, education and vocational training (Art. 38); limits on the ownership of agricultural land (Art. 44); the promotion of the cooperative movement (Art. 45); and the right of workers to participate in the management of industry (Art. 46).

2. On the eve of the referendum, Pope Pius XII described the choice before the citizens as one between those who had championed a Christian civilization and those who were out to destroy it (Magister, 1979: 65).
3. This was the request by the Pope that the Christian Democrats align themselves with the MSI and Monarchists in an attempt to prevent the parties of the lay and Marxist left from winning the Rome communal elections. DeGasperi rejected the Pope's request in fear that the move would split the party along conservative and progressive lines.
4. Article 3 established that 'All citizens have equal social dignity and are equal before the law, without distinction of sex, race, language, religion, political opinion and social condition', and Article 37: 'The working woman has the same rights and, for equal work, receives the same compensation as the working man. The conditions of labour must permit the fulfillment of her essential function in the family and assure to mother and child appropriate special protection.'
5. These were defined as farmers, owners of small and medium-sized firms, shopkeepers, artisans, etc.
6. The referendum was held to determine whether the country would make the transition from a centralized monarchy to a constitutional republic. The results showed that there was a clear correlation at the mass level between support for the left and a vote for the Republic. The same could not be said for support for the Christian Democratic Party.
7. The view that the PCI has been a status quo party when it comes to the political system but a reformist orientated party when it comes to social and economic issues was first cogently argued by Putnam (1975).
8. These positions were part of the re-formulation of the PCI political strategy undertaken by Togliatti which is referred to as the *svolta di Salerno* of 1943.

5 Decentralization of Decision-Making: New Political Actors

5.1. Institutional Decentralization as an Adaptive Response

Through the adoption of a conception of politics and inter-governmental relations as an open game (Putnam, Leonardi & Nanetti, 1985) played according to rules that can be changed by the players on the basis of short-term results and acquisition of new ideas and skills, one can begin to understand the interconnection between economic decentralization and institutional decentralization in the Italian context. Inside this interpretative framework exist players with different capacities to forge alliances and garner support, and who show diverse abilities to change the pace of the game and impose their style of play on the other players. It is in this sense that, in the Italian case, one finds the most creative political 'players' located not within the institutions but within civil society and the economy. This is, not surprisingly, the type of relationship between civil society and political institutions foreseen by the Italian Constitution.

The Italian Constitution has two fundamental characteristics. The first characteristic is *flexibility* in allocating decision-making power. Constitutionally speaking, decision-making in Italy is centred on Parliament. However, contrary to the situation that exists in other countries in Western Europe, the Italian parliamentarian is, to a certain extent, free to conduct his activities without being institutionally or politically subject to the control of the Government or even to his parliamentary party group. The individual MP's freedom of manoeuvre is buttressed by a series of structural features of the political system including:

- parliamentary rules, such as the secret ballot, that permit the evasion of party discipline and the mobilization of individual bases of support which may be separate and distinct from those mobilized by the party;
- the use of preference votes in elections to determine the assignment of seats in multi-member electoral districts, thereby making each MP responsible for the aggregation of his own basis for support; and
- the existence of a multi-party system that has never produced a party

with an absolute majority of the votes, thereby maintaining the political game, both within Government and Parliament, fluid.

The impact of these three factors has made it difficult for the Italian parliamentary game to be transformed in the adversarial relationship between Government and Opposition found in the British, American, West German and French systems. There have been numerous cases in Italian political history since World War II when it was difficult to find the Government or clearly to distinguish the Opposition. In practical terms, this has meant that Government legislative proposals have had great difficulty in navigating a clear course through Parliament without having to accept amendments and reformulations of the initial legislation proposed by representatives of the Opposition and even by members of the coalition parties. In Parliament the governing coalition faces the opposition parties on a basis of parity. Government proposals do not have privileged treatment, nor can they be made immune from modification as a part of the parliamentary deliberative process. As a result, Government has recently preferred to fall back on the expedient of ruling through government decrees rather than through legislation (Della Sala, 1987).

The reason for this state of affairs is that the political system created by the Constitution provides positive incentives for constant coalition building outside of the formal arrangements that bind some parties into governing coalitions and define others as members of the Opposition at the national or other levels of the political system. Thus, the important criterion for success in the Italian system is the gaining of position or leverage *vis-à-vis* other actors rather than total victory over them. Winners never become all-powerful, and losers are never powerless. Therefore, there is a constant need to manoeuvre for position, adapt to changing socio-economic conditions, and co-opt new political actors.

The fluidity of political relations has also been encouraged by the existence of separate levels of government based on a long tradition of autonomous and separate elections. The extensive system of local governments—i.e. 20 regional, 96 provincial and 8,010 communal governments—has multiplied the number of arenas where the political game of positioning can be carried out, and, not surprisingly, it has permitted the proliferation of diverse governing coalitions. In the 1980s, as before, it is not uncommon to find parties that are on opposite sides at the national level to be cooperating in local governments. This is the case with regard to the Communists and the Socialists coming together to form leftist juntas and Communists and Christian Democrats governing together in communal juntas—a fairly common occurence in small cities.

The second charateristic of the Italian Constitution is *multiple access points* to the decision-making apparatus. It allows for strategies of change and innovation in the rules of the game to begin from outside the institutions and, subsequently, to gain entry into the institutional order. In other words, initiatives for change in the decision-making rules often originate in civil society and then move towards the political institutions. The implication is that institutional reforms in Italy are not produced spontaneously by the institutions themselves or by technocrats working to implement a pre-determined, formal model of society (Pasquino, 1986). Instead, the inverse is usually the case. Political reforms normally take off from alternatives and concrete experiences which already exist in society. The political implications of this incremental approach to change is that legislative reforms are a way for the political institutions to catch up with reality—i.e. they codify and regulate that which already exists in society rather than create a completely new and unexperimented political innovation.

It is from this perspective that one begins to understand the trajectory of the debate surrounding, for example, the definition of area-wide planning districts and the new role of the province, which will be discussed below. While this strategy of institutional change has the limits associated with incrementalism, on balance it remains proactive rather than reactive. It provides the system with a substantial potential for institutional innovation. The system's proven capacity to respond to societal pressures offers two main political advantages. While, on one hand, the institutions do change with the times there is, on the other hand, a maximization of institutional continuity. The Italian system has consistently avoided sudden institutional breaks with the past or the generation of traumatic social costs.[1]

The key to an understanding of the relationship between economic decentralization and institutional decentralization in Italy is that of *institutional response*. This world of decentralized production has found and continues to find its own institutions. It is a reality so diversified and dynamic that it requires the existence of 'diffused forms of government' (CENSIS, 1983: 646). From a political-institutional perspective it stimulates the experimentation with institutional forms that are responsive to its own exigencies. The conclusion that we must come to is that institutional decentralization was not a chance occurrence. The politics of the 1970s have been characterized by a constant series of initiatives assumed by private-social forces and the parallel, if delayed, response by institutional players such as Parliament and other levels of government to these stimuli.

From this perspective the creation of the fifteen 'ordinary' regions[2] in 1970 was not merely the formal completion of the constitutional design but, above all, an institutional response to the demand to shake off what had become the paralysing grip of a *de facto* centralized state. The regions would accomplish this goal by eliminating the State's monopoly in the management of expanded social policies, responding to the demand for participation by diverse socio-economic groups in the determination of economic policies, and overcoming the contradictions and territorial and social inequalities created by the past system of centralized control of economic development.

The creation of the regions increased the expectation in some quarters that the new sub-national level of government would become the motor for radical social change (Allum, 1973: 236) and swiftly break the mould of the old system. In this manner the regional reform was seen by a number of Italian intellectuals as the first step in a cathartic change in the State, society and economy.[3] They could not have been more wrong. Nor was it correct to assume that regional change would *automatically* bring about other institutional changes, such as neighbourhood government. As had been the case with the regions, these other reform measures needed to mobilize their own political and social clientele and induce their own legislative policy process in order to come to fruition. No single representative institution in Italy is in a position to undertake reforms for groups that are not organized to bargain and coalesce with others or have the ability to make their views felt by policy-makers.[4]

Even though it became fashionable among Italian observers at the end of the 1970s to be pessimistic at the overall impact of the institutional reforms introduced in the 1970s, outside observers (Hellman, 1987; Sassoon, 1986) have clearly articulated how the institutional and social reforms generated in the 1960s and 1970s have substantially changed the nature and process of Italian society. A more objective and appropriate view of the dynamic of legislative reform in Italy requires that we approach institutional change from a dynamic perspective, that is as responses which need constant updating as they in turn generate new expectations and new political demands. From this perspective reforms can be seen for what they are: *processes* which must be analysed using relative criteria and whose nature is iterative and, therefore, produces change on a gradual basis. Five criteria will be used to analyse the processes of institutional decentralization:

- *synchronization* between social demand and institutional response—i.e. whether the demand is followed by a corresponding response or if, vice versa, the response changes the direction of the demand;
- *graduality* of the response—i.e. the speed with which a concrete response is formulated in reaction to the social demand;
- *continuity* of response—i.e. how long the response lasts or, stated in another manner, how long the response proceeds in the same direction of the demand;
- *impact* produced by the institutional response—i.e. the specific effect it has on changing the society; and
- *feedback*—i.e. the formulation of a new demand produced by the institutional impact and which is, once again, directed toward the institutions.

What we have articulated is an iterative process in which the two components, the social-economic and the institutional, reinforce each other. In this chapter we will use this conceptual framework and these criteria to analyse the creation and development since 1970 of two new levels of government—i.e. the region and the neighbourhood—and the debate concerning the restructuring of two levels—i.e. commune and province—which have been the traditional forms of local government. The latter debate has included experimentation with area-wide planning districts which have been conceived as a component in the management of economic and social policy-making.

5.2 The Creation of Regional Governments

The long period of incubation, 1947–1970, required by the regional reform coincided with the years of rapid post-war growth. Its protagonist was a society quite heterogeneous in terms of socio-economic differences. At the same time, it was a society with a small number of elites whose economic and political interests were served well by centralized institutional decision-making. In those early years, the most effective argument against the creation of the regions was their cost and potentially negative political consequences. The corollary argument was that it was more important to use the nation's scarce resources in the economic and social reconstruction programmes upon which the Government had embarked.

The cost argument was strongly defended by the conservative interests which produced the centrist national coalitions throughout the 1950s and stressed the need for continued central control over the management of the economic incentives in favour of large private and public industrial enterprises. In this regard, the regions would have been superfluous. They could not be expected to determine incentive policies for large industry which had become in the immediate post-war period the centrepiece in the formulation of the country's programme for economic development. The choice in favour of such economic policies demanded a strong centre (Bagnasco, 1977; Salvati, 1982). Yet, the demand for decentralized control over economic decisions was not forthcoming from the trade unions, which at the time were on the defensive and concerned with expanding their membership and increasing their ability to bargain with employers over the determination of working conditions and salary scales.[5] Nor was there a demand for the creation of regional political institutions originating from the mass of unorganized and unpoliticized southern immigrants who were flooding into Italy's large northern industrialized cities. These demands had to wait for the political events and economic and social changes of the 1960s.

To analyse the dynamics of regional decentralization, reference will be made to Table 5.1 which summarizes its evolution by making use of the criteria outlined above. The legislation creating the regions, proposed by the Government in 1968, represented a moment of strong synchronization with the social demand. The regions were seen as institutions capable of bringing power closer to the people and expanding the opportunity for popular participation in decision-making and administration. Nevertheless, the legislation creating the regions greatly limited regional autonomy. The law conceived the creation of the regions as a point of arrival (rather than departure) for regional decentralization and excluded any future development in the process. The Government's perspective was codified in the enabling decrees (*decreti delegati*) issued two years after the holding of the 1970 regional elections.

From the beginning, the regions reacted against this limited conception of their powers by giving themselves statutes (or regional constitutions) that were quite ambitious. Already in 1970 they had initiated legal battles against the state to claim greater powers of initiative and coordination in areas in which they felt they properly had primary legislative responsibility. The restrictions contained in the 1972 decrees and the delay in implementing them limited the impact that the region, as an institution, had on society during those initial years, but the strong symbolic presence of the region was highlighted by the promotion of the principles of citizen participation and of the role in planning advocated in every regional statute. While the decrees of 1972 succeeded in transferring to the regions fragmented powers which consisted, in large part, of residual activities cast aside by the ministries[6] and maintained for the ministries the more important policy matters, there was a growing societal demand to obtain for the regions more substantive and comprehensive powers.

The second period, which has been labelled 'the mobilization of the regionalist front' (Leonardi, Nanetti & Putnam, 1987), was characterized by a strong synchronization between the social demand that the regions should become more important political institutions and the institutional developments which occured. It was the period that saw the Communists enjoying a substantial increase in electoral support and role in the formulation of government policies. Communist support was of particular importance in the passage of major decentralization legislation, which began with Law 382 in 1975, providing for a massive transfer of policy-making responsibility to the regions. Law 382 set up the mechanism that in 1977 produced the 616 decrees which institutionalized the regions as real centres of policy-making.

These legislative changes mandated by Parliament reinforced the view that there should be continuity in the increase of the region's powers to develop policies. During these years, the regions were very active in formulating legislative initiatives that in many instances anticipated the decrees and

Table 5.1 The process of regional decentralization as institutional response

Analytical criteria	1968–1972	1973–1977	1978–1983	1984–
Synchronization	Strong Basic legislation	Strong Forward-looking legislation	Weak Centralizing legislation by State	Moderate Decline of centralizing legislation
Graduality	slow Movement towards first decrees	Accelerated Greater economic and social powers	Slow Lack of framework legislation	Slow Lack of framework legislation
Continuity	Blocked Law as point of arrival	Supported Prospects of greater powers	Blocked Impasse on area-wide planning district	Supported Debate on area-wide planning district and delegation of powers
Impact	Moderate Restrictions on regional activities	Strong Activism by many regions	Strong Diffusion and specificity	Strong Diffusion and specificity
Feedback	Demand for increased powers	Demand for State action	Consolidation of new powers	Definition of promotional role in development

transfer of powers from the State or preempted national framework legislation—for example, in the areas of the preservation of historic centres and delivery of health and hospital care services.

In the subsequent 1978–83 period there was a decrease in the synchronization, given the continued diversification of the socio-economic fabric and the requests for decisive and multiple regional intervention that it posed. What brought about the change was the trend displayed by the State towards intervening in a centralizing manner, almost as a means of counterbalancing the powers that it had just transferred to the regions. The tendency was clear both in terms of budgetary arrangements, where the amount of State funds not earmarked for specific policy areas decreased, as well as in the legislative arena where the State intervened with detailed and binding legislation restricting the region's autonomy in the areas, for example, of agriculture, industrial reconversion and housing.

At the same time, the absence of the State in terms of framework legislation called for by the 616 decrees slowed down the process of decentralization which lost some of its continuity and force, expecially with regard to the identification of the intermediate level of government—i.e. between the region and the communes—that was supposed to assume the responsibility for area-wide social and economic planning. Nevertheless, the overall impact of regional policy-making became stronger. Regional activity was extended to new areas of policy and, as will be seen in Chapter 6, was forced to confront new problems. Also, the impact of the region's actions became more specific in terms of their territorial and sectorial incidence. This meant that while a region's action acquired total geographical coverage and influenced a wide variety of interests, it also tended to differentiate itself from that of other regions. It is in this manner that the regional institution has consolidated itself by directly linking its activities with the specific social and economic interests that are active within its territorial confines.

During the last period presented in Table 5.1, there is a moderation of the centralizing trend by the State, a renewed interest at all levels in finding solutions to the problem of the intermediate level planning body while there is also confirmation of further progress towards decentralization with the delegation of regional powers to local governments (*deleghe*). In addition, the demand from society grows in favour of a stronger regional role in the promotion of the new development model of diffused growth. Thus, the cycle had reached the point of demonstrating the direct linkage between economic decentralization and institutional decentralization.

5.3. The Search for the Area-Wide Planning Body

In Italy, the adoption of national planning as the method of governing was discussed at length in the 1960s. The debate had articulated national planning primarily in terms of economic development goals, but economic planning was never implemented. At the beginning of the 1970s the regions took over the general concept of planning and, with it, tried to define a new approach to decision-making for themselves. The regional statutes identified planning as the method of government through which the region could develop its central role in the promotion of economic development and, at the same time, decrease the intra-regional territorial imbalances that had grown so prominent during the post war period of uncontrolled economic growth.

The regional statutes adopted the notion of planning as a *process* rather than as the formulation of a plan, which had been the common view prior to 1970. Planning as a process was to begin with the identification of problems, proceed past the selection of priorities and choice of strategies based on available resources, and arrive at a redefinition of the problems once action had taken place and its impact had been evaluated. The regions' commitment to pursue the planning process outlined in the statutes was a politically important one, even if in each case the commitment was just the point of departure. The initial commitment had to be operationalized through subsequent legislation and administrative action. During the course of the first legislature (1970–75), none of the regions succeeded in implementing economic or territorial planning. The experience with the area-wide planning districts (*comprensori di pianificazione*) was indicative of the problems that the regions faced in trying to implement their newly formulated conception of planning.

While a number of regions approved concept legislation creating area-wide planning districts and identifying their functions, the legislation often failed to define the districts' geographical boundaries, which had the *de facto* impact of delaying the implementation of the districts. This position was symptomatic of the political nature of the debate surrounding the choice of the criteria to be used in delineating district boundaries. For example, whether or not a planning district was to be centred on a major commune, or to what extent political homogeneity ought to be considered in the determination of the 'homogenous' area for a district. The difficulty was compounded by the lack of methodological clarity on how to apply the chosen criteria. The obstacles faced in the operationalization of regional planning were confirmed in the responses to interviews conducted in 1976 with a national sample of regional councillors where the interviewees stated that, while the need for planning was widely accepted, it had proved difficult to articulate and it had not yet been implemented in any region (Putnam, Leonardi & Nanetti, 1985).

During the course of the second legislature (1975-80), the attempts to operationalize planning as a comprehensive method of government continued at the level of political debate and studies but also began at the level of actual experimentation. The second legislature saw the formulation of the first comprehensive studies on the methodologies to be used in preparing area-wide, economic and territorial plans in a number of regions. Also, the time seemed to be ripe for the abolition of the province, which was increasingly viewed as a superfluous body with few, unimportant functions (INU, 1981; Cerase *et al.*, 1983). By 1980 area-wide planning districts were created in eleven out of fifteen ordinary regions. In seven regions the boundaries and composition of the districts were clearly delineated by regional legislation and members were appointed to their decision-making committees so that they could commence operation.

The concept of the area-wide planning districts first originated in the form of the Mountain Community (*Communità Montana*), conceived in 1971 by national legislation (Law 1102). The 1971 legislation required the regions to identify and empower corsortia of communes located in mountain areas for the purpose of promoting socio-economic development through the multi-purpose planning of their resources. Law 1102 stipulated that Mountain Communities had to correspond to 'homogeneous areas' and that the regions had to delineate their functions and organizational structures.

Undoubtedly, the state financing that was provided on an annual basis for the consortia of mountain communes has helped to spur their continued growth and, in a number of cases, stabilized their population base. In addition, the availability of autonomous budgets and powers were important elements in helping the Mountain Communities to increase their legitimacy in the eyes of their citizens, promote their leadership and coordination role among the member communes, and affirm their function as intermediaries in contacts with the regional government. Some observers have even spoken of the 'leading role' of the Mountain Communities in local policy-making and implementation (SPS, 1985: 201).

The Mountain Communities have not been the sole form of communal association created by the regions since 1970. There has been a generalized trend across regions to delegate to communal associations responsibilities for the administration and delivery of services at the inter-communal level. Often it is the type of association that carries out a sectorial function (*consorzio*), whether it be in health, education or transportation. In a number of cases, the region has acted under its own authority, as with the communal associations for the management of health services (*Unità Sanitarie Locali*) in fulfillment of the 1978 national legislation that instituted the national health service. At other times—for example, in the case of education—the regions have implemented more detailed national directives mandating the creation of inter-communal school districts (*distretti scolastici*). By the end of the 1970s there was a proliferation of sub-regional or inter-communal districts with their own organs, staff and budgets designed to deal with diverse sectorial policies. However, there were also the first examples of communal associations being allocated multiple service functions, as in the case of the Tuscany region (Vandelli, 1982; Pieracci, 1982; Regione Toscana, 1979).

In this context, the implementation of the concept of multi-purpose area-wide planning districts began to appear as a threat to existing interests. It was generally recognized that for the area-wide districts to have a real planning role their first task was to consolidate and rationalize the existing districts created for the management of sectorial policies. But this was rapidly becoming an insurmountable obstacle. At the beginning of the third legislature (1980–85), the experimentation with the area-wide districts was terminated by Emilia-Romagna and Lombardy, the two regions that had carried it furthest.

The causes for this change—in addition to the known and ongoing conceptual and operational difficulties—are to be found in the inability of the planning districts to aggregate political support to make the transition to the institutionally recognized status as the replacement for the province. The opposition to the planning districts originated from the provinces themselves and the existing sectorial districts and communal consortia. This opposition ran through all the parties, and after 1978 it succeeded in stalling any progress on the reform of local government that would have sanctioned the change. To a certain extent, the experience with the area-wide planning districts can be placed in the category of an abstract reform which possessed a number of well-intentioned principles but did not have the necessary clout to ensure passage. The experimentation with the area-wide planning districts remains, however, important for the experience acquired in the definition of boundaries and attribution of powers to sub-regional planning bodies and the contribution that it made to the debate on the functions of the province.

The lack of reform of local government and the conceptual and political difficulties encountered by the area-wide planning districts served to rehabilitate the political fortunes of the province which had in its favour the fact that it had operated for over a century and that it did possess its own political legitimacy based on direct popular elections. Thus, its autonomous political status contributed to its ability to redefine and strengthen its own political role. In the conflict between the area-wide planning districts and the province, the province seems to have won (D'Albergo, 1983). An increasing number of observers advocate the reformulation of the province's territorial responsibilities and political role so that the latter can become the effective centre for sub-regional planning (Giovannoni & Romani, 1984: 26).

After 1978 the debate on the new province—i.e. the general-purpose, area-wide government—began in earnest. And in 1982 it was followed by the formulation of a number of parliamentary bills designed to redefine its powers. In addition, proposals were made for the creation of metropolitan provinces for the large urban areas, such as Milan and Turin (*Regione e governo locale*, 1983; Belligni, 1981). While no proposal has yet been chosen, the province has seen its functions augmented with the delegation of powers by the region, especially in the areas of agriculture, vocational education and transportation.

5.4 The Strengthening of Municipal Functions

The province's roller-coaster existence during the last decade has been balanced by the steady growth in power and prestige of the oldest representative form of local government, the commune. The commune has found itself at the centre of the entire decentralization movement, whether it promoted the creation of the region or neighbourhood institutions. Consequently, the commune's role has been profoundly transformed in two directions. During the last twenty years, the communes have implemented decentralization at the sub-city level. These autonomous communal experiments anticipated in many instances the passage of national legislation on neighbourhood government. Also, throughout the 1970s the communes have been engaged in a struggle to maintain their role against the incursions mounted by the region, state and, more recently, province into their spheres of responsibility and activity.

The defence of communal autonomy in relation to the region has first of all centred on the institutional questions of defining their respective roles and functions, especially following the communes' steady increase in powers and responsibilities. This growth has been fuelled by three factors: the net increases in communal functions as a result of the 616 decrees, the attribution of other functions by sectorial state legislation, and the delegation of powers by the regions. The 616 decrees expanded the commune's functions by attributing to it the planning and management of many personal services—among which recreation, public aid, day care, and school aid—previously managed by state and/or private organizations. This was followed by a further transfer of responsibilities when the national health reform went into effect in 1980, calling for communes to establish USLs.

The cumulative impact of these transfers increased the visibility of the commune. The transfers involved personal services which had a direct impact on individuals and families. An example is provided by the allocation to the communes of the care for the elderly, handicapped and others needing social assistance through *ad hoc* municipal agencies. At the same time, the massive transfer of responsibilities to the commune has created serious political and administrative bottlenecks and other collateral, counter-productive developments which impinge on municipal autonomy.

There are numerous examples of these negative consequences in the health sector which account for the largest budget and where the USLs have demonstrated a tendency of becoming separate entities that do not respond well to the control exercized by the communes. One of the basic reasons for these difficulties is the lack of reform of local government which was supposed to have followed the enactment of the 616 decrees. As a consequence, functions which have been envisioned by the 616 decrees as temporary in nature have had to be taken over by the communes on a continuous basis. The communes have had to cope with these problems without adequate budgetary coverage or long-term legal and political direction.

Many institutional proposals have directly surfaced in response to these problems. Some commentators have even looked back with nostalgia to the days in which the power of the state prefects assured a direct link between the commune and central administrative-political authority. The reality is that, despite all the contradictions, the communes have seen a growth in their powers above and beyond those conferred on them by the old communal and provincial Law of 1934. The 616 decrees have changed forever the nature of the commune. It no longer manages problems of local interest alone but those of a general, social nature such as health, housing and growth management as well.

Taken together, these changes signal the transformation of the commune from an institution responsible for the management of sectorial policies to 'a general purpose government responsible for all policies within its territorial boundaries, aside from those higher-level functions allocated to the State and the region' (Zangheri as cited by Staiano, 1983: 99). The commune also increased its importance following the delegation of activities by the regions in application of the 616 decrees. Many of the functions transferred by the decrees from the state to the regions had, in turn, to be delegated by the region to lower-level governments for administration. The delegation of powers from the regions allowed the commune to reinforce its position in relation to that of the province, which was often allocated residual activities.

With regard to the issue of communal autonomy in relation to the State, the last fifteen years have focused on the financial arrangements between the two levels. At the beginning of the 1970s the commune lost its power to impose taxation, which had traditionally been one of its distinguishing marks, and it became completely dependent upon financial transfers from the State. The financial situation of the commune further deteriorated in the late 1970s when the State began to engage in spending cuts and insisted on increasingly placing restrictions on how the money transferred was supposed to be spent (Pizzetti, 1984).

The State's policy on local finances has been a contradictory one. On the one hand, the State has limited the commune's ability to tax, but on the other hand it has stepped in to pay off communal budget deficits. Without a restructuring of its financial powers that would oblige the commune to come up with the financial resources to pay for the services it provides for its citizens, at times the commune has been forced to cut back on services. Thus, the economic crisis of 1979–83 produced an expansion of communal responsibility, but it also increased the control exercized by the State over the commune through the manipulation of financial resources.

Since the economic recovery which started in 1984, a number of developments bode well for the future of communal administrative and financial autonomy. There has been a trend to restructure municipal offices and adopt new administrative practices; communes with more than five thousand inhabitants are computerizing their operations (SPS, 1985; Dau, 1982); programmes to requalify communal administrative personnel are expanding (SPS, 1984); national personnel contracts have increased the technical/professional component of the top management positions in local governments (Balducci, 1985); and there has been a reappearance in the latest government proposal on local government reform of new taxing powers for the commune (Financial Law 1988).

5.5. The Establishment of Neighbourhood Councils

The first post-war challenge to the organization of Italian local government was mounted by the spontaneous communal decentralization and neighbourhood council movement of the early 1960s. At the origin of the movement was the inadequacy of the local government structure in the face of the morphological changes provoked by the massive immigration to the larger northern cities and the industrialization trends of the 1950s and 1960s. For example, the dormitory communities that sprang up at the periphery of Milan—the so-called *coree*—were devoid not only of basic municipal services but also of local political representation and centres for social interaction.

A number of different cultural traditions, from the Catholic–communitarian to the sociological-functional to the Marxist communitarian, attempted to address these problems. These cultural movements attempted to formulate responses to the problems associated with the need to reorganize the urban social fabric, provide institutions having closer contact with the people, and permit citizens to partake in decisions regarding the local community. Communal decentralization became a national issue as a result of two developments in national politics: the student and workers movements of the late 1960s and the opening of the way to institutional reform in the 1970s.

The first component was important in placing on the political agenda the notion of 'urban rights'. This concept was interpreted as the struggle to gain access to public services that were conceived as an important part of modern urban life, such as education, transportation, employment, health, housing and cultural and recreational opportunities. The demand was for universal eligibility and for the government to provide these services to all citizens on an equal basis. As a consequence, the provision of these services on a gratuitous or subsidized basis[7] would function as a way of redistributing income and expanding the access of individuals to growth opportunities.

A second major change in perspective was the demand for increased citizen control over services which was extended to the right to participate in the decision-making process concerning service and development choices. The centralized nature of the communal administrative apparatus was seen as an obstacle to be overcome in making the policy process regarding services responsive to local needs. The immediacy of issues, such as the location of day-care facilities and centres for the aged or recreation facilities, made it appropriate that these decisions be taken at the level of the neighbourhood and the city.

Alliances were quickly forged between the grass-roots political movements of the 1960s and the commune for the purpose of taking away from the State the control of services and the determination of growth management decisions. After the initial experimentation with neighbourhood councils in Bologna, which started in 1964, in the first half of the 1970s the spontaneous experiments with urban decentralization appeared in a majority of the country's large and medium-sized cities (Nanetti & Leonardi, 1979). The movement for reform led to an alliance between the country's two major local government associations—the National Association of Italian Communes (ANCI) and the League for Local Autonomy and Power (Lega). Critical support for this movement was provided by the trade unions which were moving in the direction of accentuating in their contractual platforms issues of 'social income'—i.e. the benefits to their members derived from the availability of quality public services (Nanetti, 1983a).

The development of regional governments provided the second important context for the realization of the urban decentralization reform carried out by Law 278 of 1976. In 1970 a large number of regions inserted in their statutes clauses that extended the concept of decentralized decision-making all the way down to the neighbourhood level. Law 278 brought to fruition the social and institutional demand for neighbourhood government that had been growing steadily and could no longer be ignored by national legislators. The 1976 law transformed the system of neighbourhood organs—council, president, citizen working commissions, etc.—into articulations of the commune and, therefore, the State.

The major characteristics of Law 278 were: the adoption of the principle of political (in addition to administrative) decentralization through elected representative councils; the option for the communes to provide their neighbourhoods with budgets to carry out their activities on an autonomous basis; the means to facilitate citizen participation; and coordination between city council and neighbourhood council decisions. Nevertheless, the exact nature of the relationship between the commune and the neighbourhood was to be spelled out in subsequent by-laws to be drawn up by the communal council at the time that the neighbourhoods were created. In 1980 the first nation-wide elections of representatives to the neighbourhood councils took place. Elections were held in two-thirds (113) of cities with a population of over forty thousand. Of the 58 cities that chose not to create directly-elected neighbourhood institutions, most were in the South (Nanetti, 1983b).

However, at the same time that neighbourhood elections were being held, criticism of the 1976 reform and calls for significant changes began to surface (*Potere Locale*, 1980; *Il Comune Democratico*, 1980). Firstly, general institutional and social problems were identified which were directly related to the specific type of decentralization undertaken. One view (Barbera, 1983) was that the institutional and social reforms passed in the 1970s had enhanced individual rights but also corporatist interests in society and that more ought to be done to bring together for the achievement of common purposes new social actors and groups that had recently emerged at the local level.

Analyses of the means of participation adopted in many cities pointed out the need to recognize the existence of further social change in the 1980s which had rendered *passé* the liberal-democratic model of the neighbourhood council as a mini-Parliament dominated by the political parties, a model that had been acquired through the struggles of the 1970s. This criticism was acknowledged by the assessor for decentralization of the city of Bologna who stated in 1983 that: 'We must recognize that this phase in the experimentation with decentralization in Bologna as well as in other cities has ended, and we must now critically evaluate the cultural traditions (and assumptions) that initially gave birth to it' (Vitali, 1983: 116).

Changes have already emerged in the ongoing experiences in neighbourhood government and in the proposals to reform local government. Among the first, there is evidence of the trend to recognize the neighbourhood as the level at which personal services are actually produced, specifically to: make the neighbourhood responsible for the management of personal services and related investment decisions; determine the optimal size of the neighbourhood for the carrying out of this function; mobilize the users of services by opening up the neighbourhood organs to sectorial representation; and promote the policy of a 'bill of rights' for service users. A consensus has also emerged with regard to several local government reform proposals. There is widespread agreement that it is not feasible to continue with a uniform approach to local government powers and responsibilities, not only because of the disparate size and location of communes, but also in the light of the diverse experience with urban decentralization during the past twenty years.

Notes

1. An example of the opposite approach is offerred by the Thatcher Government's abolition of the six metropolitan county councils. This highly radical change would be inconceivable in Italy because it would upset existing institutional

balances, political equilibria among the parties, and societal channels to decision-making.

2. The term is used to distinguish them from the five 'special' regions which were identified by the Constitution in response to concerns with the rights of ethnic and linguistic minorities in border areas (Val d'Aosta, Trentino Alto-Adige, Friuli-Venezia Giulia) and with separatist movements (Sicily and Sardinia). Four of the special regions—Val d'Aosta, Trentino Alto-Adige, Sardinia and Sicily—were created through the formulation of constitutional decrees in the period between 1946 and 1949 while Friuli-Venezia Giulia had to wait until 1964 before coming into operation. The fifteen ordinary regions were legislated into existence in 1968 and the first regional elections were held in 1970.
3. These expectations may find their roots in the traditional messianic expectations characteristic of both the Catholic and Marxist cultures, which are in part reflected in the social principles contained in the Constitution—such as the right to employment and education—and the political struggles to bring society into line with the constitutional ideal.
4. A case in point is offered by the recent fate of the 'Grande Riforma'—i.e. reform of the Constitution and political system—which in six years failed to mobilize a popular constituency and, therefore, has passed from the political scene without giving birth to one single change in the political system (Pasquino, 1986).
5. The trade unions in the industrialized North were simultaneously being attacked by business—e.g. the attempt to crush the Communist-led CGIL in the FIAT plant in Turin—as well as by the state authorities led by the Minister of the Interior, Mario Scelba (Coppola, 1986).
6. According to the 'transitional rules' (*disposizioni transitorie*), which in 1948 were designed to start implementing the Constitution, a series of ministries—e.g. agriculture, public works and tourism—were supposed to have been abolished as part of the process of transferring their functions down to the regions.
7. The phrase used by groups such as Lotta Continua, Potere Operaio and others was *prezzo politico* or 'political price'.

6 Regionalization of Growth Strategies: Economic Development

6.1. The Features of Regional Planning

The regional statutes formulated by the fifteen ordinary regions affirmed the region's role as a general-purpose government responsible for a wide range of policy matters, including the economic interests of citizens. This affirmation was made despite the fact that none of the regional statutes made explicit reference to the region's functions in economic matters. The statutes incorporated the view that the region had a primary role in the development of economic policies to the point of adopting planning as the underlying factor in government activity.

Long-term comprehensive and sectorial planning—which is what the regions had committed themselves to in the statutes—is, in fact, a much broader concept than the one expressed by the list of regional legislative policy areas contained in Article 117 of the Constitution (see Table 6.1). The expansion of legislative goals reflected in the 1970 statutes is due to understandable historical and political causes. Firstly, the list of policy areas prepared in 1947 reflected, as Dossi (1983) and Bucci (1981) have argued, a rural view of the economy in which the preoccupations of an agricultural society predominated and in which social issues of equality and justice were at the centre of the political debate. The choice of policy areas listed in Article 117 completely lacked any foresight of the changes that would eventually and so profoundly differentiate the country's economic base and change the types of pressures and responsibilities placed on regional governments. When the regions did come into existence, the 1947 conception of their responsibilities for the economy was woefully out of date. Secondly, the legacy of the strictly centralized, sectorial economic policies adopted by the State in the 1950s and 1960s—for example, the highway construction programme or the expansion of the petrochemical and petroleum industry—had served to effectively preempt the development functions of the five special regions and set the precedent of State dominance that was to continue even after the creation of the ordinary regions (Bachelet, 1975).

This centralized approach to economic development ceased in the 1970s to

Table 6.1 Regional legislative policy areas as defined by the 1947 Constitution

Organization of regional offices and administrative bodies
Communal boundaries
Fairs and markets
Public charities and health and hospital care
Vocational education, training of artisans and scholastic assistance
Museums and libraries of local government bodies
Urban planning
Tourist trade and hotel industry
Trams and mass urban transit of regional concern
Thoroughfares, aqueducts and public works of regional concern
Lake ports and navigation
Mineral and thermal waters
Quarries and peat bogs
Hunting
Fishing in inland lakes and rivers
Agriculture and forests
Artisanry
Other matters indicated by constitutional laws

correspond to the nature of the problems being generated by the transformations taking place in the economy and society. The problems of the 1970s required a different and more creative form of public intervention than those that were envisioned in the 1940s. In particular, the expectations generated by the birth of the regions provided the incentive to create a broader platform of requests that defined the realm of regional planning in terms not only of the *productive sectors* but also in terms of the equally important *urban services*, the control of *territorial growth*, and the availability of *personal services*. All these were considered to be constituent elements in the definition of *growth* that was to be pursued by the region as a central goal of regional planning.

As we will see in this chapter, the possibility for the ordinary regions to make a more systematic impact on these four elements of regional planning increased with the second phase of the transfer of powers to the regions accomplished by the 616 decrees of 1977.[1] With the implementation of the decrees, a broader—both *de facto* and *de jure*—interpretation of Article 117 of the Constitution prevailed. The 1977 decrees, in effect, provided national legislative sanction for the regions' previously one-sided attempt to interpret their powers more broadly through the formulation of ambitious, forward-looking statutes in the 1970–71 period. The decrees represented a change in the way that regional powers were conceived by all levels of government.

They moved away from a restrictive interpretation towards a more inclusive approach that identified three expanding sectors as the realm of regional responsibility: social services, economic development and territorial and environmental planning. The interpretation adopted by the decrees was inherently political in nature in the sense that it incorporated a dynamic rather than static definition of the scope and content of regional planning.

A related innovation in the 616 decrees was the stipulation that the regions should legislate in an 'organic' manner in each of these three sectors. Their responsibilities lay not only in each of the specific policy areas mentioned in Article 117 of the Constitution but also in germane or complementary 'new' areas that had emerged since then and were organically linked to the constitutionally identified areas of regional concern. Thus, the formulators of the decrees undertook to creatively 'reinterpret' the constitutional provisions in light of existing problems and exigencies.[2] The results of the redefinition are presented in Table 6.2 which indicates how the three sectors, taken together, represent a broadening of the scope and direction of regional planning in Italy. This is particularly evident, for example, in the decrees' increased sensitivity towards:

- the emergence of new societal needs related to the enjoyment of natural resources or the access to cultural activities;
- the new conception of the individual which is expressed in the recognition of the role of the citizen as a participant in the delivery of a service or as the user of an integrated system of services; or
- the new conception of development-supportive resources expressed in terms of the provision of advanced services to firms or the development of occupations—as well as in terms of their limits, such as the conservation of agricultural land or alternative energy resources.

In summary, the cultural leap reflected in the decrees lay in their conception of the region's planning role as the power to promote, orientate and define specific—but also related—development activities and discarding the previously-held notion of planning as a purely regulatory function.

At the same time, the expansion of the region's planning responsibilities led the region to abandon the pursuit of the comprehensive approach to planning (*programmazione globale*). Beginning in the late 1970s, the regions moved towards a more pragmatic and management-conscious approach to planning in line with their newly developed functions. A first crude indicator of this shift is a quantitative comparison of regional legislation before and after 1978. Since 1978 there has been a decrease in the regional legislative output relative to personnel and finance problems and a parallel increase in the legislation on implementation—such as, area-wide service districts and the delegation of functions, *deleghe*, to local governments, or/and technical

Table 6.2 Reorganization by organic sector and conceptual redefinition of regional policy areas, after 1 January 1978

Sector		
Social Services	Economic Development	Territorial and Environmental Planning
Areas defined by the DPR 616		
1. Human development	1. Commerce	1. Conservation of agricultural land
2. Health and hospital care	2. Tourism and hotel industry	2. National parks and reserves
3. Vocational and artisan education	3. Artisanry and small industry	3. Land use controls
4. Right to study	4. Agriculture, forestry and mining	4. Transportation and roads
5. Cultural resources	5. Co-operation	5. Aqueducts, ports and public works
Areas of recent and future interest		
6. Recreation and cultural activities	6. Advanced services to firms	6. Environmental protection
7. Information and mass media	7. Energy	7. Natural calamity and disaster relief
8. Voluntarism	8. Credit	8. Housing
	Regional Planning	

instrumentation for regional action. In the social service sector there has been a growth in regional legislation addressing the needs for access to public information and better recreational and educational opportunities. A similar legislative growth was registered in the economic development sector, particularly with regard to tourism, cooperative enterprises, advanced services to industry, commerce and credit.

The new approach to regional planning spurred on by the 616 decrees also delineated an *endogenous model* of development policies that pays particular attention to the needs of small industry and the services connected to it and stresses the mobilization of all regional resources—i.e. institutional, entrepreneurial, manpower and infrastructural—that can be leveraged to induce a self-propelling process of development. The endogenous model is one that best fits the development perspectives of social capitalism found in Italy's diverse regions; in fact, it already characterizes Italy's more developed regions and appears to have been quite effective in achieving economic take-off and self-sustaining growth. Endogenously-stimulated growth is now seen as the plausible alternative for the less developed areas, such as the interior of southern regions, for which there has been a demonstrated failure on the part of the exogenous model to spur development, given its reliance on entrepreneurial resources from outside the region (IBRES, 1983).

6.2. Aggregating Diverse Economic Interests

The region, just like every other representative institution, is also characterized by the continuous search for political consensus. Analyses of the last fifteen years of regional policy-making have led to the identification of four *stages* of growth in the search for consensus by regional institutions:

(i) an increase in *activism* on the part of the region designed to involve in its sphere of activity the new economic interests affected by its newly acquired functions;

(ii) an increase in the *demand for interaction* with the region on the part of associations and groups that seek to protect their interests and influence the region's policy choices;

(iii) an increase in the *diversification of support* given to the region by diverse groups which depend, among other things, on the region's priorities and available resources;

(iv) but also an increase, in absolute terms, in the *actual interaction* of the many groups with the region which reflects the increased capacity of the region to satisfy the requests of a wide range of interests.

Already in 1976 data from a research project conducted in six regions and including personal interviews with a sample of regional observers (representatives of industrial, artisan, co-operative, agricultural, banking and trade union interests) confirmed that no one group had been placed at a disadvantage by the creation of the regions. In addition, it was reported that even if the trade unions and farmers had gained the most from the existence of the regions, the benefits had certainly reached a wide range of groups (Putnam, 1976). Observers of regional institutions referred to the region's planning activities as a 'positive-sum game', where advantages accrued to a wide variety of interests and where citizen participation in the activities of the regional government did not come about on an individual basis but instead took place through the membership of citizens in interest groups and the interaction of the latter with the regional authorities.

The tendency of the region to strongly interact with economic groups and respond to their interests is confirmed by data from a survey conducted seven years later—in 1983—in all twenty regions and involving representatives of the same interest groups. The percentage responding in the affirmative to the question of whether the region had a significant impact on the interests of their respective organization ranged from 43 per cent for banking representatives to 50 per cent for the trade unions to 66 per cent for industrial associations and to 72 per cent for farmers' organizations. In addition, a majority of from 62 to 67 per cent of the respondents described the impact of the region as positive in nature, which confirms the noticeable success that the region had in establishing a two-way relationship with these interest groups. In this regard, the data did not reveal major differences between North and South or between special and ordinary regions. However, noticeable differences did exist from one region to another. The detection of a regional impact ranged from a minimum of 15 per cent expressed by interest groups in Molise to a maximum of 91 per cent by those in Friuli-Venezia Giulia. Evaluations of the positive nature of this relationship ran from a strong 90 per cent in Friuli-Venezia Giulia and Basilicata to a minimum favourable rating of 36 per cent in Calabria, which represents a case unto itself.

A measure of the interaction that exists between the region and interest groups also emerged from data on the availability of the region to regular consultations with the various organizations. A large majority of agricultural, trade union and business representatives (respectively, 60, 57 and 55 per cent) confirmed that the region was available for regular consultations with their organizations. In this regard, though, there was a difference between North and South. In the North, organizations were inserted in a more diversified and regular system of consultations with the region than was available in the South. Nevertheless, even among the southern regions the percentage of representatives that reported regular consultations with the regional authorities ranged from 21 per cent in Puglia and 29 per cent in Calabria to Sicily with 73 per cent and Campania with 62 per cent, which were levels that were fairly common in the North. Friuli-Venezia Giulia distinguished itself once again from the others with 85 per cent of the respondents reporting regular consultations.

Over the years, the increased availability of the region was translated into the contacts that regional elected and administrative officials had with interest-group representatives. The thickest web of contacts, both on the part of regional bureaucrats (88 per cent of responses) as well as regional councillors and assessors (77 and 69 per cent), had been established with groups representing agricultural interests. These were followed by trade union and business representatives, respectively 67 and 60 per cent of those representatives reported to be regularly contacted by the regional bureaucrats. Representatives of the banking world had, on the whole, a lower frequency of contacts: 40 per cent reported having regular contacts with bureaucrats and 27 per cent with regional assessors.

Another index of regional accessibility and availability was provided by the data that compare the ease (or lack thereof) of establishing contacts with the State administration and its regional counterpart. Large majorities of the interest-group representatives stated that it was harder for their organizations to interact with the State administrative apparatus than with the region. On this point it is interesting to note that these sentiments were most common among trade union representatives (81 per cent), followed by the representatives of agricultural (74 per cent), business (69 per cent), and banking (65 per cent) interests.

Other research projects have confirmed that the process of regionalization of the trade unions has moved forward more rapidly than is the case with business groups. The difficulty of interest groups interacting with the State administration was reported to be slightly greater in the North. In the South the relation between interest groups and the State seemed to reflect the relative presence in individual regions of the Fund for the South and public enterprises. We can, therefore, understand the fact that interest-group representatives in Abruzzo and Basilicata—two regions in which the Fund and public enterprises are not present on a massive scale—reported the same level of difficulty in interacting with the State (87 and 82 per cent in the two regions), as was found in Piedmont (89 per cent) and Lombardy (79 per cent).

A second aspect of the relationship between the region and interest groups is measured in terms of political support given by the groups to the regional institution. In the survey they expressed themselves strongly in favour of a greater fiscal and financial autonomy of the region from the State. Leading this tide of opinion were the trade unionists (93 per cent), followed by the agricultural representatives (76 per cent), businessmen (72 per cent) and bankers (66 per cent). No differences were registered on this question between respondents operating in the South *vis-à-vis* the North or those in ordinary versus special regions. Strong favourable majorities appeared everywhere. The political significance of this position is important because of the State's control over the destination of the majority of regional expenditures and the difficulty that the region has in generating its own resources. The Italian regions do not have the power to tax their residents on economic transactions in the region.

A confirmation of the support for the granting of greater financial autonomy to the regions was offered by the large majorities in favour of expanding ever further the powers of the regions in other policy areas. Overwhelming majorities in all groups backed the idea of increasing regional powers in the areas of artisanry and industry, agriculture and protection of the environment. In regard to the first two there was the expressed desire to reduce drastically the power and size of the national ministries. In fact, the only region where only a minority of respondents were in favour of the expansion of regional powers was Calabria, with 41 per cent. Even in foreign trade—a policy area completely outside the powers currently allocated to the regions—there was significant feeling in favour of extending regional responsibilities. Businessmen were among those who expressed the most positive views in this regard (49 per cent). In response to these increased expectations—and as will be discussed in the next section—the regions have undertaken to dramatically increase their activities in these fields.

Other research has documented the work carried out by the regions in aggregating organized economic interests. Surveys conducted in the past few years by CENSIS—a private national social science research organization—have underlined how, in general, a strong relationship has developed between the local economy and decentralized levels of government. In particular, a survey of businessmen in seven provinces in the Centre–North investigated issues on which entrepreneurs co-operated with diverse levels of local government. The study found that relations between business and the regions had developed along four major fronts. The first and major area of co-operation was in gaining access to credit for business, and the second was the provision of vocational education.

The other two important areas of co-operation were those of economic planning—i.e. the definition of development objectives and the choice of specific projects for intervention—and promotional activities for goods and services produced in the region. Businessmen expressed the view that the region should further increase its role in facilitating access to conventional credit and in the creation of financial tools of its own to promote development and innovations with regard to vocational education programmes (CENSIS, 1983: 653–5).

Other studies confirm the dynamism of the region in the mobilization of interest groups in support of innovations that the region is trying to implement. Reference has already been made to the region's role during the last decade in challenging the centralizing stance of the State, for example in matters dealing with agriculture. But there has also been an increase in activity in the area of industrial policies. Through this activism the region has attempted to develop its still residual powers and extend its role in strategic sectors. Among these key sectors are business credit and finance (SPS, 1984) and the stimulation of business by working with the provincial Chambers of Commerce (SPS, 1985).

In pursuing stronger links with business the region has not, however, ignored or rejected ties with the trade unions. Recent surveys on the relationship between the trade unions and the regions have verified the existence of an intense and systematic relationship that takes the form of both bilateral (trade union–region) and trilateral (trade union–region–business) consultations on economic matters and the representation of the trade unions on public–private agencies to administer public services. In addition, it is clear that these forms of interaction with the trade unions are regionally specific—i.e. they have been developed by individual regions in co-operation with the now regionalized trade union movement.

The weakening of the trade unions' bargaining power during the years of the recession did not decrease their interaction with the region. If anything, relations have become closer because the unions have sought the region's help in resolving industrial disputes. For example, in 1977 the trade unions in Basilicata co-operated with the regional authorities in mobilizing the region's political, economic and social forces—referred to as the *Vertenza Basilicata*—in an attempt to bring the region's economic problems to the attention of the national government and public opinion (Leonardi, Putnam & Nanetti, 1987). Similar mobilizations have taken place in other southern regions. In 1987 the unions organized a general strike to focus national attention on the problems of Calabria. In other areas the regions and trade unions have worked together to define the best means to pursue the restructuring of failing industries, and co-operating in joint commissions (*commissioni collegiali*) created to monitor and orientate the labour market. In essence, there is increasing evidence that the unions see co-operation with the region as a positive-sum game (Regalia, 1985). A case study on the Umbria region confirmed the role that the recent economic crisis has had in promoting the integration of the trade unions into the regional political system (Donolo, 1983).

Research on the interaction of the regions and specific business groups provides further evidence of the existence and increased importance of the institutionalized relationship between the region and sectorial business associations (Cazzola, 1983). The process of regionalization of business associations varies extensively, both in terms of the type of economic sector and form of management. In general, the regionalization of *Confindustria* (Italy's large manufacturers' association) has taken place at a slower pace than has been the case for small business, artisan and farmers' organizations (Maraffi, 1985). Case studies conducted on the textile industry and other sectors have concluded that systematic work needed to be done in a wide variety of industries in order to verify the hypothesis that the regionalization of sectorial associations has advanced furthest in the economic sectors where the regional action has been more influential, such as, for example, in the case of the building industry (Mutti, 1985).

Finally, the region has sought support among shopkeepers by establishing a relationship with their representative associations. This has been helped by the expansion of the region's planning responsibilities in reorganizing and rationalizing both the wholesale and retail distribution networks of the commercial sector. The interaction with these associations has also increased following the region's development of vocational education programmes specific to the commercial sector. Both the Catholic and Marxist orientated co-operative movements (respectively grouped in the *Confcooperative* and the *Lega delle Cooperative*) have reorganized themselves on a regional basis similar to that of the trade unions, and the artisan associations were among the first to establish close ties with the regional governments dating back to the beginning of the 1970s.

Thus, we have seen that in the last fifteen years the existence and activities of the regions in economic matters have stimulated the reorganization of interest groups on a regional basis and the creation of a regional perspective on policy matters. This reorganization has permitted the region to identify and interact with representatives of regional interests across a broad spectrum of economic and social policies in the attempt to mobilize support for its programme and find allies in its struggle with the State over the region's authority to undertake new policy initiatives.

6.3. Promoting Regional Products and Services

Since the creation of the ordinary regions there has been a perception that, in comparison with the State, the regions have enjoyed a locational advantage in developing policies that promote goods and services produced within their boundaries. The many economic and financial forces that have served to weed out, reorganize, or force the specialization of firms—particularly during the last ten years—have been intimately linked to the resources and social conditions in each region, and the results have confirmed the centrality of each regional institution in creating a climate favourable to the consolidation of developmental activities, especially during the recent recession. The promotion of regional goods and services is a general role in economic policy that the regions have carved out and, by now, firmly established for themselves. This area of policy allows them to intervene, both with direct action in matters where they enjoy primary legislative responsibility as well as with indirect strategies in support of industrial activities.

Thus, increased pressure from various quarters has been placed on the regions to intervene economically on a broad scale. Regional growth policies now run beyond the more traditional and direct support for economic activities through subsidies and other incentives which—together with policies for the development of industrial parks—characterized the first years of regional economic policies. The demand in the regions is for policies that are centred on the provision of advanced services (*servizi reali*) to industry to contain the costs of innovation and restructuring of productive capacity and to secure new markets. For their part, the regions have demonstrated the tendency to expand their own role beyond the scope of this demand and to stimulate new productive activities. They have shown particular interest in promoting cultural, environmental and archeological resources and in offering to the public goods and services produced through the appropriate use of these resources.

Regionally-initiated promotion policies for goods and services have a strong element of 'specificity'—that is, of being different from one region to another, and also of fitting well within the region's economy and its potentials. As a corollary to the specificity of regional policies there are two other characteristics: the small scale and the multiplicity of initiatives. Regional policies for the promotion of endogenous products can be grouped into eight large categories. An analysis of each category reveals the scope, impact and potential of the region's promotional role as a factor in development. The analysis shows that the Italian regions' pursuit of social capitalism is achieved through patterns of experimentation and adjustments in policy.

6.3.1 Promotion abroad

The expansion in foreign markets has represented a common element in the success of Italian small industry. Already by the middle of the 1970s the regions of the North and Centre—where export industries are more diffused—had established a strong presence in major foreign markets (Zucchelli, 1980: 190). More recently, the increased competition from Third World countries has stimulated the identification of new market segments to which to export a greater variety of products with a high technological content, added value and of the highest quality. It is essential for these new product lines to be backed up by penetrating and refined commercialization programmes. In the absence of formal powers of their own in foreign trade, the regions are meeting this challenge through a crescendo of promotional activities and presence at international fairs and trade shows.

Particularly in the northern regions, financing has been provided for the creation of export consortia to cover activities at fairs, and to support commercial missions, market analyses and advertising initiatives. In the 1980s, the North American market has been the object of particular attention: from the consortia of wine exporters to the campaign for the trademarking of leather goods. A recent survey has shown that the export consortia that adhere to the Federexport have increased their sales by 60 per cent in the four years between 1979 and 1983 and that two-thirds of these firms are located in northern regions (SPS, 1985: 79). Also, the regions have intensified their requests to the Prime Minister's office for agreements with the government which allow them to directly conduct promotional activities abroad. Already in the period between 1977 and 1981, a few regions actively sought authorization for the conduct of promotional activities in foreign countries. Lombardy led the list with 250 requests, followed by Emilia-

Romagna with 199, and Abruzzo with 81, and the number of requests was rapidly increasing (Aniasi, 1982: 238).

6.3.2 Applied research

The need for small industry to innovate their production processes is prompting the regions to establish themselves in the field of applied research where adequate State financing is lacking (Fieschi, 1984: 38). The high cost of scientific research for small industry in fact delineates clear responsibilities of the region in defining the needs for technological innovation as well as diffusing know-how across the industry. The premise behind this public–private co-operative approach is that support for applied research ignites mechanisms within the industry itself that favour the reproduction and expansion of innovations.

New forms of co-operation with business for the development of technical innovations applied to industry are being developed on three levels: (a) the production process, where the trend is to increase the level of automation and introduce advanced technologies; (b) the characteristics of the products, where internal quality controls are mandated and the marketability of the products determined through market studies; and (c) the management of the factory, which requires the support of computer systems and the availability of younger and technically trained managers. Thus, while at the level of national policies Italy still lacks the models for systematic support for applied research that exist in other European countries (Gotti, 1984), the regions are partially filling the gap, and a few of them have produced very good results. In the early 1970s, the approach most often used was the hiring of consultants from university institutes and research agencies to work on development projects, but this more often than not produced basic rather than applied research. The regional research institutes that were created in many regions during the 1970s were also orientated towards the general problems of economic development. Instead, in the 1980s experiments were initiated in a few regions and then spread to others to create *ad hoc* research organizations with a mandate in one of the three aspects of production discussed above.

Two examples of the new research organizations are the Laboratory for Research on Artificial Intelligence in Piedmont—a first of its kind in Italy—and the Centre for the Experimentation on the Application of Advanced Computer Techniques to Industrial Design and Production. Both organizations were developed through the participation of the region, business organizations, the Polytechnic University of Turin and local governments. The latter also provides training of management cadres. In Emilia-Romagna the region provides several examples of research on product characteristics contributed by regional centres which lend such assistance to specific industrial sectors. Foremost among them is the Ceramic Centre, a university consortium in which the region participates along with the sectorial business association and the regional Association of Chambers of Commerce (Omoboni, 1984).

Also in Emilia-Romagna, the Institute for the Testing and Development of Earth-Moving Vehicles (CEMOTER), is the product of an agreement between the National Research Council (CNR), the region, business organizations, and the city of Ferrara. The Institute was created to safety-test equipment used in agriculture but also to train technicians and managers to work in agricultural enterprises. In Marche the Electronic Institute for Industrial Quality (ISELQUI) is a company created with the financial participation of the region and the regional industry which makes quality musical instruments for the purpose of carrying out research on technical innovations and also monitoring the quality of the instruments produced.

6.3.3. Access to credit

This is an area where the regions do not have primary legislative responsibility but where they have intervened by adopting two indirect strategies. On the one hand, they have placed themselves in the position of guarantors between credit institutions and business, and on the other hand, they have moved to provide credit services. The main objective of regional activity in this field is to leverage the access to credit that it provides to business to synchronize company plans with regional development programmes. A second objective is to make credit institutions more directly involved and to share in the responsibility for the preparation and implementation of regional development plans.

For this purpose a few regions have created public–private companies—in which the region holds the majority of the capital—to provide financial guarantees as well as technical and financial assistance. In Tuscany, for example, the region has intervened in the agricultural sector by creating a Guarantee Fund (*Fondo di garanzia*) which provides partial loan guarantees to protect banks that loan to farmers (individual farmers and co-operatives) and also guarantees for farmers that do not have sufficient collateral to take out loans. In the industrial sector, the region has created *Fiditoscana*, a stock company that operates for small and medium-sized industries by guaranteeing short and medium-term credit. Through this company, in particular, the region has influenced the granting of credit in the direction of its multipurpose development project: the Amiata Project.[3]

Similar policy instruments have been created in several other regions. The importance of their role is tied to the unpredictability of the downturns of economic cycles and to the difficulty in predicting—from the point of view of the credit-granting institution—the potential for success of business, especially small business. In 1983, the Association of Regional Finance Agencies (ASSOFIR) was created to share among the regions information on finance policies and development plans. Complementary to the regional initiatives on loan guarantees are programmes developed especially by the local banks that co-operate with local business organizations in the creation of revolving loan funds. The latter type of programme is much more common in northern than southern regions. Regional government relations are stronger with banks that have a 'regional' rather than a 'national' character,[4] such as the Credito Romagnolo in Emilia-Romagna, the San Paolo in Piedmont, and the Monte Dei Paschi in Tuscany.

6.3.4 Development of internal and depressed areas

In the 1980s there has been a growing awareness of the importance of advanced services to industry for the purpose of creating self-sustaining development in the internal and depressed areas of the regions. The consensus view is that regional policies must support not only the production but also the promotional and commercialization phases of production in order to make up for the diseconomies of the location and context of these areas. To this end, services supportive of growth must include the buttressing of local management cadres—in both the local government and the private sectors—through experimental policies in training and assistance.

Recent experiments undertaken by the Basilicata region move in this direction. Basilicata has focused on infrastructure and service development for industrial parks in the mountain areas hit by the devastating earthquake of 23 November 1980. In other sectors the region has prepared development projects that combine the growth potential in agriculture—for example, livestock and experimental crop production—and tourism, such as the Norman castles and the Roman sites in the region's internal areas (IBRES, 1983), to aid in the achievement of economic take-off of its internal areas. Tuscany has formulated policies to develop its depressed mountain communities that extend from Garfagnana in the north-western province of Lucca to Mount Amiata. In the latter, where the closing of the mercury mines had a heavily depressant effect on employment, the region is intervening through the implementation of the Amiata Project, which has a two-pronged objective of increasing livestock production and meatpacking and promoting the development of tourism.

Sardinia has also moved to develop its internal areas through expanding the size of farms to achieve higher levels of efficiency. Parallel to the policies in agriculture, the region is supporting initiatives to stimulate small local producers to market on a national scale gourmet and craft products typical of its internal areas. Liguria has suffered harshly owing to the crisis of the large public enterprises that brought the closure of shipbuilding facilities, oil refineries and steel plants. In recent years, the region has invested in new ideas and incentives for its re-industrialization to move towards a post-industrial phase of development. Through its three centres (Agency for Financial Credit, the Research Centre and the Centre for the Diffusion of Technology), the region has entered into partnerships with the large public enterprises (Ansaldo, the public steel industry, and Italimpianti, public works industry) to create technical units whose tasks are to design projects for the restructuring of the basic industries, the modernization of and investment in the tourist and commercial sectors, and the promotion of an advanced tertiary sector.

6.3.5 Utilization of new resources

In all regions the protection of the environment and the utilization of cultural resources are growing in importance. Environment and culture are seen by Italy's regions as untapped resources, together with the renewable sources of energy which will be discussed in Chapter 7. The economic recession of the early 1980s imposed a broader conception of environmental issues while highlighting the element of the protection/conservation of resources as a guarantee of sustained growth in the future. Also, the greater value that people today place on quality of life and the concern with the problems of youth unemployment, all combined to produce an increased appreciation of the economic potentials of the rich heritage of cultural resources.

For example, in 1985 the Tuscany region incorporated in its planning for the Etruscan Project (*Progetto Etruschi*) the estimate of the impact that the multiple-site exhibit and its permanent residuals would have on local employment and income. The *Progetto* created a system of archeological parks open to the public that was integrated into the other two systems of the protected green spaces and of the museums in the region. This approach has also exemplified the co-operation between public and private entrepreneurship and financial resources, given that the Project was the largest sponsored exhibit ever seen in Italy. The results showed that it was not just a major cultural event. The direct financial benefits were substantial, but the long-term residuals were even more so. Half of the Project's investment capital went into the restoration of 80,000 square feet of permanent display space in museums and historical buildings around the region.

Emilia-Romagna and Umbria conceive of their historic centres as development resources. In co-operation with local governments and property owners, these regions are supporting large-scale restoration projects. Molise has orientated its activities towards archeological and natural parks. The region is developing its own environmental, cultural and tourist resources which, up to now, have been under-utilized. The discovery of paleolithic sites unique in Europe, the archeological excavations of the remains of ancient Sannite settlements, and the rediscovery of the fortifications of the indigenous pastoral civilization have provided an impulse to the identification and designation of archeological parks. The region has also taken the first steps towards the creation of the regional park of the High Molise with its distinctive natural resources.

In Tuscany the multi-purpose *Progetto Arno Ambiente* has required large infrastructural investments for cleaning the waters of the river basin and for flood control purposes. In Piedmont the regional policy to save the Savoy royal family residences has produced the restoration of the Rivoli Castle near Turin—the so-called Savoy royal family's Versailles—which hosts high-level artistic events and a museum of modern art. The region has opted in favour of a private firm for the management of the facility. In Basilicata, work is under way on the *Parco dei Sassi* and the primitive churches of Matera. The programme is restoring an urban environment that has been revitalized by the return of artisan activities.[5]

6.3.6 Applied vocational education

Vocational education is one of the few areas over which the regions have had extensive control since the early decrees of 1972. However, for several years their efforts in this area hardly displayed any innovativeness. Rather, they remained confined primarily to the financial support of the apprentice programmes which the regions had inherited from a variety of state and state-supported institutions. With the broader mandate that the regions received in 1977, quite innovative policies began to appear in the area of vocational education that tried to address the challenges of industrial restructuring, the pervasive youth unemployment problem, and the changing labour market. Since then, most regions have created agencies—*osservatori*—to monitor the labour market, but in a few regions distinctly different strategies are being pursued in vocational education, including the participation of the business community in its planning and financing.

An example of the latter is provided in Emilia-Romagna by the Centre for Vocational Education which is administratively located within the Assessorate for Public Education of the city of Modena. It operates as a service agency to local business. Its main objective is to define the skills required by new professional positions that will meet the changing needs of the local economy—such as the application of computer graphics to colour pattern designs for fabrics—and then implement vocational education and retraining programmes in close co-operation with the business community. In many other regions policies are targeted towards the promotion of entrepreneurship and include the support given to youth co-operatives in the agricultural and service sectors, the placement with the financial support of the regions of apprentices for on-the-job training in various firms, and training in the arts as best exemplified by the creation of the successful regional ballet company and school of Reggio Emilia.

6.3.7 *Promotion of typical products*

Regional policies for the promotion of products are actively being pursued by all regions. Understandably, they display particularly strong traits of regional specificity. Examples of promotional activities from Tuscany and its marble-mining industry range from the construction of an exhibition hall to the organization of international fairs and conferences to the commercialization of marble products abroad. Piedmont, Lazio and other regions are promoting the specialization of their wine products with initiatives that go from the advertising of wine district itineraries, to the recently approved legislation protecting the consumer from fraudulent wine products. Lombardy is concentrating on business and convention tourism, while other regions—such as Umbria and Abruzzo—are promoting agriculturally-orientated tourism, *agriturismo*, for the purpose of upgrading their rural housing stock and life in small rural villages. Still others, like Emilia-Romagna, are promoting various forms of mass tourism, *turismo sociale*, for example involving vacation packages to regional resorts for pensioners and the handicapped. In addition, regions are undertaking the systematic collection of data on their own resources through the compilation and updating of inventories of typical resources and products, such as livestock production and fisheries.

Promotional activities also begin to involve products from the regions' internal areas. In Sardinia, a recent development is the creation of consortia of small producers for the commercialization on the continent of products typical of Sardinia's interior. In Basilicata the region has recently launched the successful commercialization of quality-controlled products (*D.O.C.*) from the interior Vulture area—e.g. the highly regarded Aglianico wine that had never been commercially distributed outside the immediate area of production. At the other end of the spectrum are the regions with a highly developed agriculture. In the 1980s the tremendous success story involves the marketing of food products from the Padania area which has been labelled the 'food valley' of Italy. It is centred on the Parma province.[6] Its products have established their presence in the richest world markets where they are creating a new culinary style.

6.3.8 Provision of advanced services

The high demand for advanced services that is associated with the modernization of industrial and agricultural firms has generated regional responses in the form of stock companies endowed with public and private capital. These companies are present above all in the northern regions. Already in 1972, the owners of small and medium-sized industries in Lombardy had asked for regional policies in support of technological innovation. Since then, the region has created several *ad hoc* stock companies, from Lombardy Resources which lends technical assistance to local government in the area of management and personnel services, to Finlombarda Leasing that operates in the renting of office space and equipment, to Lombardia Informatica that provides computer services.

The Marche region has an Agency for Technical Assistance to Business and another company that gathers information on the industrial productions and market patterns of the region. In Emilia-Romagna ERVET (Agency for Economic Development) was one of the first created not merely as a research centre but as an instrument for implementing policies. Approximately five hundred companies belong to ERVET. They co-operate in the development of sectorial service centres, for example in the areas of toolmaking, shoes, knitting and computers. Tuscany has also been pursuing a policy of supporting typical sectors of production that are of great importance at the level of the local economy, by backing them with support services. For example, the company SOGESE was created to improve the quality and expand the number and size of fairs and expositions.

6.4. Inter-regional Co-operation Agreements

Another area where the regions are venturing to experiment with new forms of activity is that of inter-regional relations, particularly among regions sharing borders. Several regional statutes had foreseen the feasibility of inter-regional agreements. One statute, Emilia-Romagna's, had formally adopted as one of its objectives the development of the South—singling it out as a condition for the fulfillment of its own development objectives—thus recognizing the linkage between the two in terms of overall national development. During the 1970s, State laws and EEC directives had promoted inter-regional co-operation, even though they restricted it to well-defined matters. Examples of these types of agreement are the inter-regional consortia for the training of agricultural technicians (that were created in response to EEC directives) and the creation of the inter-regional Institutes for the Prevention of Livestock Diseases foreseen by State law in 1975.

Looking at inter-regional co-operation activities promoted autonomously by the regions, it is possible to identify two basic motivations underlining their growth. The first is the political motivation of regions to preserve their individual autonomy from the State, through mutual co-operation. The second motivation involves the necessity to resolve problems that spill over the confines of any one region. At the level of inter-governmental relations, the centralizing tendency that has characterized so much national legislation since the late 1970s and which has attempted to regulate in detail those very policy areas that pertain to the region has provided the regions with an incentive to seek co-operative responses to reaffirm their legislative autonomy. Particularly significant in this regard is the course of events associated with the formulation by the regions of the criteria to be used in the classification of the hotel industry—a minor policy area which the Ministry of Tourism deemed to be in its jurisdiction. The response of the regions was unprecedented and of significant political value. They took the dispute to the Constitutional Court as a legal struggle against the State, where it was adjudicated in their favour.

But it is on the level of inter-regional management of issues that one finds the most interesting examples of policy co-operation that are motivated by the pursuit of common objectives and that, in turn, arise from the sharing of problems. Often they are problems that do not lend themselves to a rapid resolution, and neither does the implementation of the projects that are developed. This is particularly true for the large-scale projects with multiple objectives and multiple programmes whose investments depend in large part on the State. On this level of inter-regional relations one identifies three general objectives for inter-regional cooperation: (1) inter-regional planning; (2) expansion of economic activities; and (3) exchange of resources.

6.4.1 Inter-regional planning

Related to this objective are the most numerous examples of inter-regional co-operation agreements. Among them, four are large projects of multi-functional planning of resources that have advanced to different stages of implementation. These are: the Po River Project, the Project for the Adriatic Coast, the Project of the High Adriatic of the Alpe-Adria Consortium, and the Ionian–Europe Project. There are also many more examples of sectorial planning initiatives that usually involve two regions at the time and which concern a specific issue. Moreover, from their inception the regions have participated in inter-regional meetings, conventions and studies as a way of working towards more concrete agreements. Of particular importance have been those organized by Piedmont, Lombardy and Emilia-Romagna on problems of immigration, transportation, social services and the integration of industrial activities.

Undoubtedly, the most ambitious inter-regional project that has required the greatest amount of energy and that institutionally speaking, has proceeded the furthest is the Po River Project (*Progetto Po*), involving the cleaning of the waters of the Po River, the restructuring of the flood control systems along its riverbeds and the use of the river's resources. The first concrete steps were taken by the four regions crossed by the river (Piedmont, Lombardy, Emilia-Romagna and Veneto) soon after the 1977 transfer of responsibilities for river navigation to the regions. Firstly, an agreement for the management of internal navigation was ratified in 1979 while work began on the creation of an inter-regional consortium or agency. A second important step was completed in 1981 by the agreement among the four regional presidents that created a Unitary Committee to propose policies and to be assigned a joint technical planning office. This second agreement expanded the initial focus on problems of internal navigation to the multi-faceted problems of pollution, use of the river's resources for the production of energy, fish farming, and other economic activities.

The four regions began to collect data from studies that had been completed on the river, information on the responsibilities of public agencies and on the activities of citizen groups concerned with the river. A third step was the search for funding for this type of project. Requests for financing were addressed to the national Fund for Investment and Employment (FIO),[7] but with limited results. Subsequently, the legislative initiatives of the Emilia-Romagna and Lombardy regions creating the four-region consortium for the management of intersectorial problems had to be postponed. The continuous resistance on the part of the State to the expansion of regional responsibilities through a broad interpretation of the 616 decrees translated, in this particular case, into the opposition to the consortium on the basis that it would emasculate the authority of the State office (*Magistrato del Po*) in charge. Also the refusal of FIO to finance the more costly infrastructure remains the main obstacle to the realization of inter-regional projects of this scale.

The project for the restructuring of the Adriatic coast has had an even more difficult time than the Po Project, also in terms of arriving at an agreement among the regions concerned. In this case, representatives of the four regions involved in the Adriatic Coast Project (Emilia-Romagna, Marche, Abruzzo and Molise) meet to co-ordinate the set of projects which are then independently submitted to FIO for financing. The environmental issue of concern is the process of eutrophication of the Adriatic waters—i.e. the red algae produced by the dumping of phosphate detergents and the chemical phosphate industrial waste discharged by the Montedison, the large petrochemical plant at the port of Marghera near Venice. The principal instrument for the resolution of this problem remains the adoption of the national level of environmental legislation which would prohibit the use of phosphate detergents and the dumping of waste by Montedison. But other problems that the Project has to address are the construction of man-made reefs and platforms to halt beach erosion and the replenishing of the fish stock off the coast. Up until now, the conclusions drawn by the conferences organized by the regions to bring pressure on the Government have not got beyond the bill-drafting stage.

Also on environmental problems of the Adriatic, the Friuli-Venezia Giulia region took the first steps by organizing a conference to involve the other regions which gravitate on the upper Adriatic (Veneto but also the Yugoslavian regions of Slovenia and Croatia) in the development of an anti-pollution strategy for this area. The objectives are to protect the economic importance of the upper Adriatic which provides up to half of the Adriatic's total fish catch and, at the same time, to guarantee its continuing attraction to tourists. The prospect is that the programme to be developed will be managed by the constituted International Alpine–Adriatic Community whose goals extend to improved transportation and trade, and to cultural exchanges with the Yugoslav regions. At the southern end of the Italian peninsula another ambitious project with a broad mandate is the Ionian–Europe Project which has been at the study stage for a few years and which involves the regions of Basilicata, Puglia and Calabria in developing the Ionian coastline, centring on the Graeco–Roman coastal areas of Metaponto and Sibari for international tourism.

With the creation of the FIO, sectorial initiatives in inter-regional planning have multiplied, and it is this type of smaller-scale development project that has been favoured. Projects have been financed for the cleaning-up of Lake Garda (involving Veneto and Lombardy), the expansion and modernization of the Ligurian port of Voltri (Piedmont and Liguria), and the flood-control works for the Ofanto River basin (Campania and Puglia) and the Sinni and Noce Rivers (Basilicata and Calabria). Other projects involve new roads such as the new truck route between Tuscany and Emilia-Romagna

6.4.2 Economic expansion

Inter-regional co-operation initiatives underline and accompany the growth and diffusion of multi-regional economic activities. In the 1980s, the existence and the consolidation of multi-regional enterprises is an established fact that principally involves the two sub-Apennine western and eastern growth corridors that also penetrate into the southern regions. These are not large enterprises. They are medium to small-sized firms that are moving towards a multi-regional dimension according to the strategy of 'short steps' (Formica & Totola, 1980: 8). For example, the November 1980 earthquake that hit Basilicata and Campania provided the impetus for this trend. In this context the inter-regional agreements stipulated between the Emilia-Romagna and Basilicata regional governments have a particular significance in that they have attempted to set off a series of self-propelling processes in the interior areas of Basilicata through three types of co-operation provided by the small industrial sector of Emilia-Romagna: direct technical assistance to small industry and artisanry, assistance in the organization of local entrepreneurial associations, and investments in new plants. Direct co-operation between the two regions had begun before the earthquake. After the earthquake, an agreement between the two regional governments called for technical assistance and aid in the reconstruction and creation of industrial parks in the earthquake zone. Similar agreements followed between Basilicata and other northern regions—e.g. Friuli-Venezia Giulia.

6.4.3 Exchange of resources

Inter-regional co-operative initiatives are also created when diverse but complementary resources exist on both sides of the regional boundaries that could be profitably brought together. In planning the uses in Puglia of water supplied by Basilicata the two regions have faced the negotiation from positions that have at times been difficult. Nevertheless, the possibility of co-operation between the two regions provides the Basilicata region with the prospect of getting some economic benefit in return for the supply of water which is so vital to Puglian agriculture. Basilicata's ability for bargaining directly with the Puglia regional government and the economic interests directly benefited by the water rather than having the negotiations routed through a national agency gives the region greater leverage in ensuring a positive economic return and a reversal of Basilicata's traditional role as the supplier of scarce resources for the development of other southern regions.

Notes

1. The importance of the decrees goes beyond the confines of the fifteen ordinary regions. Indirectly, they also had an impact on the five special regions because, by putting the two types of regions on a more equal footing, the decrees contributed to a growing sense of solidarity among the twenty regions in their relations with the State (Putnam, Leonardi & Nanetti, 1984).
2. This reformulation was carried out by the Giannini Commission which was created in 1975 to prepare the first draft of the decrees on the transfer of state powers to the regions as required by Law 382 which was passed by Parliament in July 1975. In Article 1 the Law specifically stipulated that the identification of

policy areas to be transferred to the regions by the decrees must be carried out by organic sectors and not in a piecemeal fashion on the basis of the responsibilities attributed to ministries, local State organs, or public agencies. The definition of organic sectors had to be based on objective criteria and must ensure that the region could engage in a systematic and rational form of planning in the policy areas that the Constitution had attributed to it (Barbera & Bassanini, 1978: 128).

3. The *Progetto Amiata* is a multi-year development project that targets for development the sub-regional area in the south-west of Tuscany centred on Mount Amiata, which is located in the province of Siena.
4. Regional banks are not present over the entire national territory. The most noticeable examples of national banks are the Banco di Roma, Banco di Napoli, Credito Italiano, Banca Nazionale del Lavoro and the Banca Commerciale.
5. The *Sassi* is the older area of Matera built directly into the rock and inhabited by thousands of people until the late 1940s when new public housing was constructed elsewhere in the city.
6. It extends to cover the provinces on both sides of the Po River.
7. Fioisa technical unit created within the Ministry of Budget and Planning to evaluate investment projects for funding purposes according to cost-benefit and other technical criteria. The unit has been the subject of controversy stemming from charges of political interference from the Ministry in the evaluation process.

7 Sub-Regional Service Districts: Efficiency of Service Delivery

7.1. Urban Services for Economic Growth

The objective adopted for the 1986 regional transportation plan in Emilia-Romagna—promotion of the region's economic development through the modernization of the rail, air, motorway and water transportation systems—is emblematic of the current approach to urban services. In effect, the conception of a close relationship between urban services and economic development policies and the support that the former have provided to economic recovery is not restricted to Italy but is common to all advanced, industrialized societies. A series of studies recently conducted by the OECD has revealed that the increase in the efficiency and efficacy of urban services is a central element of the economic recovery policies and of adjustments to the structural changes in the international economy made by member states (OEDC, 1985a, 1985b, 1983a, 1983b, and 1982).

These economic adjustments require national governments to redistribute resources by investing in infrastructures and services and regional and local governments to target their investments to sustain and attract business by diminishing production and marketing costs. In the European countries where regional-local governments receive the bulk of their resources from national governments, the cuts in national allocations have translated into a decrease in the resources available for locally determined economic development and social service programmes. In contrast to their counterparts in the United States, sub-national governments in Europe do not always have the ability to impose new taxes. As is illustrated in Table 7.1, a substantial part of regional and local budgets in the OECD countries goes to pay for services, and in a number of countries the governments cannot at their own discretion reduce services (Sharpe, 1981). Therefore, the budgetary crunch experienced by sub-national governments in the late 1970s and early 1980s has operated as a major force in stimulating sub-national governments to search for solutions that promote efficiency.

As discussed in Chapter 5, during the same period, Italian sub-national governments experienced a major increase in responsibilities without a

Table 7.1 Local and regional government expenditures by functional sector, in some OECD countries (%)

		General Adminis-tration	Transport and Communi-cations	Infrastruc-ture and Economic Development*	Social Services Health	Education and Culture	Public Order/ Safety
Australia	(1981)	20.4	26.2	29.8	4.7	16.6	1.9
Denmark	(1979)	4.0	4.8	53.3	30.7	5.1	0.1
France	(1980)	12.4	15.4	27.6	21.9	20.2	2.5
Germany	(1980)	7.1	10.4	28.9	31.5	19.3	2.8
Iceland	(1977)	6.4	23.4	29.4	20.9	18.3	1.6
Luxemburg	(1981)	13.9	19.9	28.7	6.2	27.7	3.6
Switzerland	(1981)	8.8	10.3	22.4	20.5	32.0	4.3
United States	(1981)	5.2	6.7	17.1	15.3	47.3	8.4
Italy	(1982)	7.1	7.8	39.6	36.6	7.9	1.0

* Includes expenditures in the area of housing, water supply and street lighting; expenditures for economic development and energy; and miscellaneous expenditures.

Source: OECD, 'Recent Trends in the Provision of Urban Services', mimeo., 18 April 1985, p. 8 and ISTAT, *Annuario statistico italiano, 1984* p. 320.

corresponding increase in budgetary allocations. The Italian case also highlights the difficulties in providing urban services according to uniform criteria. The Italian legislation on communal functions does not recognize any distinction between large and small communes and, until recently, it did not allow for the development of alternatives in service delivery. Not surprisingly, this built-in rigidity has contributed to the existence of large differences in the availability of public services among the three geographical areas (North, Centre, South) and among communes of different size. A 1979 study revealed that the per capita service expenditure on basic services of the small communes—i.e. those with populations below five thousand—was a little more than half that of the larger communes. The lower level of expenditure was not derived from a higher level of efficiency achieved by their delivery system but from the fact that poorer services were provided and a large amount of funds remained unspent—i.e. the accumulation of *residui passivi* (*Italia delle Regioni*, 1981). These unresolved tensions between local government responsibilities and social and economic needs in urban versus rural settings underline the problem of how fairly and effectively to distribute national resources. Small communes need to be ensured the ability to fulfill their administrative functions while larger cities must be permitted to respond to rapidly evolving needs.

A second aspect of local delivery of services in Italy is the productivity of investments and the control exercized over expenditures. A 1979 study conducted by CESPE,[1] ranking the regions on an index of efficient production of urban services showed that the larger southern regions consistently ranked lowest. The study also found that the larger communes in the South provided fewer services than did their counterparts in the North and Centre and that their per capita cost of services provided was much higher than elsewhere. The implications of these conclusions are consistent with the data presented in Chapter 2 on the higher number of local civil servants employed per resident in the South *vis-à-vis* the North. The traditional role of local government employment in the South has been, firstly, to alleviate unemployment and, then, to provide services to the citizens. There is, however, a growing awareness in the South that this indirect approach to local government services has only served to retard rather than promote local economic development. More recently, complementary analyses carried out by CESPE and CENSIS—using 1983 data to construct 'distress' and 'well-being' indexes as, respectively, positive and negative indicators for quality of life—arrived at similar conclusions. They showed that the biggest gap between North and South is, above all, in the provision of services more than in the levels of income or private consumption (*TEST*, 1983).

An emerging trend in OECD countries is the attempt to use the urban service policies of sub-national governments to positively affect local socio-economic and financial conditions. In Italy, this trend has emerged very strongly, and the regions have found themselves at the centre of the demand for greater efficiency in service provision originating from two opposite directions. On the one hand is the pressure applied by the reduction in financial resources allocated by the national government. On the other is the increase in the social demands addressed to the region. The regions have responded through innovative service policies. In this chapter the attention is on the region's attempt to spur the rationalization and innovation in the provision of infrastructural services.[2] Chapter 8 will analyse the impact of regional innovations in land use regulations and growth management at the communal level, and Chapter 9 will focus on the link between innovative regional activities and the quality of social services at the sub-communal level.

In terms of infrastructure services, the regions have introduced innovations in four policy areas to increase the component of social capital supporting the local economy. The first area is the rethinking of the *institutional* structure of decision-making for urban service policies, including a major expansion of the scope of decentralization. The goal here is to make decision-making more flexible and responsive to local conditions. The second area is the experimentation with new forms of *management* for the service authorities to increase their efficiency. The introduction of *technological* and programmatic innovations constitutes the third area, and its aim is to improve service productivity and responsiveness. Finally, new roles are to be provided for *consumer* groups for the purpose of more effectively controlling the quality of services.

7.2. The Role of Communal Associations

Institutional innovations by regional policies in infrastructure services centre on ways to aggregate communes and allocate service responsibilities to the new level of management. But to appreciate the extent and significance of regional experimentation it is necessary to recall the inadequacy of the existing legislation and how it still constrains the region's action. The 1934 legislation regulates how local governments can organize themselves to provide services and the 1925 legislation regulates public service authorities.

In line with the Italian legislative tradition of the single function consortium—for example, the consortium for revenue collection—the Unified Provincial and Municipal Code of 1934 identified the voluntary membership consortium as the form for the aggregation of local governments (communes and provinces) into associations. The Code regulates this type of consortium by defining its characteristics of sectorial specificity, autonomy and voluntary membership which have, with the passage of time, demonstrated their limitations (Villone, 1984). For example, these consortia have proved to be obstacles to the planning of multi-functional services and have not been accountable to the member communes. The content of the 1925 law on the local public service authorities is largely incompatible with the 1947 Constitution (Article 43) and the spirit of the regional reform, especially its stipulation of regional decision-making autonomy.

For a long time, the need has existed to change the legal foundations for the organization and management of public services. Strong pressure to change the legislation has been applied by the public services organization—the Confederation of Local Government Public Services (CISPEL)—the regions, the provinces and the communes, but there has been little progress on a mutually acceptable revision of the legislation. In the absence of a reform law on local government and public services, the regions have nevertheless acted to improve the efficiency of urban services by promoting the creation of sub-regional service districts which operate through *ad hoc* communal associations.

7.2.1 *Area-wide transportation districts*

Transportation is a sector in which the regions have been quite active, and where they have proceeded to create single-function, sub-regional service districts as the first step in restructuring transportation services. The regions have been prompted to intervene by the demand for the greater flexibility in services and by the large deficits incurred in the 1970s by local transportation authorities. In the early 1970s the regions had adopted in their policies, for cogent budgetary reasons, a definition of transportation services that distinguished between intra-city and inter-city services.[3] Being responsible only for inter-city transportation services, the regions were not forced to absorb the huge deficits accumulated by the large urban transport systems that were left to the State to eliminate.

With the passage of the 616 decrees, the regions' approach to transportation services changed to reflect their expanded role in this sector and the need to plan for an integrated system of transportation services. Leadership in this direction came from the legislative initiatives taken by a few regions—for example Abruzzi, Emilia-Romagna, Lombardy, Piedmont, Umbria and Veneto—that provided for: the identification of area-wide transportation districts (*bacini di traffico*) encompassing intra-city and inter-city services,[4] the creation in each district of an *ad hoc* consortium of urban and suburban local governments in charge of the actual delivery of the services, and the co-responsibility of the region in making up the deficits subsumed into the new transit consortia.

Other important issues regarding transportation planning are tied to the ongoing expansion of small and medium-sized cities. As pointed out in Chapter 2, large cities are no longer the main centres of attraction for immigration; they have been substituted for in this role by the small and medium-sized cities. During the 1970s this shift in population was accompanied by the growth and geographical diffusion throughout the smaller centres of many services in response to health, educational and cultural-recreational needs. The improvements in services occurred especially in the small and medium-size cities in the Centre-North of the country which, in turn, accelerated the dispersal of population.

The population changes have had numerous impacts on transportation services. There is an increasing demand to circulate within these smaller urban centres whose boundaries are expanding owing to the preference for lower-density urban developments. The demand is also growing for services connecting the smaller centres and linking them to the metropolitan centre. The multiple demand for transportation services in the smaller centres is very different in nature from that which articulates the transportation needs of people in the larger cities. In particular, in the small and medium-size cities the number of orgin and destination points increases. So do traffic flows and the average distances that have to be covered in making inter-city connections (De Blasio & Tarulli, 1979). In the context of smaller cities, the provision of public transportation poses unique problems of cost, integration of the various service modes, and flexibility in the use of transportation vehicles. All these factors underline the need for planned operations that go beyond the level of individual cities and incorporate innovative management approaches that make use of new service producers. Umbria, for example, has successfully experimented with taxi driver co-operatives to service the region's many small cities.

In 1981, the national framework legislation on transportation adopted the principle of integrated transportation planning articulated through transportation districts. The law also created the National Transportation Fund (*Fondo Nazionale Trasporti*) which pulled together the financial resources targeted for local transportation. Distribution of resources would no longer be conducted on the basis of legal authority (i.e. region or commune) but of function. The distributional formula that was chosen was coherent with planning at the level of the transportation district. However, difficulties have emerged in applying the law: above all, in the absence of national transportation planning. The framework legislation foresaw, in fact, that the transportation planning conducted by the regions would be based on a general national transportation plan. The regional transportation plans (PRTs) were supposed to become operative only after they had been integrated into the National Transportation Plan (PGT). However, the latter has yet to see the light of day.

The lack of a National Transportation Plan has not only created delays at the regional level, but it also raises questions of the future compatibility between the PRTs and an eventual PGT. While over half the regions have defined their transportation districts, only a small group—which includes Piedmont, Lombardy, Emilia-Romagna and Lazio (for bus transport)—has developed PRTs. However, the regions have opted for different types of district authority to be empowered to plan their transportation system. The choice of the consortium of communes has been adopted by Lombardy, Puglia, Umbria and Tuscany. Emilia-Romagna, Liguria and Abruzzo have, instead, preferred the province as the district authority responsible for transportation planning. The debate still has to be resolved between the supporters of the province and of the consortium.

7.2.2 Multi-purpose communal associations

The persistent problem of the small size of the majority of communes in relation to the spectrum of services that they are legally obliged to provide was addressed by the 616 decrees. The decrees allowed the regions to create multi-purpose communal associations in which local governments were obliged to take up membership. Communal associations became responsible for the planning and delivery of a number of services at the level of smaller multi-purpose service districts. The decrees also adopted a definition of efficiency in service delivery that is linked to the effective response to needs and increased control by the users. Therefore, the new model for local government associations had to respond to multiple needs for services of the population living within a service district. The two models of multi-purpose communal groupings that are most common today are the Mountain Community and the Communal Association.

Since 1978, State and regional laws have increasingly identified the Mountain Community as the associational model defining the service district for communes in mountain areas. The Mountain Community has accumulated service functions in the areas of health care (when its boundaries coincide with those of the USL), administrative oversight of communes, park administration and water pollution. On the heels of the 616 decrees, the process of delegating regional powers has priviledged the Mountain Community rather than the single mountain commune. In fact, the Mountain Community is approaching the model of the fully-fledged general-purpose government, making it the most comprehensive form of communal association to date.

The second type of communal grouping is represented by the multi-purpose Communal Association which, unlike the Mountain Community, is not promoted by state law as a new level of government. Communal Associations have been created by regional legislation and attributed more specific functions. Tuscany was the first region to create Communal Associations whose boundaries overlap with those of the USLs, school districts and other service districts. Umbria and Marche have followed with similar legislation. In the latter, the region was subdivided into twelve Communal Associations and twelve Mountain Communities for purposes of allocating infrastructural investment funds and for the planning and management of infrastructure and social services. A third type of communal grouping is the Mega-consortium. It is the association that corresponds to the largest service district, approaching in size the provincial dimension. Examples of Mega-consortia can be found in the administration of irrigation projects and water distribution services, such as the Reno River Water Consortium that brings together fifty-four local governments which share the multiple use of the river's water resources, or the Intercommunal Consortium of Reggio Emilia among forty-two communes for the distribution of water and natural gas (Ciarlo, 1984).

7.3 New Management Models and Criteria

The region's search for innovative solutions in service delivery to increase productivity has also been translated into support for experimentation aimed at the reorganization of the service authorities which provide services at the district or communal level. Firstly, experimentation has been conducted within the existing management models foreseen by the 1925 law. These include municipal service authorities (*azienda municipalizzata*), the consortium authority (*azienda consortile*), the *ad hoc* municipal department (*gestione in economia*), and contracting-out to third private parties (*appalto*). Secondly, it also involves the promotion of new management models to accommodate new needs and involve new service producers.

The municipal service authorities in Italy are a powerful political and economic sector, particularly in the North where they have established a strong presence. In recent years, their number has grown in fast-changing southern regions such as Abruzzo (CENSIS, 1983). The customer volume of the municipal service authorities is surpassed only by the national electric company (ENEL), and their volume of business is, in fact, greater than that of the national telephone company (SIP) and the state railroad system (FFSS). The burgeoning deficits which the authorities experienced throughout the 1970s made it imperative to find new solutions either through radical restructuring or the imposition of private management models. In the 1966–77 period the gap between costs of production and revenues had increased eightfold so that by 1977 the deficit incurred by the municipal service authorities equalled 47 per cent of their total expenditures (Cerea & Paola, 1979).

Actions during the last ten years to restructure the authorities and to reduce the costs of production have led to a noticeable improvement in their balance sheets. Improvements were registered, for example, in the level of the deficits in the operating budgets which, from an average of 14 per cent in the period 1972–76, dropped to 6 per cent in 1981. By the early 1980s the municipal service authorities had achieved very positive results in the ratio of personnel costs to revenues from the sale of services. For example, in 1982 sale revenues covered 97 per cent of the expenditure for personnel, up from the 84 per cent level covered in 1980.

The improved overall picture for the authorities in containing the cost of producing services and increasing investments has to be broken down according to types of service. The best results were achieved in transportation and refuse collection where in 1981 and 1982 there were cost reductions of, respectively, 83 and 58 per cent and increases in investments of 24 and 87 per cent. However, in spite of these improvements, the bulk of the losses is still incurred in the urban and inter-city transportation services. In 1983 all the losses in transportation represented 81 per cent of the total deficits of the municipal service authorities, but over half of them were concentrated in the metropolitan areas of three regions: Lazio (particularly Rome), Calabria and Sicily (particularly Palermo) (SPS, 1985). Another indicator of the increased productivity in services has been the reduction in the per capita number of work hours lost to employee absenteeism which dropped from 196 (5 weeks) in 1980 down to 166 (4.1 weeks) in 1983. In the same period, a large increase was registered in the value of the service produced per worker, which—accounting for inflation—almost doubled from the 15 m. lire in 1980 to 29 m. in 1983. This trend has involved the entire range of services supplied by municipal service authorities, but it has had its highest increases in refuse collection and disposal (157 per cent), intra-city transportation (106 per cent), and inter-city transportation (88 per cent).

Several factors have contributed to the achievement of these results. Firstly, the improvements should be, in part, attributed to the introduction of new management tools for the operation of the authorities. These include the adoption of multi-year and annual programme plans and multi-year budgets, innovations which had been proposed in 1977 by the association of municipal service authorities but which the State only made mandatory in 1981. The innovations attempt to achieve a fit between the broader service policy goals of local governments and the operational choices, inspired by criteria of efficiency, made by the municipal service authorities. In the process of elaborating the multi-year programme plan, the local government specifies the general objectives for each service—for example, where to expand, how to allocate user costs, which qualitative improvements to consider—and the municipal service authority has a number of years in which to operationalize service changes in line with these political and economic objectives.

A second factor contributing to the improvements is the introduction of new accounting methods brought into the management of the municipal service authorities by certified accountants (*revisori dei conti*) whose responsibility is to prepare the three-year budget and set productivity targets that the authority has to meet (SPS, 1985). A third factor is the contribution made by the newly created Productivity Observatory (*Osservatorio della Produttività*). The Observatory is the operational research organization for the association of service authorities which studies, defines and updates the parameters of efficiency and productivity in each service. Its purposes are to identify operational inefficiencies and develop programmes to aide the authorities in overcoming them. The Observatory operates, therefore, as a management consulting service for municipal service authorities; it also feeds data to the certified accountants on changes which should be made in the management of the authorities (CISPEL, 1984).

In general, small communes do not avail themselves of the option of the municipal service authority but prefer to manage their public services through their own government departments and pay for them out of their general operating budget (*gestione in economia*). This approach has presented a problem of escalating costs tied to the quantitative growth in the services which the communes have to provide and the demand from the public for new services. Therefore, it is even more important for the region to promote the formation of consortia among the smaller communes in order to plan and manage services, especially those with a higher technological component for which production costs are prohibitively high, such as the new technology used in waste disposal. At the national level the debate on how to successfully promote service consortia has identified the need to move away from making budgetary allocations to communes on the basis of their previous expenditure patterns—referred to in Italy as the *spesa storica*. For example, a proposal from the National Commission for the Study of Local Finance[5] would put into place a new system for allocating financial resources to local governments based on the evaluation of their ability to actually deliver the services to their citizens and only 20 per cent of the transfers would be on the basis of past expenditures.

To some extent the shift to consortia for the provision of services has been slowed down by the many administrative obstacles placed in the path of consortium authorities by the restrictive regulations contained in the 1925 and 1934 legislation and opposition from the national government. For example, the participation in consortium authorities is restricted to communes and provinces while other public entities, including the region, are excluded (Tessarolo, 1980). In contrast, the new model of the stock company (*società per azioni*) has gathered support because of its operational flexibility and the perspective that it offers for public–private partnerships. It has become the preferred solution in Lombardy for the management of transportation services. National data for 1981 and 1982 show a decline in the number of consortium authorities from 66 in 1981 to 51 in 1982, but an increase from 20 to 25 in the number of stock companies during the same period. The 1985 government reform bill on the reorganization of public services proposes other new management options such as: contracting-out with another commune, province or municipal service authority (*servizio in concessione*) or the public–private option on the variation of the private stock company with a majority of public capital but with the participation of financial institutions and other private interests.

A proposal for a new management option offered by CISPEL is concerned with reconciling two needs: local government political autonomy and efficient management of services. Based on the premise that the municipal service authority should be allowed to market its service and operate at an efficient level, the proposal argues that a legally binding contract (*contratto*) should be established between the authority and the local government. The authority would respond to the demands from the local government, which reflect the local government's service goals and choices, with its own proposal containing price structures and costs. At the end of the negotiations, the contract would sanction the agreement reached by the two sides, including the specification of the costs assumed by the local government if it wants to offer the service at a subsidy. But the local government maintains the right of access to all data on the costs of production incurred by the municipal service authority.

Finally, it should be pointed out that the innovations in the management of services are induced not only by economic considerations but also by the expansion of the objectives and content of a particular service. For example, the traditional service sector of refuse collection now provides a wider range of services which include, in addition to the traditional refuse collection and street-cleaning operations, new services for the disposal of industrial wastes, water purification, and snow removal. Presently, the cost of these services represents the second largest expenditure in the communal budget after transportation.

7.4. Technological and Planning Innovations

In the regional debate on service policies the search for the optimal level at which to manage different services is one of the main issues. It is also important because it is closely related to the issue of technological and planning innovations which alter the modes for the actual delivery of services. Technological and planning innovations affect services currently offered as well as the introduction of new services. With regard to traditional services, refuse disposal is one in which major technological innovations have been introduced. The objective is to improve the service both in terms of the frequency of pick-ups and environmental safeguards in refuse disposal operations. Since the mid-1970s local government awareness of environmental issues has grown reflecting the heightened sensitivity towards air, ground and water pollution. Thus, there has been a parallel increase in the number of communes that directly handle sanitation services. Two national surveys covering the period 1977–82 documented the increase in the number of communes which directly manage the service either through a municipal service authority or by participating in a consortium authority. Correspondingly, there has been a sharp decrease in the contracting-out of the service to private firms.

The survey data also indicate that the methods to dispose of waste are changing in favour of the more environmentally sound ones. While the dumping method was still prevalent (76 per cent) among the communes, by the end of the period under consideration almost twice as many communes were using the covered landfill method (47 per cent by 1982, up from 25 per cent in 1977) versus the open landfill (down to 29 per cent in 1982 from the 51 per cent in 1977). In general, dumping remains the prevalent method of refuse disposal among medium and small-size cities. The use of incinerators has increased (to 13 per cent of the communes by 1982), including those which recover natural gas and energy from the combustion process and those which have the facilities for product recycling and the production of compost. Another trend is the separate collection of different types of refuse, which in 1982 was being carried out in approximately one-third of the Italian communes by public as well as voluntary operators. In the regions of Lombardy, Emilia-Romagna and Veneto almost all the communes had introduced this type of collection (CENSIS, 1983).

A few particularly significant experiments by local governments will now be analysed for the purpose of illustrating the impact of technological and programme innovations on service efficiency. The commune of Modena (population 180,000 in 1981) is in the vanguard in the successful application of new technologies to its refuse collection and disposal services. In 1982 Modena's municipal service authority patented a system for collecting household refuse based on the mechanical loading and unloading of refuse containers through an electronic system that allows for the reduction of the refuse crew from three to two employees. Experiments are under way with a totally mechanized method of refuse collection that would reduce the crew to one. Modena has also undertaken to expand its sanitation services by adding an educational and information component for its citizens. Underlining these plans is the premise that expenditure on the environment is productive because of its employment potential and the recovery of scarce resources. As the Emilia-Romagna region has underscored through its policies on the need to recycle paper, glass and other materials, Modena has responded with programmes to decrease the use of plastic bags, to move to automatically-loaded refuse bins, and to increase environmental education in schools.

The high cost of refuse collection and disposal has focused attention on the recovery of resources. In this service area, once again, it has been municipal service authorities that have moved to introduce the best disposal plants available. However, given the initially high investment cost and the lack of a national policy of resource recovery, the economic viability of the smaller disposal plants remains limited and so does the prospect for constructing many more resource recovery plants. The number of regional initiatives is still low, but there are examples of regional-municipal collaboration in the disposal of hazardous waste which are extremely advanced and which show strong potential for application in other cities.

The 1982 national legislation on energy conservation attributed the cost of the disposal of chemical and toxic wastes to the producer. The region is now institutionally responsible for the designation of sites and the preparation of hazardous waste disposal plans, while the implementation can be contracted out to local service authorities or private companies. Implementing an agreement with the Emilia-Romagna region, the city of Modena has just constructed an integrated incinerator/water purification plant system where the latter uses the power produced by the incinerator. Moreover, the new Inter-provincial Centre for the disposal of toxic waste serves a wide area which includes the entire province of Modena and a number of communes in the adjoining provinces of Reggio Emilia and Bologna. The management of both Centres and their services is carried out by Modena's municipal service authority.[6]

Another example of successful technological and planning innovation in service delivery is provided by the municipal service authority of Brescia (population 207,000 in 1981). Back in 1972, the city prepared and started to implement a plan for *teleriscaldamento*, the system of centralized heating through the use of hot water serving the entire city. The heat usually lost—that is, the low and medium temperatures that are derived from the transformation of thermal to electric power—is recuperated in this system to heat water which is then supplied to the city's dwellings and business through a pipeline network (Silveri, 1979). The territorial limitations of the heat distribution system make it ideal for the urban scale, and in 1982 the Brescian system was already making a profit. The service is managed by the local municipal service authority which provides all of the city services: from natural gas, electricity, hot water and heat to transportation, water and refuse collection and disposal. In the 1980s *teleriscaldamento* is being introduced to heat homes and businesses in many medium and large northern cities and also in Rome.

In addition to the better utilization of existing resources, a last but important theme related to service efficiency is the search for alternative energy sources. The regions have so far limited themselves to *ad hoc* legislation responding to local demands for financing specific local projects. This approach is certainly not a substitute for setting an energy policy and selecting region-wide projects in the areas of solar energy, energy recovered from refuse and other renewable sources, or the use of alternative fuels in urban transportation. As the examples above have illustrated, interesting experimentation in these areas is found in the co-operation between the local and the regional levels of government.

7.5. The Impact of Consumer Groups

The effort to achieve greater efficiency in urban services implies that serious consideration has also to be given to another method of pursuing this objective—that is, the promotion of citizen monitoring of the municipal service authorities or the municipal departments that provide the services. Since the early 1980s, it has been the municipal service authorities, through their association, that have taken the lead in articulating the economic benefit of citizen oversight of service operations. The premise is that costs are likely to increase and the quality of service to decrease in the absence of institutionalized forms of control on the part of consumers.

A consequence of these two eventualities—increased cost and decrease in quality—is the likelihood that the wealthier consumer will opt out of public services whenever possible. Although the market option is possible in some services, like health, transport and education, it is still quite limited in Italy today; moreover, it does not exist in the case of other services such as telephone service and refuse disposal. In most cases public services in Italy are offered in a monopoly situation, whether the producer is the municipal service authority or the local government department, or the private operator who has contracted with the commune. Therefore, it is argued by the municipal service authorities that efficient delivery can only be guaranteed through the existence of citizen control and political pressure and that the municipal service authority model best lends itself to it. Municipal service authorities have promoted experimentation with citizen control carried out at the regional, district or city, and neighbourhood levels.

In 1980 their association adopted a statute for municipal service authorities that specifies the responsibility of the authorities to ensure a 'full and accurate' flow of information to the public on their operations. Among the measures which the statute prescribes, a very significant one is the participation of the neighbourhood councils in the preparation of the authority's programme plan and budget, and in the review of the authority's year-end account. The statute also mandates municipal service authorities to undertake informational activities in the schools and to provide information to and receive feedback from trade unions, business and other associations. Statistical and budgetary information is produced and distributed as a synopsis of the yearly account of the authority's performance which also incorporates comparisons with the performance of municipal service authorities in other cities and comparisons with national averages.

Other initiatives which the municipal service authorities have undertaken are the organization of public conferences at the communal and regional levels which are scheduled at regular intervals and the creation within each municipal service authority of a consumer relations office. In addition, there are proposals that would give consumers an even greater voice. One such proposal would allow consumers to recall (*revoca*) managers of municipal service authorities who have performed poorly (Sarti, 1981), but, so far, this has not been implemented. Another formulates a Bill of Rights (*carta dell'utente*) for consumers of public services which proposes norms to protect the consumer and guarantees them right of oversight. A number of regions, including Emilia-Romagna and Veneto, have implemented this proposal through their own legislation.

Notes

1. A national social science research organization.
2. A common distinction that is made by the public administration literature is between *infrastructure* services—e.g. refuse collection and disposal, transportation, water supply, etc.—and *social* services—e.g. health care, education, public aid, etc. The same distinction between types of services will be maintained in this study.
3. Inter-city services include both the service between the main city and any number of towns in its metropolitan area as well as the service linking smaller towns.
4. The boundaries of area-wide transportation districts are identified by using a multiplicity of criteria—e.g. origin-destination data, employment and development patterns, and municipal boundaries.
5. The membership of the Commission is composed of local government associations, representatives of the national government, and of the Census Bureau (ISTAT).
6. This facility is the first of its kind and size to be managed by a municipal service authority. The region provided most of the money for construction. Smaller contributions to the cost were made by the city and the EEC. The facility is expected to pay for itself in five to six years.

8 Communes and Development: The Management of Urban Growth

8.1. Instruments for Development and Control

Since the end of World War II, Italian communes and regions have assumed an increasingly central role in controlling urban growth, while the role of the State has correspondingly declined. Control of urban growth has come under the sponsorship of the region, which has made urban planning a primary municipal function. Two innovations have accompanied this change: one is cultural-conceptual while the other is operational in nature. On the one hand, over the forty-year period there has been a re-definition of the very concept of 'urban growth', to underline the view that growth is qualitative and that it is intimately tied to the conservation of urban centres. On the other hand, new tools have been developed which allow the communes not just to *control* growth by restricting it (i.e. through land use regulation) but also to *manage* growth by guiding it (i.e. through development policies and programmes).

The history of urban planning policies in Italy in the post-war period is riddled with conflict. Urban planning began within the political and economic context of the reconstruction, from which it adopted the national vision favourable to fast growth (Nanetti, 1972). The cultural isolation that had characterized the Fascist period produced local officials inexperienced in matters of city administration and unprepared to meet the challenge of rapid urban growth. Nor did city administrators possess adequate tools to control growth. Nevertheless, the history of urban planning policies underlines the institutional growth of the commune, particularly in the last fifteen years. As observed by Cassese (1978), since 1970 and in conjunction with the institutional growth of the regions, the communes have demonstrated a significant ability to experiment in areas that have been added to their responsibilities and have shown a new political activism in developing their relations with the central government and the regions.

The coming of age of Italian communes, with regard to the control of development, has gone through various phases, each characterized by its own political and social movements, cultural debates and choice of policy and implementation tools. The first phase is that of the mushrooming expansion of the larger cities, often at the expense of the smallest communes, and of the massive internal migration from South to North and from the rural areas to the city. Between 1951 and 1961 approximately 17 million people became part of the internal migration wave that, for the most part, hit the large cities (Ferraresi & Tosi, 1979). During the same period, Italy's population increase of 3 million people was almost completely concentrated (91 per cent) in the provincial capitals, and the four largest cities—Rome, Milan, Naples and Turin—alone absorbed two-thirds of the total (Campos Venuti, 1967).

During the first phase, the communes were confronted by the limitations imposed upon them by planning legislation: the 1942 urban planning law (*legge urbanistica*) No. 1150 and the decree No. 154 of 1945 on the reconstruction plans (*piani di ricostruzione*) for cities damaged by the war. Law 1150 restricted the commune to a passive role. While it was responsible for the development of the master plan (*piano regolatore generale*) whose land use controls were legally binding, the commune could not set its own development priorities. The 1942 law was an improvement over previous legislation in that it extended the geographical reach of the master plan to cover the entire commune, that is, both the urbanized as well as the undeveloped areas. But the law soon proved very difficult to apply. In fact, having made what in terms of planning principles is a sound distinction between the master plan and site plans (*piani particolareggiati*),[1] the law correctly subjected the implementation of the master plan to the availability of public financing of the infrastructure foreseen in the site plans. However, in so doing the law erred politically: it presumed revenues which the communes did not have. In other words, the law provided no incentive and, indeed, imposed further costs on the communes if they chose to exercize control over their own growth. The consequence was not the halting of growth but rather the circumvention of the law itself and providing free reign to the developers.

Several factors contributed to this state of affairs. Given the inertia of the Fascist Parliament during the war period, the enabling decrees for the 1942 law were never approved. The decrees were essential for facilitating the implementation of the act under the statutory law system which applies to Italy. The lack of such procedures forced the communes to absorb the entire financial burden for implementing the site plans. The commune had to provide the infrastructure for private developments as well as buy land for public facilities and services at close to market prices. The fiscal dependence of the communes on the State, coupled with the meagre communal budgets in the early post-war years, created a *de facto* situation in which private developers were able to claim the right to build in areas identified by the master plan for development—even in the absence of site plans—and impose *post facto* on the communes the cost of communal infrastructure and services. This *laissez-faire* approach to urban development was further strengthened when the courts began to reject the commune's right to block private development in areas lacking site plans.

Secondly, governmental decree 154 of 1945 linked the formulation and the content of reconstruction plans—which in most cases were targeted to the central areas of the cities—to the land use provisions in the master plan. Reconstruction plans called for a great degree of detailed planning and, in essence, were site plans but on a larger scale. Unfortunately, the same loophole that existed in the 1942 law reappeared in the 1945 decree. In the absence of the master plan, the reconstruction plan simply had to comply with 'provisions of the (1942) urban planning law'. Therefore, the same disincentives had a bearing on the communes' control over the reconstruction projects as were present in their control over the new development projects. While the existing legislation created disincentives for communal control, government reconstruction loan programmes created strong incentives for private development (Samonà, 1960). The end result was that in the 1940s and 1950s both facets of growth—reconstruction and new development—too often emphasized quantity at the expense of quality.

The ideas for development held by the communes that did prepare master plans were culturally in line with what has been called the 'myth of reconstruction'—that mixture of the reminder of the losses suffered because of the war and the imperative to overcome them as quickly as possible (Costa, 1978). Almost always, they translated into unrealistic plans relying on projections of residential, commercial and industrial expansion that were many times greater than the existing base. For the most part, the plans did not contain estimates of infrastructure and service costs, nor was there a financial component to the plan that indicated where the funds would come from to pay for the incurred costs. However, during the first years, only a handful of communes engaged in the preparation of a master plan.

More commonly, communes chose to formulate and adopt a building programme (*programma di fabbricazione*)—less demanding technically and financially—to control development. The building programme only applied to the undeveloped areas, thereby dealing with them separately from the overall territorial context of the commune. This approach skewed even more the perspective on development in favour of the areas of new growth. These areas were already being promoted by the existence of incentives, such as the twenty-five year property tax exemption for new construction, provided by the post-war national housing legislation. To the extent that it did, the building programme regulated growth in a simplistic manner without relating it to the analysis of demographic or employment patterns.

The second phase in the process of acquiring the ability to control territorial development by the communes began around the middle of the 1950s. It was the period when the first signs of a change in attitude appeared, in opposition to the gigantic growth projections proper of most master plans of the first phase, and which led to the call for a new approach and more effective legislation. For example, at the beginning of the 1960s, communes located all around the city of Bologna—which were all of the same leftist political colouration—began to adopt master plans that were aimed at containing suburban sprawl and pacing private development with the commune's ability to finance the needed service infrastructure. Based on objectives of 'minimum private sector expansion' and 'maximum public sector expansion', the plans were accompanied by more credible financial projections of how to cover the cost of future public infrastructures and services.

This was the same period in which the National Institute of Planners (*Istituto Nazionale di Urbanistica*, INU) proposed a sweeping reform of the 1942 urban planning law. INU viewed the old law as incapable of restraining (and in some ways it even facilitated) the abnormal expansion of the peripheral areas of cities and providing them with adequate city services. The reform supported by INU never materialized, but in 1962 the law on public and subsidized housing (No. 167) for the first time gave the communes the ability to make concrete development choices in line with the general objectives of their own plans.

The first commune to implement the provisions of law 167 was the city of Bologna, which developed plans for public and subsidized housing and used the funds made available by the programme to expropriate large and highly desirable areas. The city's goal was the development of new, lower middle-class neighbourhoods equipped with all the necessary services. Many other communes followed. These types of communal initiatives brought to the fore the debate on municipal services which centred on the adoption of minimum standards for public services. Modena's 1965 master plan, which formally adopted a standard of 50 square metres of parkland per inhabitant, represented the beginning of a tendency by many communes to abandon the purely regulatory approach to development issues and move towards a planning approach formulating development priorities through the choices of infrastructure location. In other words, it signalled a significant movement away from the narrower goal of growth control in favour of growth management. This approach was formally sanctioned by a ministerial decree (No. 1444) in 1968 that mandated that master plans incorporate minimum service standards and maximum residential density standards (Campos Venuti, 1978).

During the 1960s, a corollary development issue concerned the interrelationship among all of the parts of what were emerging as metropolitan areas through the expansion of the principal city in the area. The need to respond to the metropolitan trend led to the first experimentations with intercommunal planning that had been foreseen, however ineffectively, by the 1942 urban planning law (Rodella, 1967). For the most part, the attempts made relied on objectives that were too general and implementation procedures that were politically unsophisticated. In the case of the Milan metropolitan area, the very first proposals for the Milan Intercommunal Plan were actually formulated in 1951 and 1955, but they failed, owing to lack of support from the heterogeneous political coalitions as well as to the fear that the smaller communes always had of Milan's hegemonic presence.[2]

Between 1955 and 1960 the collaboration between parties of the centre and of the left produced the 1963 Intercommunal Plan which was modified several times in succeeding years. The Plan focused too narrowly on the analysis of social and economic changes to the detriment of the problems of transportation and location of industries. It proposed the concept of the 'regional city', *città regione*—i.e. the extension of urban amenities to all the towns, thus avoiding any locational choices. The concept itself inevitably reduced the importance of the area-wide level in controlling growth.

In the case of Turin, the first efforts to propose an intercommunal plan at the beginning of the 1950s also failed, and the city had to wait until 1964 to have its Intercommunal Plan adopted. It was an extremely generic plan in its approach to development goals for the metropolitan area. Any specificity in the plan was merely the summation of the various communal plans contributed by the towns participating in the intercommunal planning process. Intercommunal level planning was *de facto* relinquished to the city of Turin when the other communes accepted the premise that the master plan of Turin was not subject to change. Revisions of the Plan in 1967 tried to focus on objectives of alternative locational choices and growth patterns and on realistic means for the implementation of the Plan. Nevertheless, the contribution of the other communes was overshadowed by the leading role of Turin, and their participation in the intercommunal planning process remained limited.

In Bologna, background studies for the intercommunal plan had been conducted in the period between 1952 and 1955 in conjunction with the studies for the city's master plan. Then, as discussed above, between 1962 and 1963 the communes in the metropolitan area adopted master plans which shared common objectives of controlling private development and containing the costs for infrastructure and social services. They also pursued common implementation strategies, such as the acquisition or donation from private developers of areas to be reserved for the development of public services. Later, private donation of land by developers had to be dropped when the Ministry of Public Works and the State Administrative Court (*Consiglio di Stato*) ruled against it (DeCarlo, 1964 and 1965).

Throughout the 1960s, the operational difficulties experienced by all the intercommunal experiments in attempting to control urban growth contributed to reviving the political battle of the communes for a new urban planning law, a demand that was also one of the main programmatic goals of the national Centre-left coalition. This second phase in the planning experience of the communes was brought to an end by two contrasting episodes. The first was the partial modification made in the 1942 law with the approval of the so-called '*legge ponte*', the transitional urban planning law of 1967 (No. 765) that introduced mandatory development standards (*standard urbanistici*), differentiated by typology of commune, and regulated the physical characteristics of buildings as well as the size and location of the areas reserved for municipal service infrastructure and amenities. Consequently, the 1967 law required all communes to adopt the two planning instruments for the control of urban growth: the master plan (including its site plans) and the building programme as well. The law also provided that the issuance by the commune of building permits should be tied to the payment by the developer (to be covered within a three-year period) of the estimated cost for basic infrastructure (*costi di urbanizzazione primaria*), such as sewer and road connections.

Shortly thereafter, in 1968, a Constitutional Court decision invalidated those parts of the *legge ponte* that limited the increase in land values by allowing communes to hold the areas which the master plan set aside for public uses and which the commune would expropriate as the plan was implemented through the preparation of specific site plans. Following the Court ruling, the compensation to be paid to property owners by the communes for the areas set aside for services reached astronomical levels. Just when the communal plans had to adopt mandatory development standards, therefore, the decision of the Constitutional Court placed into question the feasibility of the more directive approach of growth management.

Law 765 even worsened the impact on the communes by providing a temporary loophole. It allowed a twelve-month moratorium when it was possible to build without consideration for the new legislative provisions. The amount of construction jumped fivefold in comparison to that of any previous year. It must also be stressed that the 1967 law was applied sparingly. In the South ten years later only seven communes had asked for the payment of infrastructure costs by private developers.

The third phase in the evolution of urban planning policies begins with the birth of the regions, which institutionally were attributed the policy area of urban and territorial planning. In response to the problems caused by uncontrolled urban growth, mass movements arose in the late 1960s in the urban areas to press for citizen participation in development decisions, the reorganization of cities to make them more liveable, and the right to city services and to adequate housing (*diritto alla città*). In the 1970s the regions played a fundamental role in promoting the notion of the commune's responsibility to plan its development. Regional governments undertook to lend technical and financial assistance, particularly to the small and medium-size communes, to help them develop and adopt plans and building programmes. For example, in 1972, 64 per cent (167) of the communes in Puglia did not have any type of plan; in 1975 that figure had declined to 27 per cent (69) of the communes. Another telling example is offered by Lazio. In 1972, 83 per cent (308) of its communes did not have a plan. Two years later, the level had been cut to 11 per cent (Putnam, Leonardi & Nanetti, 1985).

Equally important was the impact of the innovative planning legislation that was produced, first by a few regions and later adopted by others, and which even found its way into national legislation. The urban planning law which Lombardy passed in 1975 was the most comprehensive piece of such legislation produced during the first legislature. The law introduced, for example, new implementation tools for the communal plans, such as the work programmes (*programmi di attuazione*), detailing the schedule and financial coverage of the actual development projects, a notion that was later incorporated into national legislation (No. 10, 1977). Despite prodding from the regions, the State did not come up with a comprehensive rewriting and updating of its planning legislation. Different national government coalitions continued to extend the life of the emergency legislation (No. 1187) passed in 1968 and aimed at alleviating the critical situation for the communes created by the Constitutional Court decision. The 1968 legislation allowed the communes five years from the approval of the master plan to reimburse owners of land held in areas designated for expropriation.

In the mid-1970s, particularly innovative experiments appeared at the communal level, reflecting the legacy of ideas generated by a fifteen-year long debate on development issues, and breaking new ground. The experiments began to move away from the issues of urban expansion by concentrating on issues concerned with the reorganization and conservation of existing urban centres. Among the most significant was the experience of Pavia where the creation of neighbourhood government went hand-in-hand with the process of preparing the new master plan. The point of departure of the Pavia experience was the 1974 Municipal Service Plan (*Piano dei servizi*), whose objective was to protect the undeveloped areas in the central part of the city. The Plan was based on detailed studies of small neighbourhood areas, measuring their population and economic resources, and housing and service needs. In 1976 Pavia adopted a new master plan which put a freeze on all private construction in the city centre, allowed for moderate growth in the peripheral neighbourhoods, and zoned for agricultural use the remaining outlying areas. The plan encountered difficulties in its implementation, especially because of the lack of adequate financial resources for its ambitious public service goals (Campos Venuti & Oliva, 1978), but its directive policies of growth management remained in place. Other large—including Milan and Rome—and small communes followed Pavia's example in the following years with varying levels of success.

Another prominent effort at growth management by a commune that began to receive close attention in those years was that of the city of Bologna whose innovative policies had been developed over a fifteen-year period. Here, the guiding principle was the search for a functional balance between the city centre and its periphery, thereby breaking the dependence of the former on the latter. To this end, the plans adopted by Bologna aimed at containing the pattern of private development based on rising building land values and expanding public infrastructure. Urban policies in Bologna made maximum and systematic use of all existing legislation—from public and subsidized housing to pre-school education. The city's administrative apparatus was restructured and upgraded, and the city promoted a political and administrative form of decentralization. Characteristic of the Bologna experience was the comprehensiveness, continuity over time, and extent of implementation of its planning policies. In comparative terms, these characteristics made the Bologna experience in urban planning the most significant case in Italy.

The 1977 decrees (No. 616) certainly reinforced the role of the regions and communes *vis-à-vis* the State in the area of urban planning. For example, they transferred from the State to the regions the setting of development (planning and building) standards. But, even more, the commune's effectiveness in growth management was enhanced by the provision of the 1977 law (No. 10) regulating the right to build (*edificabilità dei suoli*). The fundamental change that the law made was the separation of the right of ownership of property (which is protected by the Constitution) from the right to build on it, which the law attributed to the commune.[3]

The mechanism created by the legislation to operationalize the right of the commune to decide how the property should be used was the 'concession' (*concessione*) to build. The owner is required to seek and obtain from the commune the *concessione*, which obligates him to assume the cost of basic infrastructure related to the project (*oneri di urbanizzazione primaria*) and to contribute to the cost of the new services and amenities for the area (*oneri di urbanizzazione secondaria*), according to the parameters that are set by each region. The law put the communes and regions in a position to engage in long-term planning since it mandated the formulation of multi-year development work programmes (*programmi pluriennali di attuazione*) and limited the concessions to projects located in the work programme areas.

The implementation of the law has encountered problems at the communal level.[4] The most glaring deficiencies—in terms of resistance to the preparation of the multi-year work programmes and to unwarranted revisions of local plans—cropped up in the South. In this part of the country, many communes continued to endorse ineffective approaches—for example, the growth projections contained in the new master plan for Reggio Calabria—and to weaken existing plans, as in the case of Messina and Catania where repeated revisions of the master plans whittled away already limited parkland. In addition, southern cities more so than others continued to display their traditional limitations: for example, the lack of statistical information that the communes have tried to remedy through the computerization of their facilities.

8.2. From Historic Preservation to Urban Conservation

The commitment of the communes and the regions to more effective planning policies has not been limited to the control of new growth, but, in time, it has shifted its focus to the protection of the existing urban centres. Historic centres were singled out as a planning issue in the 1960s. Over the last twenty years, the nature of the debate on the future of historic centres has changed from considering them separately—as a special section of the city—to a broader approach which relates them to the city as a whole and to its regional context. This cultural change imposed a new view of the essence of the growth of cities that brought together, in a relationship of interdependence, the quantitative and qualitative aspects of the expansion of the peripheral areas and the transformations of the historic centres. It represented a gradual process of change which unfolded through various temporal phases, each characterized by innovative ideas and the search for more effective technical tools to implement them, and ultimately expressing the concept that the protection of the historic centres requires interventionist policies and not just restrictive controls.

A national conference held in Gubbio in 1960 on the theme of the protection and restoration of city centres represented a watershed in this evolution. It sanctioned the rejection of the activities of 'modernization' which, during the period of the reconstruction and the 1950s, had torn down buildings and widened roads inside the historic centres. In opposition to this view and practice, the conference proposed the concept of historic preservation (*risanamento conservativo*) and the adoption of two objectives: (1) the protection of the artistic treasures and monuments and the integrity of the urban structure of older cities, and (2) the improvement of the quality of life in them. In fact, the conference underlined the impossibility of achieving the second objective without accomplishing the first.

These principles were expressed in a 1962 legislative proposal of the National Association of Historic Centres that integrated historic preservation with the urban planning policies of the commune. The commune was mandated to prepare a historic preservation plan in conjunction with the adoption of its master plan or to revise the latter in case of incompatibility between the two. The Association's proposal also articulated general policy criteria and binding technical principles that were to underpin the formulation of the historic preservation plan.

But it was later, with the urban planning law of 1967 (No. 765), that the communes obtained from the State the power to impose binding regulations on private development for the protection of their historic centres. The 1967 law lifted, for example, the provision that had limited communal action to works of consolidation and restoration of monuments and buildings; at the same time, it gave communes the power to protect from development the available areas in the historic sections of cities even in the absence of the master plan. In fact, it was the first time that planning legislation had specifically articulated issues of historic preservation in terms of retaining the structural characteristics of the existing residential areas and not just the preservation of monuments (Carozzi & Rozzi, 1971).

A stimulus to the adoption of comprehensive preservation policies on the part of the communes came from *ad hoc* State laws regarding the protection of historic centres in particular conditions of hardship. The special national law for the rescue of Venice (1973) required the formulation of an area-wide plan for the integration of historic preservation projects with general social and economic objectives. The policy adopted by the Veneto region in 1974 provided for the creation of two stock companies, with the majority of capital owned by the region, to implement restoration and preservation projects in Venice and Chioggia (Amorosino, 1975). Also of importance was the special law for the reconstruction of the historic centre of Ancona which had been severely damaged by the 1972 earthquake. The city, empowered to operate with great flexibility and on a wide range of policies, was able to make use of the most advanced construction technologies and to cut through administrative red tape, thereby achieving good results, which included bringing back to the rehabilitated historic neighbourhoods the population that had lived there before the earthquake.

Despite the fact that these laws tended to highlight the special nature of individual cases, they nevertheless underlined the move to a different phase in the debate on historic centres. The move was in the direction of articulating and protecting the social value of historic centres in relation to their external areas, and to shift to the broader principle of urban conservation (*conservazione attiva*) or the application of policies designed to maintain the physical, social and economic context of the historic centres. The debate switched from the perspective that had denied the value of the older centres and endorsed their modernization, to its exact opposite: the rediscovery of the centre's function not only as a cultural but also as a social and economic force of attraction. The best examples of urban conservation policies are the plans for the cities of Bologna, Brescia, Pavia, Modena and Ferrara—a few of which will be discussed below.

The 1969 Bologna plan was the first to utilize an innovative analytical methodology that identified building typologies according to which each structure in the historic centre was then classified for the purpose of intervening with differentiated and appropriate action (Cervellati & Scannavini, 1973; Comune di Bologna, 1979). The planning approach that underlines the Bologna plan is, undoubtedly, that of urban conservation, with the main goal of halting the displacement of working-class families and their economic activities from the historic centre (Cervellati & Miliari, 1977).

The principal means for achieving this goal was the *convenzione*, a legally binding agreement between the city administration and private property-owners which brought the two parties into close co-operation in the implementation of conservation projects, designed strictly in adherence to the specifications for the particular typology of the building, and also in fulfillment of the social objectives of the plan. For this purpose, the *convenzione* incorporated a mix of anti-displacement clauses but also financial incentives for property-owners to rehabilitate their buildings (Moggio-Gattei, 1977). In 1974 Pavia moved in the same direction, with amendments to its master plan intended to create incentives for the retention of industrial activities in the historic centre by restricting any change of zoning of industrial sites from manufacturing to recreational uses as public parkland only.

In recent years, there has been a natural extension of the concept of conservation beyond the perimeter of the historic centre to include the first outer ring of older neighbourhoods (*periferia intermedia*), in an attempt to better achieve the goal of containing the processes of change that displace the working-class and artisan activities from the centre and replace them with traditional and new service sector activities. Also, the movement for urban conservation has now spread from the cities to the smaller towns in the metropolitan hinterland where it has been enhanced by the new planning powers given to the communes by the 1977 law (No. 10).

The most recent debate on the communal policies for urban conservation has further articulated the theme of the quality of life throughout the urban area. One proposal argues that urban conservation policies need to be differentiated and improved upon by seeking a *specific* identity and role for each neighbourhood and each historic centre. Cervellati (1984) proposes that this search for identity should proceed all the way up to paying attention to the visual details (*arredo urbano*) that give a place its character (Ruggeri & Zanzani, 1981). In fact, the debate is prompted by the large sites—found in most cities—that have lost their original function and have become marginal—such as old industrial complexes, car racetracks and commons (*aree demaniali*)—and by the problem of re-fitting them for alternative uses (*riuso*). Under the current conditions of zero or negative population growth in many northern Italian cities, this policy approach proposes that further restrictions be placed on expansion outward for the purpose of concentrating resources towards improving the quality of life within the urbanized areas. Such a proposal to 'plan for quality' has recently been endorsed by the city of Leghorn.

8.3. The Local Promotion of Housing

The increased role of the commune in the promotion of housing has coincided with the deepening of the housing crisis and with the implementation of regional decentralization. During the fifteen-year period between 1951 and 1966 there was a strong increase in home ownership, which rose from 40 to 51 per cent of the total housing stock.[5] Correspondingly, the rise in demand (particularly in areas of high immigration) increased rents in what was a shrinking rental market. The growth in the gap between the supply and demand of housing occurred despite very high levels of housing construction. In the decade between 1959 and 1968, 3.3 million dwellings were built, in comparison with the total increase in population of 3.2 million. However, it is also true that there was still a backlog of more than one family sharing apartments. In comparison with the 1950s, the level of public financial support for housing in the 1960s declined substantially and the funds that did exist were concentrated on new housing in peripheral zones which did not have adequate services.

It was in the 1960s that the housing crisis took on a new dimension, not just as a mere shortage but because of critical shortages of housing for working-class, urban families. The crisis deepened with each successive wave of immigration that was directed toward the large industrial cities of the North, in addition to Rome and other metropolitan areas in the South. The social tensions created by the housing shortage exploded at the end of the decade with the occupation by right-to-housing groups of vacant apartments in a number of cities around the country and with the first general strike, on 19 November 1969, protesting the shortage of housing and demanding new housing programmes (Buratto & Lelli, 1975).

This series of events forced the government to intervene and approve a number of band-aid measures until it could pass the conceptually innovative housing law of 1971 (No. 865). Law 865 is important since, firstly, it established a link between housing needs and programmes and the social and economic objectives of the master plan, thus recognizing the commune's primary role in housing and the legislative support provided by the region to the commune. At the State level, the law created the Housing Committee (*Comitato Edilizia Residenziale*, CER) for the distribution of State funds for housing among the regions on the basis of a plan that was to take into account regional housing needs. The selection of housing sites was the responsibility of the region, which was to fulfill its responsibility in co-operation with other levels of local government. Generally, the sites were to be chosen within the areas set aside and acquired through the provision of the 1962 law on public and subsidized housing. Those authorized to bid for the construction contracts were the reorganized Public Housing Agencies (IACP) and co-operatives, but not private developers.[6] The limitations produced a relatively small number of housing units and, within a few years, forced the passage of an emergency plan for the financing of subsidized housing.

An important characteristic of the 1971 housing law was the power it gave the regions to select sites for public investment in housing in consultation with the communes, while the communes reserved the function of acquiring the sites and of stipulating builders' contracts that determined the cost of housing and the level of rents. However, it is commonly acknowledged that a major shortcoming of the law was the limited funds made available by the State (Regione Umbria, 1977). For example, with regard to subsidized housing, the State was not forthcoming in adjusting the level of support to bring it into line with the rise in inflation, thus greatly reducing the commune's ability to take full advantage of the law.

Despite these programmes, the housing crisis deepened in the 1970s, owing to a different set of factors. In addition to the traditional ones—such as the gap between the cost of housing and family income—the new factors contributing to the crisis were: changes in the world economy that raised the cost of building materials and the impact on housing of the cost of expanding urban services. In 1978 the government responded by adopting a ten-year housing plan (law No. 457) which pooled all the public resources for housing to fund four-year programmes prepared by the regions and to be implemented through two-year projects. The regions had to estimate housing needs for the period, survey current residents of public housing to establish eligibility, and ultimately allocate funds for new construction among the communes. For the first time, the law stressed the priority of rehabilitating the existing housing stock rather than engaging in new construction. In 1983 the CER report on the level of implementation of the housing plan over the first six years found great variation from region to region. The worst record was registered in some of the southern regions. Generally, in the second and third project period there was an increase in the ability of the regions and their communes to prepare the housing projects and complete the construction on time.

The need on the part of the regions and communes to intervene rapidly in response to the demand for affordable housing had become critical by the end of the 1970s, when the shortage in rented housing became a real emergency following the virtual disappearance of the rental market on the heels of the passage of the national rent control law (*equo canone*) in 1978 (No. 392). For some years, the dramatic rise in eviction notices and the continuously high levels of inflation and interest rates, which prevented many from making the move to home-ownership, combined to create social tension, especially in the metropolitan areas where most of the evictions took place. The legislative response to this housing emergency—for example, the special plans (*piani straordinari*) of 1980 (law No. 25) and of 1982 (law No. 94)—strengthened the role of the commune in housing in relation to that of the regions since the State transferred funds directly to the communes. Following the housing emergency, many of the larger communes have restructured their departments by creating housing assessorates and housing offices. The latter formulate categories for prospective public housing tenants, assign dwellings to those evicted, and monitor the demand, particularly for public housing.

For their part, some communes have demonstrated a great capacity to innovate and experiment with housing plans to meet emergency situations. In Brescia, the construction by the commune of the San Polo neighbourhood used the funding mechanism of the rotating fund, in which the initial investment by the commune was used to build the first batch of units whose subsequent sale helped to finance the purchase of other tracts of land and the construction of additional housing. The neighbourhood includes a majority of owner-occupied, subsidized properties and the others are rented public housing units. The project was carried out, in addition to the commune, by the IACP, by co-operatives, private contractors, and even by some residents who built their own homes. It used binding agreements between the commune and builders to keep costs at almost half those found on the private market. The neighbourhood is a mixed-use project (*progetto integrato*) and in addition to its diverse housing—from the small apartment to the town-house—it contains an industrial park for small business, and commercial and service areas.

In Modena, in 1983, the city administration put together a different approach by creating a stock company, whose majority share is owned by the city, which attracts private savings to be invested in rented housing. Together with the stock company, the city created a service agency for the management of the newly built rented housing. The premise is to eliminate the barriers to investment in this sector on the part of small investors by shielding them from the concern of managing the property. The investor receives 'housing shares' for the twelve-year period of the investment, at the end of which the building is sold and the investor is repaid in full and given his share of the building's appreciation.

A third approach is that of the city of Bologna, and it addresses the high cost of housing, especially for young couples and other first-time home buyers. The Bologna proposal concentrates on the goal of splitting the cost of production or restoration of a dwelling between the city and programme participants, for example having the city pay for the basic structure and the participant for the cost of completion. Finally, in Milan, the city's policies for preserving the existing housing stock, which go back to the 1960s, include the stipulation of agreements with private developers for rehabilitation projects. One innovation introduced in 1981 is the 'special convention', according to which, in a building that is being rehabilitated, a percentage of the apartments are reserved for the former tenants, while the developer sells or rents the others on the open market.

Notes

1. The master plan is the general zoning and infrastructure plan which identifies the areas (zones) where different kinds of development (e.g. residential, commercial, industrial, etc.) are allowed, subject to the specifications of the site plans. The site plan is the approved detailed development proposal encompassing the specifications of the location, typology and volume of buildings, street layout, supporting infrastructure, etc. for an area.
2. Up until 1975 Milan was governed by a centrist (up to 1960) or centre-left (from 1960 to 1975) coalition, while the surrounding communal governments were of many different political colourations; many in fact were governed by leftist (PCI-PSI) coalitions.
3. Article 42 of the Constitution states that: 'Private property is recognized and guaranteed by law, which determines the methods of its acquisition and enjoyment and the limitations designed to assure its social function and render it accessible to all. In cases prescribed by law, and on the basis of compensation, private property may be expropriated for reasons of the general interest.'
4. On the other hand, the regions have moved expeditiously to determine the cost categories and the parameters for updating them for the different sizes of commune.
5. The total housing stock also included a growing percentage of vacation homes built as investment properties.
6. Three types of public sector involvement in housing were developed in Italy over the years: (1) *edilizia sovvenzionata* or public housing built directly with public funds by the IACP after 1972 and a variety of public agencies until 1972; (2) *edilizia agevolata* or subsidized housing built by co-operatives and private developers with lower-cost mortgage loans subsidized by the State; and (3) *edilizia convenzionata* or low and moderate cost housing built according to an agreement (*convenzione*) between the commune and public or private developers and usually involving land cost write-downs or land donation by the commune.

9 Neighbourhood Councils: Social Service Delivery at the Grass Roots

9.1. Participation in the Management of Social Services

The 1970s represented a watershed in the conceptualization of the role of the social services in Italian society. Previously, the dominant forms of delivery had been controlled by the State, where the major objective was often to provide employment in the public sector, or by private, religious or Church-affiliated institutions that used service provision as a means of penetrating society and carrying out their evangelical mission. Particularly in the latter case, services assumed the connotation of 'charity' extended to the needy and of instruments for doing 'good deeds'. On the heels of the social mobilization of the 1960s and 1970s there came an evolution in Italian cultural norms that was nowhere as evident as in the redefinition of social services and the respective roles in their delivery of the private and the public sector. In turn, this change of orientation stimulated the growth of three major policies and institutional developments: (1) the municipalization of service delivery; (2) the de-institutionalization of assisted groups; and (3) the formal recognition of the sub-communal level as the optimal point for the delivery of a broad range of social services.

The municipalization of social services was brought about through the 1977 regional decrees (No. 616) and the 1978 law (No. 833) that created a national health care system. Together, these two measures represent the most innovative steps in the decentralization of the social policy process by identifying in the commune or communal consortia the level of government that is responsible for the management of services and for limiting the provincial level of government to a residual role. Subsequent state and regional legislation has promoted the delivery of social services as part of locally-based and integrated systems rather than favouring the growth of separate services responding to different needs. Additionally, the municipalization of service delivery has meant the abandonment of the notion of social services as charity to be provided for the needy. The new conception incorporates the principle of universal access so that social services are to be provided to all members of society as a right.[1]

At around the same time there has been an affirmation of the cultural and political movement that seeks to de-institutionalize assisted groups in opposition to the notion that these groups should be isolated from society and placed in institutions, which had been the preferred solution in the past for state-run services. The de-institutionalization movement has pointed towards alternative forms of assistance that focus on prevention and promote the social integration of marginalized groups in the territorial community to which they belong.

Likewise, the creation of neighbourhood government (law No. 278, of 1976) and the role of the elected councils in the formulation of communal social service policies has strengthened in two ways the neighbourhood level in the organization of services. Firstly, neighbourhood government has had the impact of diffusing services throughout the city. Secondly, its political and administrative organs provide a variety of opportunities for citizen participation, and they are the terminals to which demands are addressed and new services articulated. Where neighbourhood institutions are missing, cities have had difficulty in implementing new approaches to the expansion and delivery of social services (Nanetti, 1983a). This has led to a considerable amount of differentiation of what one finds at the grass-roots in one city *vis-à-vis* another. Thus, Italian cities vary greatly in terms of the quality and quantity of services offerred to their citizens.

Despite the profound change in the institutional and cultural context of social service policies, there remain radical territorial imbalances in the wide differentiation from one region to another in the availability of services. Profound geographic inequalities in the distribution of services are still the norm and the southern regions and peripheral areas around large cities find themselves in a particularly disadvantageous position. These imbalances even exist in service areas in which the State has been active for a long time, such as that of day-care centres where, between 1971 and 1983, the State has financed 55 per cent of the infrastructure and service expenditure (CENSIS, 1983). For example, in 1983, while Emilia-Romagna which has one of the lowest birth-rates in the country had one day-care centre for every 278 children, Campania had one day-care centre for every 12,245 children, and the country's highest birth-rate.

Correspondingly, there are regions that have achieved, from a quantitative as well as a qualitative point of view, levels of public services that are among the highest in Europe. It is, above all, within this highly developed environment—which is still limited to some of the northern and central regions—that the qualitatively new demand for social services has emerged with regard to programme content, schedule flexibility, diversification of services and participation of users in service management. Today in Italy there exists a strong positive correlation between the level and quality of public services and the demand from citizens to participate in their management. There is also a positive correlation between experiences with neighbourhood government, which entail the delegation of real powers from the commune to the neighbourhoods, and citizen participation in the management of public social services (Nanetti, 1985).

The period of mass mobilization of the late 1960s and early 1970s saw a rapid increase in the participation of service users in public assemblies and political debates on broad service policy issues and the experimentation with self-management. This type of participation has subsided (Ranci, 1985), and in the 1980s the new approach to citizen participation emphasizes personal involvement and actual work with smaller groups on single issues or a few germane service issues. Citizen participation in service management thus translates into: (1) co-management (*cogestione*) of service infrastructures and programmes that are already provided at the neighbourhood level and (2) co-production (*coproduzione*) of services, or the contribution of neighbourhood residents to the creation of new services that are not yet available.

Since 1977, the process of delegating functions from the communal to the neighbourhood level has been particularly accentuated in the area of social services where there is already a clear tendency towards new modes of citizen participation. In particular, in cities where neighbourhood governments have been elected there is an increased recognition of volunteer groups which operate autonomously but also in co-operation with the neighbourhood-elected councils (Bersani, 1984; Zanniboni, 1982). In these cities, citizen participation in the management of services should appropriately be defined as volunteer work, which is an *integral* component of public service delivery. Numerous examples can be cited.

In the area of leisure and sport activities, it is common for groups of residents—in co-operation with the neighbourhood councils—to be in charge of preparing schedules for the use of neighbourhood facilities such as swimming pools, playgrounds and gyms; to supervise their maintenance; organize competitive events; and co-ordinate courses offered by volunteers (IREF, 1985). More recently, neighbourhood councils—based on the examples of those in Modena, Reggio Emilia and Ferrara—have begun to systematically use resident pensioners in the upkeep of gardens and public buildings and involve them in the socialization activities of children in day-care centres and nursery schools. In Reggio Emilia the neighbourhood councils co-ordinate the activities of these volunteers with the appropriate city departments to ensure transportation for the volunteers and to provide them with token payment.

Volunteers are also involved in the construction of new recreation facilities. They contribute their labour to projects co-ordinated by the neighbourhood council. The most notable examples are those of neighbourhood parks created out of vacant lots, the preparation of vacant sites to be used as fruit and vegetable gardens, and the rehabilitation of farmhouses and other buildings whose presence has a particular significance for the social history of the neighbourhood and represents an element of continuity, identity and aggregation for the residents of the neighbourhood. In these cases, the buildings are targeted for use as multi-purpose neighbourhood centres. Once the new neighbourhood facilities are planned and built, their management and use are co-ordinated by committees of volunteers and neighbourhood councillors. The cities of Florence, Bologna and Pesaro have been particularly active in promoting these facilities for the elderly and neighbourhood volunteer activities.

Service management by citizens has also occurred in public social services targeted to user groups with special needs, such as the elderly, children and the handicapped. Examples include groups whose work is co-ordinated by the hospitals and USL in the neighbourhood, which offer exercise programmes for preventive and therapeutic care; groups that work with children in schools on hygiene and health education; and others that do programme planning in gerontology centres and family planning clinics. In the area of pre-school education the contribution of parents normally takes place at the level of the school and is most often a contribution to the definition of programme content.

The participation of residents in the management of services is also found in the area of cultural services. After the initial phase in the mid-1970s of developing basic infrastructures such as neighbourhood libraries and reading centres, concern in recent years has turned to a re-definition of their role as multi-purpose structures and to the expansion of neighbourhood programmes to include theatres, art studios and film clubs. Most of these activities are promoted and co-ordinated by neighbourhood volunteers.

In the 1980s neighbourhood institutions have demonstrated a particular attention to the young by trying to involve them individually and as groups in the planning and management of youth centres. A comprehensive approach to youth services has been taken by the city of Forlì. Service planning and programming is carried out by neighbourhood management committees, half of whose membership is made up by the young and the rest by staff and other volunteers. Many of these programmes are aimed at youth socialization, while others deal with problems of drug addiction, apathy and emargination (Montanari, 1982). A number of cities have developed services specifically targeted at youth: the informal meeting centres in Turin, leisure-time centres in Milan, and the more structured programmes of the youth centres in Bologna. In Trieste social meeting centres have been conceived as facilities for the rehabilitation of drug addicts.

The value of volunteer management of services has to be judged beyond its civic contribution to include the actual monetary value of the work provided, given that the number of clerical employees available to the neighbourhoods for management tasks is quite limited. On the other hand, in a city like Bologna, with a population of half a million, in 1983 neighbourhood facilities included sixteen libraries, twenty youth centres, twenty-three gerontology centres, and thirty-eight sports complexes, in addition to numerous public parks, day-care centres, cultural facilities and other services. In today's context of tighter communal budgets, the contribution to the management of services by users has become indispensable and local and neighbourhood governments are actively promoting these partnerships. Thus, the rise of voluntarism has coincided with the crisis of the Welfare State and the decrease in the State's ability and willingness to pay for the expansion of the social agenda.

9.2. Voluntarism in the Social Services

For both conceptual as well as operational reasons, it is useful to make a distinction between participation in the management of a public social service and the production of a social service on the part of volunteer associations. As has been pointed out, the participation in the management of a public service is also a volunteer activity, but, at the same time, it represents an *integrating* component of the service which remains a service offered by a public agency. Instead, the experiences discussed below deal with services produced by the non-profitmaking sector (*privato sociale*) that operates autonomously from the commune and plays three different roles as producer of services:

— *complementary*, when the service by the non-profitmaking sector complements a public service, such as the home care by a volunteer organization that is complementary to the public hospital care provided to the elderly;
— *supplementary*, when a public service is not provided and the service offered by the non-profitmaking sector is the alternative to services provided at full cost by the market; and
— *alternative*, when the non-profitmaking sector provides a different service from that offered by the public sector, often because of the former's capacity to experiment with new approaches but also because of different views on what the goals of the service should be, such as in the case of family planning clinics.

Since the beginning of the 1970s, there has been a tremendous growth of voluntarism in the social service area. Its growth has been documented by surveys and by the visible proliferation of groups and activities. As is common practice in Italy for the debate of new concepts in social action, a large number of highly visible conferences have brought to the attention of the public and local administrators the phenomenon of voluntarism. CARITAS, a large network affiliated to the Catholic Church, undertook a study in 1976 and 1977 to make an inventory of Catholic social service organizations staffed by volunteers. The effort was followed by the organization of biannual national conferences on the role of voluntarism in different regional and local contexts and the reasons for its growth and prospects. In 1985 a national centre for the collection of documentation and the dissemination of information on voluntarism was created in Lucca.

In recent years, state laws have more explicitly incorporated the non-profitmaking sector into the delivery of services, although to date framework legislation is still lacking which would accommodate voluntarism as an unpaid service to society. Several issues need to be addressed by such legislation, including the status of volunteers as an unpaid workforce in order not to conflict with labour laws, the setting of minimum quality standards for services rendered, and the monitoring of these activities. Certainly, the growth of voluntarism is another example of how Italian civil society debates an issue, experiments with policies, and finally promotes a legislative response. In terms of single policy areas, the first response by the State began with the recognition (law No. 772, 1972) of volunteer services to be performed at home or abroad by conscientious objectors. Other national legislation also foresaw a role for volunteer social workers in penal institutions (law No. 754, 1975), support work by volunteers in the rehabilitation of drug addicts (law No. 683, 1975), and the recognition of a role for volunteer associations in the national health system (law No. 833, 1978), particularly in the preventive and educational service areas.

It has been the more advanced regional legislation organizing the USLs, however, that has given the largest role to individuals and volunteer associations and has best incorporated their services in the mental health, gerontological and physical handicap care sectors. In the 1980s the first comprehensive regional laws regulating volunteer service in the health and social service fields were passed by, for example, Marche, Campania and Veneto. Other regions promoted the role of volunteers in disaster relief (Emilia-Romagna)[2] and in the protection of cultural and environmental treasures (Lombardy). To these should be added regional legislation, which has developed inventories of voluntary associations as a data base for service planning proposals (Veneto). In addition, the volunteer movement has organized itself at the regional level with the creation of federations of the lay, volunteer organizations (Paracone *et al.*, 1978).

In spite of the attention paid, it has been difficult to quantify in precise terms the extent of voluntarism in Italy. Estimates have put the numbers at more than three million volunteers—or one in every nineteen people—organized into over fifteen thousand associations. More than half the volunteers operate within large associations, such as the Red Cross and CARITAS, approximately one-fifth work with neighbourhood groups, and one-fourth in organizations at the city and regional level. More men than women are volunteers, and most come from middle and upper-middle class backgrounds. Voluntarism is more present in the North; in the South volunteers are scarcer in the larger rather than in the smaller cities. In general, the phenomenon is more typical of smaller cities (IREF, 1985).

While studies confirm the concentration of voluntarism in the more traditional welfare services—this is also the conclusion of local studies conducted in Forlì (Belli, 1982) and Rome (ACAP, 1980)—at the same time the volunteer movement has expanded into service areas that attempt to meet new social needs that are not adequately met by the public sector. In other words, the self-propelling dynamic of voluntarism is based on the sensitivity that the movement displays for emerging needs as well as its openness to experimentation with new solutions. As a result, in the 1980s one finds voluntarism in a vast array of services: disaster relief, consumer protection, cultural promotion and environmental protection have been added to the areas of welfare, education and health. What follows are particularly significant examples of volunteer services that cover the range of needs that are now met and the diffusion of the phenomenon from one urban context to another.

In most large cities there are groups that make use of full-time volunteers: the Abel Group in Turin operates with approximately one hundred full-time and a number of part-time volunteers and works with drug addicts and prostitutes. Among the activities of the group are a telephone hot-line, half-way houses and drug rehabilitation centres. In Genoa the Solidarity Centre works in the area of drug rehabilitation but also has the goal of prevention, especially in the schools where volunteers participate in seminars and debates organized by the students on the subject. Volunteers in the city of Bergamo have set up a centre for assistance to drug addicts which operates half-way houses and smaller family-size living arrangements for drug addicts undergoing rehabilitation and finds them new employment. In Rimini the Saint Patrignano Community has developed a long history of rehabilitating young drug addicts who come there from all over the country, providing them with job training, and placing them in artisan jobs in the surrounding smaller towns.

In Florence the Equipe of Hope co-ordinates the work of thousands of volunteers working with unmarried mothers, the elderly, handicapped and drug addicts. Florence also has Community Commitment, a group that is active in the rehabilitation of convicts. In Turin and other Piedmontese cities a network of volunteers works for the care of abandoned children and the elderly living alone. Cremona has a group that is made up of employees of small, artisan firms that has dedicated itself to providing handicapped and disadvantaged children with vocational education.

The flourishing of these spontaneous activities has created the pressure to increase the level of communication and co-ordination across city and regional boundaries and to verify more systematically the extent to which local experiences can be adopted elsewhere. One of the first initiatives of co-ordination within the larger urban context of Rome was a city-wide organization that since 1973 has managed the activities of the volunteers affiliated to the Saint Egidio Community working in fourteen working-class neighbourhoods and the city's historic centre. There are also volunteer associations that have been present for centuries in a particular region, such as the Misericordie in Tuscany. They now co-ordinate their activities with those of the regional and local governments and provide services that are complementary to those made available by the public sector: for example, transport for the handicapped, an ambulance service and supervisory work in day-care centres and old peoples' homes. Similarly, throughout Lombardy, the Our Family association has been operating since the turn of the century in the area of rehabilitation of delinquent children and child neuro-psychiatric care.

Contrary to expectations, it has been difficult to define the role of volunteer organizations within the national health system through the stipulation of *convenzioni*, as foreseen by the 1978 law. The multiplication of co-operation initiatives between volunteers and USLs was undoubtedly slowed down by the organizational difficulties encountered by many regions in the creation of the USLs themselves. Following the granting of recognition to conscientious objectors, and the growth in their number, it is now possible to incorporate these volunteer activities into local health and social service planning. For example, the city of Forlì has constituted a co-ordinating committee to match conscientious objectors with neighbourhood health service requests. An agreement with the Ministry of Defence now also allows the objectors to work in youth centres.

Voluntarism has increased rapidly in the environmental protection sector, as witnessed by the growth in membership of large and established organizations such as Italia Nostra and WWF, and the restructuring of their programmes to emphasize local conservation activities and mass education programmes in schools as well as through the electronic and print media. In addition, local groups organize guided tours of particularly important environmental areas, such as those of the regional chapter in Puglia to the primitive Christian Church sites and the ravines where they are located.

The growth of voluntarism has also been registered in the area of cultural resource development with the creation, during the past fifteen years, of numerous regional and local organizations. The mission of many of the new associations and groups is directly tied to the conservation of local traditions, monuments and archeological sites. For example, the association Glicerio Longa has built an ethnographic museum of popular culture in the Alps. These associations have particularly strong ties with, and receive financial support from, local banks, industrial associations and philanthrophists (Tavazza, *et al.*, 1985).

Disaster relief services have always been operated almost exclusively through volunteer organizations in the absence of the public sector. Traditionally, volunteer activities have concentrated on the direct assistance to families affected by natural disasters. During the 1966 flood in Florence volunteer activities contributed from all over the world spread to include the salvaging, drying and restoration of artworks. These activities caught the attention of public opinion and since then have been awarded a prominent role in the safeguarding of cultural and artistic treasures. The role of volunteers in disaster relief expanded on the heels of the experience with earthquakes in Friuli-Venezia Giulia (1976), in Basilicata and Irpinia (1980), and the terrorist bombing of the Bologna station (1981). The subsequent creation of the Ministry for Disaster Relief and regional and local programmes to train volunteers reflect the increased importance of these issues.

The growth of volunteer groups has inevitably focused the policy debate on the nature of their relationship with local and regional governments and the need to provide volunteer activities with a clear legal base (Lipari, *et al.*, 1980). In some regions the stipulation of a formal *convenzione* is the means that has been adopted to regulate this relationship. This has been particularly important for the many organizations operating in the area of welfare and health services. In addition, there is the concern of keeping these organizations abreast of and promoting their participation in the formulation of public policies.

9.3. Co-operatives and Mutual Aid Societies

In this period of extreme dynamism of service policies reflected in the search for new forms of delivery, it is important to discuss the contribution made by service co-operatives (*cooperative di servizi*) and by mutual aid societies (*società di mutuo soccorso*). Since the early 1970s, service co-ops have experienced a remarkable growth. Although they still cover a relatively limited range of services, they are present, firstly, in welfare services—including social work, vocational education and health care—followed by monitoring of health conditions in the workplace. Service co-operatives are co-ops in which the members produce services rather than goods. But there are also examples of mixed service co-ops in which some members are producers while others are consumers of services. Another recent development is represented by a mode of service delivery in which there is the participation of both service co-operatives and volunteer associations as, for example, in the case of transportation for the handicapped in Bologna provided by a consortium of volunteer associations and co-operatives.

The reasons for the creation of service co-operatives vary. They range from the particular social and political views that members hold about the objectives of their own profession and the nature of social problems to acknowledging the inability of public bureaucracies to fill a specific need.

The first service co-operatives began to appear in the early 1970s, but undoubtedly their development has been accelerated by the contingent factor of the increased difficulty experienced by communes—starting in the late 1970s—in adding or replacing personnel because of the imposed hiring freeze. On the other hand, considering the range of new service producers, a distinction needs to be made between service co-ops and volunteer associations. The service co-ops have built on the special recognition and promotion that the Constitution gives to the co-operative enterprise because it is seen as directly pursuing an important social objective: group solidarity.[3] Therefore, the co-op is not a volunteer enterprise in that it does not contribute unpaid services, but it is a non-profitmaking enterprise. In Italy service co-ops are an extension of the powerful co-operative movement that already exists in the areas of housing, agriculture, public works and retail trades.

Service co-ops are smaller in scale than their traditional counterparts. They began operating through annual contracts with communes and, more recently, in some cases moved to longer-term contractual agreements. Co-ops provide home help for the elderly, services to the handicapped—ranging from transport to summer camps to teacher's helpers in the classrooms where handicapped children are admitted—house management services for the handicapped, etc. This mode of activity has expanded to the workplace with the creation of doctor co-ops contracting for orthodontist services and for monitoring and diagnostic services, particularly with special-risk workers. But it has also entered newer areas of services in which communes have little or no experience of their own: the co-ops are experimenting with greater freedom in new forms of rehabilitation of drug addicts and their integration into the labour market and the care of abandoned children.

All these co-operatives are manned, to a large extent, by service professionals. The strength of this mode of service delivery lies in the culture of social solidarity that derives from the traditions of the co-operative movement coupled with the efficiency that comes from its entrepreneurial dimension which is small in scale and particularly suited to respond to greatly differentiated needs. The potential for co-ordination between service co-ops and volunteer organizations in service delivery is strong. One condition is the clarification of the relationship between the co-ops and local government to incorporate these services into general communal service planning (Barilli, 1983).

With mutual aid societies one enters into another dimension of voluntary action. Mutual aid societies have a long historical tradition in Italy.[4] In the past, they operated among self-employed groups, such as artisans and retailers, for which they provided medical insurance services and unemployment compensation. Today's mutual aid societies build upon that tradition and have adapted it to meet new needs. Thus, the needs they attend to are not those of the relatively permanent new class of poor and marginalized groups such as the homeless and drug addicts. Rather, their recent growth has occurred in areas of need that have been identified in the day-to-day life of the modern, nuclear working family for which public services do not exist. Nor should they exist, since these needs are of a temporary and idiosyncratic nature for which service co-ops would be too costly: for example, the care of the family when the mother is temporarily hospitalized, the provision of sitters for children and companionship for the elderly at home or in hospital, etc.

In these cases, mutual aid societies are organized on the principle of solidarity—i.e. self-financed and self-managed—as well as prevention. Groups of families and other users constitute themselves into a mutual aid society and pay a small fee to cover the operating costs of the services which the society offers free of charge to members. Mutual aid societies have appeared in particular geographic areas, especially in the North, where they build on the experience of these traditional organizations, or they may often be extensions of existing aid societies. These new bodies see themselves as occupying a space between that of service co-ops and totally volunteer services. The mutual aid solution was given a boost by law 833 on the institution of the national health system when it recognized the complementary role to be played by mutual aid societies in the health field.

In the Italian case there is a positive correlation between the performance of politically decentralized institutions and non-profitmaking volunteer activity in all its forms (Stoppino, 1985). A first conclusion is that these two factors are mutually reinforcing. In this sense, a 'third' sector is emerging—one that has a special relationship with the public sector, not of being financed but of being stimulated by it. The current debate surrounds the issue of what should be the stimulus role of the public sector. The consensus seems to be that the public role should not be purely regulatory in nature—that would lead to unwanted institutional rigidity and the dampening of volunteer activities—nor play a purely observer's role. Instead, the public sector—regions and communes—role should be one of:

(i) Retaining a service planning function—i.e. the overall assessment of service needs and responses. This does not consist only in the direct public provision of services but includes the setting of minimum standards for the overall quantity of services offered to the public, setting minimum quality standards of content and personnel, independently of the type of provider, for each type of service, monitoring the providers of services, and protecting the rights of the users/consumers of services.

(ii) Engaging in medium and long-term planning of services to facilitate the ability of non-profitmaking providers to experiment and innovate by ensuring them reliable financing.

(iii) Devising with non-profitmaking providers means, contractual and otherwise, to define the terms of mutual responsibility.
(iv) Optimizing the use of existing public facilities by non-profitmaking providers to lower their costs.
(v) Educating the public to the existence of non-profitmaking providers by disseminating information, such as lists of certified non-profitmaking and co-op organizations.
(vi) Financing professional training and retraining programmes for volunteers in addition to public personnel; and
(vii) Ensuring the reimbursement of out-of-pocket costs incurred by volunteers.

Notes

1. In actuality, although there has been progress made in the direction of municipalization as a result of the abolition of many state agencies that in the past delivered social services, to date national reform legislation to organically define the planning and management principles in the area of social services at each level of government is still missing.
2. Of particular concern in the Emilia-Romagna region has been the relief provided to victims of right-wing terrorist bombings, such as the series of bombs exploding on trains travelling between Bologna and Florence—e.g. 1974 and 1985—and the 1980 bombing of the railway station in Bologna.
3. Article 45: 'The Republic recognizes the social functions of co-operatives based on mutual solidarity and not for private gain. The law promotes and favours their increase through appropriate means and guarantees, through appropriate overseeing, their character and goals.'
4. A history of the role played by mutual aid societies in nineteenth-century Italy as mass service organizations and the building blocks for the nascent trade union movement is covered in Hostetter (1961).

10 Conclusions

The twenty years that have passed since the watershed experience of the 1968–69 period have changed the Italian scene in a profound manner. This study has shown that the challenges and demands that welled up from society twenty years ago served to significantly change the country in the 1970s and 1980s in six important aspects:

(i) The protest movements of the 1960s and the institutions' response in the 1970s acted to accelerate the crisis of the Welfare State by moving towards an implementation of the social agenda contained in the 1947 Constitution. This meant moving away from particularistic policies to protect well-organized interests and to more universalistic coverage and meeting the needs of less structured groups in society whose interests had previously been overlooked.

(ii) The country searched for a solution to the Welfare State crisis by moving ahead into a second phase of post-industrial development, referred to in the present study as social capitalism or the use of public policies by sub-national governments to support private economic initiative and assist in the broad distribution of private wealth and initiative in society.

(iii) The society was forced to come to terms with a number of human development issues that had been ignored, such as divorce, abortion, parity between the sexes before the law and in the workplace, etc.

(iv) The state was profoundly restructured through a significant form of diffusion of power which had previously been concentrated in the national government and the ruling Christian Democratic Party. The diffusion of power saw the return of Parliament as an important centre for decision-making, and diffusion also meant the empowerment of the trade union movement and other groups which had previously been denied an active role in economic decisions.

(v) Diffusion of power also meant the process of decentralization of power from the national to the sub-national levels. The process was set in motion in 1970 with the creation of the regions. It continued in the mid-1970s on the heels of the 616 decrees with the strengthening of the role of the communes and provinces in policy-making and administration, and the creation of neighbourhood government and the experimentation with various forms of communal associations to manage new services and rationalize existing delivery systems.

(vi) The 1970s witnessed a profound change in the nature of the political system by the integration of the Catholic subculture into the democratic system of values and the Communist Party into the policy-making process. The political system was finally provided with the means of responding to demands from groups in society that had been relegated to traditional roles.

At the same time that the country underwent these institutional and political transformations, the economy witnessed a process of sustained diffusion of enterprises, the reorganization of industrial production, and the creation of new development corridors along the Adriatic and the Apennines. The 1970s saw a proliferation of small and medium-sized industries in the North-east and Centre. In a parallel fashion, the old 'industrial triangle' experienced a process of de-industrialization and technological transformation that significantly changed the nature of large industrial urban areas. These changes in the North were accompanied by equally dramatic changes in the South: the end of emigration, economic take-off by a few of the smaller regions, and the search for an endogenous form of development.

What distinguished the economic growth and development witnessed in the 1970s and 1980s from that which had taken place during the 'economic miracle' of the 1950s has been the central role played by sub-national governments. This study has shown how the social capitalist model of development requires an integrated and planned form of public intervention in order to sustain the diffused form of capitalism that has manifested itself in Italy during the last two decades. The importance of the role of sub-national governments is based on the notion that what is important in sustaining a capitalist form of diffused enterprise is not only economic policies favouring private enterprise but also social and cultural policies that provide support and create incentives for diffused entrepreneurship (i.e. propensity for becoming an entrepreneur) in the fabric of society. It should be remembered that the three-dimensional model discussed in Chapter 1 referred to the symbiotic relationship among the three corners of the triangle: institutional decentralization, economic decentralization and the social-historical fabric. The nature of the relationship denies regional and local institutions the choice of a *laissez-faire* position and commits them to a continuing process of policy conceptualization, experimentation and proposition to meet changing demands.

As we have seen in the individual chapters covering the activities of three levels of sub-regional government—area-wide districts, communes and neighbourhoods—the relationship between infrastructure and social services and economic activity has been widely accepted on a conceptual as well as practical basis as a necessary element in guaranteeing continued economic growth. In this light, for example, the role of the sub-regional service districts in rationalizing service delivery is seen as a central element in economic recovery and providing the necessary service infrastructure to stimulate the development of new activities. In a parallel fashion, the role of the communes in managing urban growth and the neighbourhoods in delivering personal services become important in providing the mix of social and economic infrastructures that characterize Italy's social capitalist form of development.

One way of conceptualizing the institutional ramifications of the demands placed on sub-national governments by the social capitalist model of development is to conceive sub-national governments as performing a series of implicitly, as well as explicitly, recognized roles that thrust the decentralized institutions into a constant and growing relationship with the socio-economic environment.

The nine roles discussed below reflect the systemic tendencies that we have observed in the activities of regional and sub-regional levels of government. These roles need to be translated more fully by each regional and sub-regional level of government into, firstly, formal administrative-institutional functions and, then, with the appropriate legislation, expanded into planning policies. Five of the roles relate to the interplay between the institutions and groups and forces that lie within the regional boundaries—and can therefore be considered as 'intra-regional' in nature—while the other four define the role *vis-à-vis* actors outside of regional boundaries—that is, 'extra regional'.

The five intra-regional roles begin with the region and other levels of government as *mediators* among competing groups. This role translates into the seeking of consensus and the aggregating of diverse interests. Mediation is an increasingly important role in the light of the multiplicity of economic and social groups and of the competing demands that are placed on the political institutions for support. It is facilitated by the ongoing regionalization of interest groups and the development of a regional conception of socio-economic problems.

The second role for the sub-national institutions is to *promote* socio-economic activities through systematic analyses of the regional/local economy, identification of development objectives and the preparation and implementation of multi-year development programmes. This role translates into the activation of either a directive or indicative style of planning. Recent examples of the role are the better multi-year programmatic budgets that link regional capital expenditures to three- to five-year development programmes, marketing studies, promotion of fairs, etc.

As *experimentors*, the region and other levels of government are cast in the role of supporter of new economic enterprises and activities. This role is essential because of the increased need to diversify products and services, and it provides the necessary link between the conceptualization and passage of new policies to meet local needs. We have seen the translations of this role in, for example, regional sponsorship of pilot projects and innovative financing techniques for new businesses to take the region beyond traditional incentive programmes to influence development.

The regions and local governments have placed themselves in the role of *providing* consumer and advanced services. The role translates into, for example, the sponsorship of associational forms among user firms, the rationalization and consolidation of service districts, and the contracting-out of technical assistance for local government. The stimulus for decentralized institutions to undertake this role is the multiplication of single-purpose service districts and the growing demand for advanced services.

In fulfilling the role of *monitor* of policy outputs and outcomes, the regional government (more so than other levels of government) has become responsible for the systematic assessment of the impacts of its actions, particularly as experimentor and provider. Activation of the monitor role brings with it a technical upgrading of the bureaucracy and refinement of methodological and research tools. Current examples of the role are the undertaking of an annual evaluation of impacts of planning programmes by the region and other levels of government.

The four, extra-regional roles place a greater emphasis on the region *vis-à-vis* other local governments, but they also require the joint participation of other levels of sub-regional government. The first extra-regional role is that of *co-ordinator*. The role is operationalized by the regions working in partnership with other regional governments in securing inter-regional agreements and/or facilitating inter-regional projects among private groups/interests, as well as among local governors, such as in the examples of the Po River and the Adriatic coastline projects.

In the role of *ombudsman*, the region operates as the defender of regional/local interests in dealing with multinational and other non-locally based large enterprises. The role depends on the region's ability to engage in formal negotiations with large enterprises for the protection of its citizens' interests.

The role of the region as a *contributor* requires it to be brought in as an acknowledged participant in state and EEC policy initiatives which impact on regional interests. A case in point is the activities of the Conference of Regional Presidents and prospective contacts/offices in Brussels that have institutionalized the role of the regional governments in speaking for their regional communities.

Finally, the region has to act as the *interpreter* of state and EEC initiatives to make them fit regional/local exigencies through their own legislation. This political role is becoming increasingly important owing to the need to ensure the effectiveness of regional development policies. Examples are provided by the possible regionalization of the Fund for the South and a better region-specific translation of national laws.

These nine roles, of course, do not exhaust the possible tasks that the regional and local governments will be required to improve upon by the future evolution of the capitalist development model. The expectation is that as time goes by the fit between the contours and content of institutional and economic decentralization will increase and, therefore, require an even greater effort in fine-tuning policies to the exigencies of the local environment. This study has shown that the 1970s and first half of the 1980s were indeed years of crisis with regard to both the structure as well as the conceptualization of traditional social and economic forms, but the crisis has been overcome. We have seen the formulation of a new model of development and the experimentation and evolution of novel forms of institutional and socio-economic growth.

References

ACAP, 'Ricerca sul volontariato di matrice religiosa e laica operante nel territorio romano' in Tavazza *et al.*, 1980.

Acquaviva, S. & Santuccio, M., *Social Structure in Italy*, Boulder, CO, Westview Press, 1976.

Alberoni, F., 'Movimenti e istituzioni nell'Italia tra il 1960 e il 1970' in Graziano & Tarrow (eds), 1979.

Alborghetti, G. (ed.), *Casa, urbanistica: Le proposte dei comunisti*, Rome, Edizioni delle Autonomie, 1981.

Alessandrini, P. (ed.), *Lavoro regolare e lavoro nero*, Bologna, Il Mulino, 1978.

Allum, P.A., *Italy: Republic Without Government?*, New York, W.W. Norton, 1973.

Almond, G.A. & Verba, S., *The Civic Culture*, Boston, Little, Brown and Co., 1963.

——— (eds), *The Civic Culture Revisited*, Boston, Little, Brown and Co., 1979.

Amato, G., *Una Repubblica da riformare*, Il Mulino, 1980.

Amato, P., 'Calabria tra occupazioni e riforma (1943–1960)' in Renda (ed.), 1979.

Ammannati, L. *et al.*, *Gli enti locali sub-regionali*, Milan, Franco Angeli, 1985.

Amorosino, S. (ed.), *Venezia: Dalle parole ai fatti*, Padova, Marsilio, 1975.

Aniasi, A., *Rapporto 1982 sullo stato delle autonomie*, Rome, Istituto Poligrafico dello Stato, 1982.

Antonelli, C. e Balcet, G., *Piccola impresa come sistema*, Roma, Buffetti, 1980.

Bachelet, V., *Legge e attività amministrativa nella programmazione economica*, Milano, Giuffrè, 1975.

Baget Bozzo, G., *Il partito cristiano e l'apertura a sinistra*, Florence, Vallecchi, 1977.

Bagnasco, A., *Tre Italie: La problematica territoriale dello sviluppo italiano*, Bologna, Il Mulino, 1977.

——— 'Il contesto sociale' in Fuà & Zacchia, 1983.

——— & Pini, R., *Sviluppo economico e trasformazioni sociopolitiche dei sistemi territoriali a economia diffusa: Economia e struttura sociale*, Milan, Quaderni della Fondazione Giangiacomo Feltrinelli, N. 14, 1981.

——— & Trigilia, C. (eds), *Società e politica nelle aree di piccola impresa: Il caso di Bassano*, Venezia, Arsenale Editrice, 1984.

——— (eds), *Società e politica nelle aree di piccola impresa: il caso della Valdelsa*, Milan, Franco Angeli, 1985.

Balbo, L. & Chiaretti, G., *La scuola del capitale*, Padova, Marsilio, 1973.

Balducci, M., *Governo locale e analisi comparata*, Milan, Franco Angeli, 1985.

Balloni, V., 'La direttrice adriatica allo sviluppo industriale del mezzogiorno', *Economia Marche*, N. 6, 1979.

Barbera, A., 'Consigli di quartiere: Spunti per le riforme', *Regione e governo locale*, September–December 1983.

_____ & Bassanini, F. (eds), *I nuovi poteri delle regioni e degli enti locali*, Bologna, Il Mulino, 1978.

Barilli, L., 'Relazione introduttiva' in Convegno regionale 'Forme nuove di intervento nell'assistenza socio-sanitaria', Bologna, 20–21 gennaio, 1983.

Barkan, J., *Visions of Emancipation: The Italian Workers' Movement Since 1945*, New York, Praeger, 1984.

Barnes, S.H., *Political Representation in Italy*, Chicago, University of Chicago Press, 1979.

Barsotti, O., 'La domanda di doppio lavoro da parte delle imprese e delle famiglie', in Gallino, 1985.

Bartole, S., 'Il caso italiano', *Le regioni*, No. 3, 1983.

_____, Mastragostino, F. & Vandelli, L., *Le autonomie territoriali*, Bologna, Il Mulino, 1984.

Bassanini, F., *Le Regioni fra Stato e comunità locali*, Bologna, Il Mulino, 1976.

Basso, Lelio, *Due totalitarismi: fascismo e democrazia cristiana*, Milan, Garzanti, 1951.

_____ *Il principe senza scettro*, Milan, Feltrinelli, 1958.

Battaglia, Adolfo *et al.*, *Dieci anni dopo, 1945–1955*, Bari, Laterza, 1955.

Bedeschi, G., *La parabola del marxismo in Italia, 1945–1983*, Bari, Laterza, 1983.

Belli, M., 'Il volontariato e i servizi sociali' in Ellena, 1982.

Belligni, S. (ed.), *Governare la democrazia, problemi di rappresentanza nelle aree metropolitane*, Milan, Franco Angeli, 1981.

Bersani, P., 'L'esperienze dell'Emilia-Romagna nel quadro di una politica nazionale per l'infanzia. Il valore di un processo collaborativo tra istituzioni e società civile. Trasformazioni e tendenze', presentation at the international seminar of the Emilia-Romagna Region/OECD-CERI on 'Partecipazione e gestione dei servizi nella trasformazione dello stato sociale. Quali prospettive per l'infanzia?', Bologna, 17–19 October 1984.

Birnbaum, L.C., *Liberazione della donna: Feminism in Italy*, Middletown, CN, Wesleyan University Press, 1986.

Blackmer, D. & Tarrow, S. (eds), *Communism in Italy and France*, Princeton, NJ, Princeton University Press, 1975.

Blades, D., 'The Hidden Economy and National Accounts', in OECD, *Occasional Studies*, Paris, OECD, June 1982.

Boffi, M. *et al.*, *Città e conflitto sociale*, Milan, Feltrinelli, 1972.

Bortolotti, L., *Storia della politica edilizia in Italia*, Rome, Editori Riuniti, 1978.

Brosio, G., 'I rapporti finanziari tra governo centrale e governi locali' in Martinotti (ed.) 1985.

Brusco, S., 'Flessibilità e solidità del sistema: l'esperienza emiliana', in Fuà & Zacchia (eds), 1983).

Bucci, F., 1981, 'Il rapporto Stato-Regioni', *Lazio ricerche*, No. 1–2.

Buratto, F. & Lelli, M., *La città come rapporto sociale*, Bari, DeDonato, 1975.

Caciagli, M. (ed.), *Democrazia cristiana e potere nel mezzogiorno*, Rimini, Guaraldi, 1977.

Calice, N., 'Movimento contadino e trasformazioni sociali e politiche in Basilicata nel secondo dopoguerra' in Renda (ed.), 1979.

_____ *Il PCI nella storia di Basilicata*, Venosa, Edizioni Osanna, 1986.

Calise, M., *Il sistema DC*, Bari, DeDonato, 1978.

_____ *L'amministrazione dello stato*, Milan, Giuffrè, 1976.

Cammelli, M., 'Sindacato e istituzioni: la presenza del sindacato nei collegi della pubblica amministrazione', *Prospettiva sindacale*, **xiii**, 2, 1982.

_____ (ed.), *Le istituzioni nella recessione*, Bologna, Il Mulino, 1984.

Campos Venuti, G., *Urbanistica e austerità*, Milan, Feltrinelli, 1978.

_____ *Amministrare l'urbanistica*, Turin, Einaudi, 1967.

_____ & Oliva, F., *Urbanistica alternativa a Pavia*, Padua, Marsilio, 1978.

Candeloro, G., *Il movimento cattolico in Italia*, Rome, Editori Riuniti, 1972.

Canosa, F., *Bianca, rossa, verde: La cooperazione in Italia*, Bologna, Cappelli, 1978.

Canosa, R. & Federico, P., *La magistratura in Italia dal 1945 a oggi*, Bologna, Il Mulino, 1974.

Cantelli, P., *L'economia sommersa*, Rome, Editori Riuniti, 1980.

Capecchi, V. *et al.*, *La piccola impresa nell'economia italiana*, Bari, DeDonato, 1978.

Carozzi, C. & Rozzi, R., *Centri storici: Questioni aperta*, Bari, DeDonato, 1971.

Carrillo, E., *Alcide DeGasperi: A Long Apprenticeship*, Notre Dame, University of Notre Dame Press, 1965.

Cassese, S., *Burocrazia ed economia pubblica*, Bologna, Il Mulino, 1978.

_____ *L'amministrazione dello stato*, Milan, Giuffrè, 1976.

Catanzaro, R., 'The Mafia' in R. Leonardi & R.Y. Nanetti (eds), 1986.

Cavazzuti, F. & Giannini, S., *La riforma malata. Un servizio sanitario da reinventare*, Bologna, Il Mulino, 1982.

Cazzola, F. 'L'associazionismo istituzionalizzato' in Fedele (ed.), 1983.

Cella, G.P., 'L'azione sindacale nella crisi italiana' in Graziano & Tarrow (eds), 1979.

CENSIS *XVII rapporto sulla situazione sociale del paese, 1983*, Milan, Franco Angeli 1983.

_____ *Gli anni del cambiamento*, Milano, Franco Angeli, 1982.

Cerase, F. *et al.*, *L'istituzione dimezzata*, Rome, Ediesse, 1983.

Cerea, G. & Pola, G., 'Note su alcuni insoddisfacenti aspetti economici della municipalizzazione', *Pavia Economica*, March–June 1979.

Cervellati, P., *La città post-industriale*, Bologna, Il Mulino, 1984.

_____ & Miliari, M., *I centri storici*, Florence, Guaraldi, 1977.

_____ e Scannavini, R. *Bologna: Politica e metodologia del restauro*, Bologna, Il Mulino, 1973.

Chase Econometrics, 'The Long Term Italian Outlook', paper presented at the conference on 'Changing Political and Economic Realities in Italy', Roslynn Hilton, Roslynn, VA, 2 December 1986.

Chiarante, Giuseppe, *La Democrazia cristiana*, Rome, Editori Riuniti, 1980.

Ciarlo, P., 'Organizzazione sovracomunale e Regioni' in FORMEZ, 1984.

CISPEL, *Servizi pubblici locali*, Notiziario mensile, May 1985.

_____ *Metodologia e parametri di efficienza nelle municipalizzate*, Quaderno No. 4, Rome, CISPEL, 1984.

Comune di Bologna, *Risanamento conservativo del centro storico di Bologna*, Bologna, Graficoop, 1979.

Confindustria, *Impresa e realtà regionale*, mimeo., 1980.

Contini, B., 'Economic Dualism: The Second Economy' in DiPalma, G. & Siegelman, P. (eds), *Italy in the 1980s: Paradoxes of a Dual Society*, San Francisco, CA, World Affairs Council of Northern California, 1982.

Coppola, A., 'Il paesaggio politico' in *Profili dell'Italia repubblicana*, Rome, Editori Riuniti, 1985.

Council of Ministers, 'The Family in Italian Society', *Italy, Documents and Notes*, April 1986.

Crescenzi, R. & Magrini, G., *La politica industriale: Le regioni e gli enti locali*, Rome, Edizioni delle Automie, 1983.

D'Albergo, E., 'Il rapporto tra Stato centrale e Regioni a statuto ordinario', in Cerase, 1983.

D'Amico, R. *Regionalizzazione e sistema amministrativo*, Catania, CULC, 1982.

D'Antonio, M., *Sviluppo e crisi del capitalismo italiano 1951–1972*, Bari, DeDonato, 1973.

Dau, M., 'L'introduzione dell'informatica nelle amministrazioni comunali', *Il comune democratico*, January–April 1982.

——— *Decentramento urbano e governo della città: Una ricerca comparata sulle dieci maggiori città italiane*, (mimeo.), 1983.

DeBlasio, G. & Tarulli, E., 'Il trasporto pubblico nelle piccole città: problemi e prospettive', *Pavia Economica*, March–June 1979.

DeCarlo, G. (ed.), *La pianificazione territoriale urbanistica nell'area bolognese*, Padua, Marsilio, 1965.

——— (ed.), *La pianificazione territoriale urbanistica nell'area torinese*, Padua, Marsilio, 1964.

DeFelice, F., 'La formazione del regime repubblicano' in Graziano & Tarrow (eds), 1979.

DeLutiis, G., *Storia dei servizi segreti in Italia*, Rome, Editori Riuniti, 1984.

Del Monte, A. & Raffa, M. (eds), *Tecnologia e decentramento produttivo*, Turin, Rosenberg & Sellier, 1977.

Della Sala, V., 'The Role of Decree Legislation in the Italian Parliament', paper presented at ASMI conference on 'The Reform of the Italian State', London, November, 1986.

Dente, B., *Governare la frammentazione*, Bologna, Il Mulino, 1985.

DiLalla, M., *Storia della democrazia cristiana, 1962–1968*, Casale Monferrato, Marietti, 1982.

DiPalma, G., *Surviving without Governing*, Berkeley, University of California Press, 1977.

Donolo, C., 'I dilemmi del sindacalismo regionale' in Fedele (ed.), 1983.

Donati, P., 'Nuovi bisogni di mondo vitale, ristrutturazione delle reti familiari e strategie socializzative per la prima infanzia', paper presented at the international conference Emilia-Romagna Region/OEDC-CERI, Bologna, 17–19 October 1984a.

——— *Riposte alla crisi dello stato sociale*, Milan, Franco Angeli, 1984b.

Dossi, E., 'L'intervento delle Regioni nell'economia: Poteri, criteri, e limiti' in Cerase *et al.*, 1983.

Ellena, A. (ed.), *Volontariato ed istituzioni*, Milan, ISAMEPS, 1982.

Ellwood, D., *Italy 1943–1945*, Bath, Leicester University Press, 1985.

Fadiga, A.L., *Il sistema scolastico italiano*, Bologna, Il Mulino, 1972.

Falconi, C., *Gedda e l'Azione Cattolica*, Florence, Parenti Editore, 1958.

Fanfani, Amintore, *Le origini dello spirito capitalistico in Italia*, Milan, Società editrice

Vita e Pensiero, 1938.
_____ *Persona, beni, società*, Milan, Giuffrè, 1945.
Fedele, M. (ed.), *Il sistema politico locale*, Bari, DeDonato, 1983.
Ferraresi, F. & Tosi, A., 'Crisi della città e politica urbana' in Graziano & Tarrow (eds), 1979.
Ferrari, S., *Concordato e costituzione: Gli accordi del 1984 tra Italia e Santa Sede*, Bologna, Il Mulino, 1985.
_____ 'The New Concordat between Church and State' in Leonardi & Nanetti (eds), 1986.
Fieschi, R., 'Ricerca, produzione, sviluppo: Interazioni da costruire' in Simili (ed.), 1984.
Filippucci, C. & Lugli, L., *I servizi per le industrie in un sistema di piccole e medie imprese*, Milan, Franco Angeli, 1985.
Flanagan, R.J., Soskice, D.W. & Ulman, L. (eds), *Unionism, Economic Stabilization and Incomes Policies: European Experience*, Washington, DC, Brookings Institution, 1983.
Flores, M.., 'Governo e potere nel periodo transitorio' in Flores *et al.*, 1983.
Flores, M. *et al.*, *Gli anni della Costituente*, Milan, Feltrinelli, 1983.
FORMEZ, *Modelli associativi intercomunali per la gestione dei servizi*, Naples, FORMEZ, 1984.
Formica, P. & Totola, M.G. (eds), *La regione nella economia e nella politica economica*, Bologna, Editrice CLUEB, 1980.
Foschi, F., *Gli anziani nella comunità*, Rome, Edizioni Cinque Lune, 1975.
Frankel, P.H., *Mattei: Oil and Power Politics*, New York, Praeger, 1966.
Frey, L. *et al.*, *Occupazione e sottoccupazione femminile in Italia*, Milan, Franco Angeli, 1976.
Fuà, G. *Occupazione e capacità produttive: La realtà italiana*, Bologna, Il Mulino, 1976.
_____ *L'industrializzazione del Nord Est e nel Centro* in Fuà & Zacchia (eds), 1983.
_____ & Zacchia, C. (eds), *Industrializzazione senza fratture*, Bologna, Il Mulino, 1983.
Furlong, P., 'The Changing Role of the Vatican in Italian Politics' in Quartermaine & Pollard (eds), 1985.
Galli, G., *La sfida perduta: Biografia politica di Enrico Mattei*, Milan, Bompiani, 1976.
_____ *Storia della D.C.*, Bari, Laterza, 1978.
Galli, G. & Nannei, A., *Il capitalismo assistenziale*, Milan, Sugar, 1976.
Gallino, L. (ed.), *Il lavoro e il suo doppio*, Bologna, Il Mulino, 1985.
Ganapini, L., 'I pianificatori liberisti' in Flores *et al.*, 1983.
Garelli, F., 'Quanti sono i bioccupati in Italia?', in Gallino (ed.), 1985.
Ghini, C., *Il voto degli italiani*, Rome, Editori Riuniti, 1975.
Giannola, A. *et al.*, *Crisi industriale e sistemi locali nel mezzogriorno*, Milan, Franco Angeli, 1985.
Gianotti, R., *Trent'anni di lotte alla Fiat (1948–1978)*, Bari, DeDonato, 1979.
Gibelli, A., 'La ricostruzione organizzativa della CGIL 1945–1947' in Flores *et al.*, 1983.
Giovannoni, G. & Romani, M., 'La provincia nella legislazione della regione Emilia-Romagna', *Regione e governo locale*, January–April 1984.

Gizzi, E., *Manuale di diritto regionale*, Milan, Giuffrè, 1981.

Gotti, E., 'Politiche regionali per l'innovazione tecnologica delle piccole e medie imprese' in Simili (ed.), 1984.

Graziano, L. & Tarrow, S. (eds), *La crisi italiana*, 2 Vols, Turin, Einaudi, 1979.

Greater London Group, *The Future of London Government*, (mimeo.), 1985.

Guidorossi, G., *Gli italiani e la politica*, Milan, Franco Angeli, 1984.

Hellman, S., 'Italy' in M. Kesselman & J. Krieger (eds), *European Politics in Transition*, Lexington, MA, DC Heath, 1987.

Hildebrand, G.H., *Growth and Structure of the Economy of Modern Italy*, Cambridge, MA, Harvard University Press, 1965.

Hostetter, R., *Italy: School for Developing Countries*, Ithaca, NY, Cornell University Press, 1961.

IBRES, *Mezzogiorno interno: Il caso Basilicata*, Naples, Guida, 1983.

Il comune democratico, August–September 1980.

Inglehart, R., *The Silent Revolution*, Princeton, Princeton University Press, 1979.

Ingrao, P., *Masse e potere*, Rome, Editori Riuniti, 1977.

INU *Regioni, programmazione, pianificazione territoriale*, Rome, Edizioni delle Autonomie, 1981.

IREF *Rapporto sull'associazionismo sociale, 1984*, Rimini, Maggioli Editore, 1985.

IRPET *Letture di analisi e programmazione dello sviluppo regionale*, Florence, IRPET, 1984.

IRSPEL, *Roma e il suo hinterland*, Milan, Franco Angeli, 1984.

——— *La pianificazione dei trasporti nelle regioni italiane*, Franco Angeli, 1985.

ISTAT, *Statistiche sociali, 1975*, Rome, ISTAT, 1975.

——— *Statistiche sociali, 1981*, Rome, ISTAT, 1981.

——— *Compendio statistico italiano, 1983*, Rome, ISTAT, 1983.

——— *Annuario statistico italiano, 1984*, Rome, ISTAT, 1984.

——— *Le regioni in cifre, 1985*, Rome, ISTAT, 1985.

——— *Annuario statistico italiano, 1985*, Rome, ISTAT, 1985.

——— *Le regioni in cifre, 1986*, Rome, ISTAT, 1986.

Istituto di Studi Giuridici, *Diritto e urbanistica nella nuova disciplina dei suoli*, Bologna, Il Mulino, 1978.

Italia delle Regioni, July 1981.

Kahn, A.J. & Kamerman, S.B., *Social Services in International Perspective*, Washington, DC, US Department of Health, Education and Welfare, 1976.

Kogan, N., *The Government of Italy*, New York, Thomas Y. Crowell, 1962.

——— *A Political History of Italy*, New York, Praeger, 1983.

Lange, P., 'The End of an Era: The Wage Indexation Referendum of 1985' in Leonardi & Nanetti (eds), 1986.

———, Ross, G., Vannicelli, M., *Unions, Change and Crisis*, London, Allen & Unwin, 1982.

——— & Tarrow, S. (eds), *Italy in Transition*, London, Frank Cass, 1980.

Lanzavecchia, G., 'L'evoluzione delle infrastrutture: Un approccio tecnologico' in Fuà & Zacchia (eds), 1983.

LaPalombara, J., *Interest Groups in Italian Politics*, Princeton, Princeton University Press, 1964.

——— & Spreafico, A. (eds), *Elezioni e comportamento politico in Italia*, Milan,

Comunità, 1963.
LaRosa, M. & Minardi, E., *I servizi sociali tra programmazione e partecipazione prima e dopo la 833*, Milan, Franco Angeli, 1985.
Lawson, K. (ed.), *Political Parties and Linkage: A Comparative Perspective*, New Haven, Yale University Press, 1980.
Legnani, Massimo, ' 'L'utopia grande-borghese'. L'associazionismo padronale tra ricostruzione e repubblica' in Flores *et al.*, 1983.
Leonardi, R., 'Educational System and the Job Market in Contemporary Italy', paper presented at the First Europeanist Conference, Washington, DC 29–31 March 1979.
_____ 'Political Party Linkages in Italy: The Nature of the Christian Democratic Party Organization', in Lawson (ed.) 1980.
_____ & Nanetti, R. (eds), *Italian Politics, A Review*, Vol. 1, London, Frances Pinter Publishers, 1986.
_____, Nanetti, R. & Putnam, R., 'Devolution as a Political Process: The Case of Italy', *Publius*, Winter, 1981.
_____, Nanetti, R. & Putnam, R., *Il caso Basilicata: Istituzionalizzazione e cambiamento in Basilicata, 1970–1986*, Bologna, Il Mulino, 1987.
_____ & Wertman, D., *The Politics of Decline: The Italian Christian Democratic Party*, London, Macmillan, 1988 forthcoming.
Lipari, N., 'Volontariato e pubblici poteri: La legislazione nazionale e regionale e le convenzioni con gli enti pubblici' in Tavazza *et al*, 1980.
Livraghi, R., 'Differenziali salariali, flessibilità del lavoro, e occupazione femminile', in Frey *et al.*, 1976.
Loewenberg, G. & Patterson, S., *Comparative Legislatures*, Boston, Little Brown, 1978.
Longhi, V., *Elementi di diritto e procedura parlamentare*, Milan, Giuffrè, 1978.
Magister, S., *La politica vaticana e l'Italia, 1943–1978*, Rome, Editori Riuniti, 1979.
Mannheimer, R. & Sani, G., 'Electoral Trends and Political Subcultures' in Leonardi & Nanetti (eds), 1986.
Manzella, A., *Il parlamento italiano*, Bologna, Il Mulino, 1977.
Maraffi, M., 'Business Organizations, Regional Governments, and Industrial Policies in Italy', paper presented at the conference 'Political Adjustments to Economic Problems at the Local Level in Britain and Italy', European University Institute, Florence, 27–28 February 1985.
Mariucci, L., *La contrattazione collettiva*, Bologna, Il Mulino, 1985.
Martinelli, A., 'Organised Business and Italian Politics: Confindustria and the Christian Democrats in the Postwar Period' in Lange & Tarrow (eds), 1980.
Martinotti, G. (ed.), *Politica locale e politiche pubbliche. L'esperienza delle giunte di sinistra*, Milan, Franco Angeli, 1985.
Menapace, L., *La Democrazia cristiana*, Milan, Mazzotta, 1975.
Meny, Y. & Wright, V. (eds), *La crise de la siderurgie européene, 1974–1984*, Paris, Presses Universitaires de France, 1985.
Merritt, R.L. & Leonardi, R., 'The Politics of Upper Secondary School Reform in Italy: Immobilism or Accomodation?', *Comparative Education Review*, October 1981.
Miglio, Gianfranco *et al.*, *Verso una nuova Costituzione*, Milan, Giuffrè, 1983.

Ministero dell'Interno, 'Ordinamento dei servizi pubblici degli enti locali. Schema di disegno di legge' (mimeo.), 1985.

Ministero del Lavoro *Rapporto della Commissione nazionale per i problemi della famiglia*, Rome, Ministero del Lavoro, 1983.

Moggio-Gattei, A. (ed.), *Regime dei suoli e convenzioni urbanistiche: L'esperienza di Bologna*, Modena, Levi, 1977.

Montanari, F., 'Verifica e prospettive del "Progetto Giovani". I Centri Giovanili di Circoscrizione' in Ellena (ed.), 1982.

Mutti, A., 'Representing Business Interests at the Local Level: Some Remarks on the Italian Textile Industry', paper presented at the conference on 'Political Adjustments to Economic Problems at the Local Level in Britain and Italy', European University Institute, Florence, 27–28 February 1985.

Nanetti, R., *Urbanization in France and Italy*, Monticello, IL, Council of Planning Librarians, 1972.

——— 'Il "governo" di quartiere in Italia: Gli scopi e i risultati', *Regione e governo locale*, September–December 1983a.

——— 'The Politics of Neighbourhood Institutions', *West European Politics*, July 1983b.

——— 'Neighbourhood Institutions and Policy Outputs', *International Journal of Urban and Regional Research*, March 1985.

——— & Leonardi, R., 'A New Power Equation: The Emergence of Neighbourhood Representative Institutions in Italy', *Urban Law and Policy*, No. 2, 1979.

Nobis, E., *Il Governo invisibile*, Rome, Editori Riuniti, 1956.

OECD, 'The OECD Urban Programme', (mimeo.), September 1982.

——— *Urban Capital Finance*, Paris, OECD, 1983a.

——— *Urban Growth Policies in the 1980s*, Paris, OECD, 1983b.

——— 'Community Involvement in Urban Service Provision', Proceedings of the OECD-Sweden seminar held in Upplands Svasby, 28–39 May 1985a.

——— 'Recent Trends in the Provision of Urban Services', (mimeo.), 18 April 1985b.

Omoboni, G.C., 'Sistema produttivo emiliano, ricerca tecnologica e istituzioni regionali' in Simili (ed.), 1984.

Orfei, R., *L'occupazione del potere*, Milan, Longanesi, 1976.

Orlando, G., 'L'impatto sull'agricoltura visto da un economista agrario' in Fuà & Zacchia (eds), 1983.

Paci, M. (ed.), *Famiglia e mercato del lavoro in un'economia periferica*, Milan, Franco Angeli, 1980.

——— 'I confini dello stato sociale', paper presented at the conference on 'The State and Social Regulation in Contemporary Italy', Rockefeller Center, Bellagio, April 1986.

Paracone, C., 'Il volontariato anni '80: Realtà e contraddizioni di un fenomeno di rilevanza culturale e politica' in Tavazza *et al.*, 1982.

——— *et al.*, *Servizi sociali: Autonomie locali e volontariato*, Turin, Fondazione Giovanni Agnelli, 1978.

Partito, Comunista Italiano, *VIII congresso del PCI*, Rome, Editori Riuniti, 1957.

Pasquino, G., 'The Debate on Institutional Reform' in Leonardi & Nanetti (eds), 1986.

Penniman, H.R. (ed.), *Italy at the Polls: 1976*, Washington, DC, AEI, 1977.

Perego, F. (ed.), *L'urbanistica della sinistra in Campidoglio*, Rome, Edizioni delle Autonomie, 1981.

Pieracci, S., 'Appunti sul ruolo delle associazioni intercomunali in Toscana', *Il comune democratico*, January–April 1982.

Pizzetti, F., 'Aspetti del sistema politico amministrativo: contrazione di risorse e rapporto centro-autonomie locali' in Cammelli (ed.), 1984.

Poggi, G., *Catholic Action*, Stanford, Stanford University Press, 1967.

Podbielski, G., *Italy: Development and Crisis in the Post-War Economy*, Oxford, Clarendon Press, 1974.

Pontarollo, E., *Tendenze della nuova imprenditoria nel Mezzogiorno degli anni '70*, Milan, Franco Angeli, 1982.

Potere Locale, March–April 1980.

Prandi, A., *Chiesa e politica: la Gerarchia e l'impegno politico dei cattolici italiani*, Bologna, Il Mulino, 1968.

Putnam, R.D., 'The Italian Communist Politician' in Blackmer & Tarrow (eds), 1975.

——— 'Notes on Regional Observer Interviews' (mimeo.), 1976.

——— 'Communiqué on Regional Councillor Interviews', 1986.

———, Leonardi, R. & Nanetti, R.Y., 'Indagine sul governo regionale del Friuli-Venezia Giulia', paper presented at the conference on 'Regione Friuli-Venezia Giulia: Un'esperienza di vent'anni', Trieste, 6–7 July 1984.

——— Leonardi, R., & Nanetti, R.Y., *La pianta e le radici*, Bologna, Il Mulino, 1985.

Quartermaine, L. & Pollard, J. (eds), *Italy Today: Patterns of Life and Politics*, Exeter, University of Exeter, 1985.

Ragionieri, E., 'La storia politica e sociale' in *Storia d'Italia*, vol. IV, Tomo III, Turin, Einaudi, 1976.

Ranci, E., 'Il ruolo della partecipazione sociale nella programmazione e attuazione dei servizi' in LaRosa & Minardi (eds), 1985.

Regalia, I. 'Sindacati e governi periferici in Italia: Andamenti e forme di un'interazione pervasiva', paper presented at the conference on 'Political Adjustments to Economic Problems at the Local Level in Britain and Italy', European University Institute, Florence, 27–28 February 1985.

——— 'Non più apprendisti stregoni? Ipotesi sull'interazione fra sindacati e istituzioni a livello periferico negli anni '80', paper presented at the CONGRIP/Stato e Mercato conference on 'The State and Social Regulation in Contemporary Italy', Bellagio, Rockefeller Center, April 1986.

Regini, M., 'Labour Unions, Industrial Action, and Politics' in Lange & Tarrow (eds), 1980.

Regione e governo locale, May–June 1983.

Regione Toscana, *Istituzione delle associazioni intercomunali*, Grosseto, Tipo-lito Vieri, 1979.

Regione Umbria, *Casa e centri storici*, Florence, Vallecchi, 1977.

Renda, R. (ed.), *Campagne e movimento contadino nel mezzogiorno d'Italia dal dopoguerra ad oggi*, vol. 1, Bari, DeDonato, 1979.

Restifo, G. (ed.), *Storia del Parlamento italiano*, vol. 19, Palermo, Flaccovio Editore,

1983.
Ricci, P., 'Enti pubblici e vigilanza governativa' in Ristuccia (ed.), 1977.
Ristuccia, S. (ed.), *L'istituzione governo: Analisi e prospettive*, Milan, Comunità, 1977.
Rodella, D., *Legge urbanistica e piani di ricostruzione*, Milan, Pirola, 1967.
—— *Legge urbanistica*, Milan, Pirola, 1971.
Rodotà, S., 'La circolazione delle informazioni nell'apparato di governo' in Ristuccia (ed.), 1977.
Rossi, E., *I Padroni del vapore*, Bari, Laterza, 1955.
Rossi, M., *Da Sturzo a DeGasperi*, Rome, Editori Riuniti, 1985.
Ruggeri, A. & Zanzani, M. *Rinascimento urbano*, Venice, Marsilio, 1981.
Rugiandini, A. (ed.), *La managerialità nelle imprese italiane*, Bologna, Il Mulino, 1985.
Rusca, R., 'Lo stato dell'arte della programmazione e interpretazione dei sistemi regionali di trasporto in Italia: Il quadro complessivo' in IRSPEL, 1985.
Salvati, M., *Stato e industria nella ricostruzione*, Milan, Feltrinelli, 1982.
Samonà, G., *L'urbanistica e l'avvenire della città*, Bari, Laterza, 1960.
Sani, G., 'Mass Level Response to Party Strategy: The Italian Electorate and the Communist Party' in Blackmer & Tarrow (eds), 1975.
—— 'Mass Constraints on Political Realignment: Perceptions of Anti-System Parties in Italy', *British Journal of Political Science*, **6**, No. 1 (January) 1976.
—— 'The Italian Electorate in the Mid Seventies: Beyond Tradition?' in H.R. Penniman (ed.), 1977.
—— 'The Political Culture of Italy: Continuity and Change' in Almond & Verba (eds), 1979.
Sarti, A., 'La partecipazione dei cittadini e degli utenti al miglioramento dei servizi pubblici' (mimeo.), CISPEL, September 1981.
Sartori, G. (ed.), *Il parlamento italiano, 1946–1963*, Naples, ESI, 1963.
Sassoon, D., *Contemporary Italy*, London, Longmans, 1986.
Saville, L., *Regional Economic Development in Italy*, Durham, NC, Duke University Press, 1967.
Scalfari, E. & Turani, G., *La razza padrona*, Milan, Feltrinelli, 1974.
Scamuzzi, S., 'Chi è il bioccupato?' in Gallino (ed.), 1985.
Scoppola, P., *La proposta politica di DeGasperi*, Bologna, Il Mulino, 1977.
Senato della Repubblica, *Dossier di documentazione sulla disoccupazione giovanile*, vol. 1, Rome, Senato della Repubblica, 1976.
Seroni, A., *La questione femminile in Italia, 1970–1977*, Rome, Editori Riuniti, 1977.
Settembrini, D., *La chiesa nella politica italiana, 1943–1963*, Pisa, Nistri–Lischi Editore, 1964.
Sharpe, L.J. (ed.), *The Local Fiscal Crisis in Western Europe*, Beverly Hills, CA, Sage, 1981.
Silveri, L., 'Il caso dell'Azienda Servizi Municipalizzati di Brescia: realizzazioni e prospettive di risparmio energetico', *Pavia Economica*, March–June 1979.
Simili, R. (ed.), *Ricerca e sviluppo: Il ruolo delle regioni*, Ancona, Il lavoro editoriale, 1984.
Singlemann, J., *From Agriculture to Services*, Beverly Hills, CA, Sage, 1979.
Speroni, D., *Il romanzo della Confindustria*, Milan, Sugar Co., 1975.
Spotts, F. & Wieser, T., *Italy, A Difficult Democracy*, Cambridge, Cambridge University Press, 1986.

SPS, *Primo rapporto sullo stato dei poteri locali, 1984*, Rome, Editoriale TEST, 1984.

_____ *Secondo rapporto sullo stato dei poteri locali, 1985*, Rome, StilGraf, 1985.

_____ *Terzo rapporto sullo stato dei poteri locali, 1986*, Rome, StilGraf, 1986.

Staiano, S., 'Il decentramento infracomunale nei progretti di riforma delle autonomie', *Regione e governo locale*, September–December 1983.

Stoppino, M., 'Il cambiamento funzionale dei consigli circoscrizionali comunali e la partecipazione popolare: il caso di Milano' in Martinotti (ed.), 1985.

SVIMEZ, *Un quarto di secolo nelle statistiche nord-sud, 1951–1976*, Milan, Giuffrè, 1978.

Tamburrano, G., *Storia e cronaca del centro-sinistra*, Milan, Feltrinelli, 1971.

Tavazza, L. *et al.*, *Volontariato, società e pubblici poteri*, Bologna, IDB, 1982.

_____ *Volontari per l'arte e per l'ambiente*, Turin, Fondazione Giovanni Agnelli, 1985.

Teodori, M., Ignazi, P. & Panebiano, A., *I nuovi radicali*, Milan, Mondadori, 1977.

Tessarolo, C., 'Consorzi tra enti locali e aziende consorziali per la gestione di servizi pubblici' (mimeo.), CISPEL, February 1980.

TEST, October 1983.

Thwaites, A.T. & Oakey, R.P. (eds), *The Regional Economic Impact of Technological Change*, London, Frances Pinter Publishers, 1985.

Treu, T. *et al.*, *Sindacalisti nelle istituzioni*, Rome, Edizioni Lavoro, 1979.

Trigilia, C., *Sviluppo economico e trasformazioni sociopolitiche dei sistemi territoriali a economia diffusa: Le subculture politiche territoriali* in Quaderni della Fondazione Giangiacomo Feltrinelli, No. 16, 1981.

_____ *Small-Firm Development, Political Subcultures and Neo-Localism in Italy*, EUI Working Papers No. 85/189, Florence, European University Institute, 1985.

Truini, A., 'Ruolo e funzioni degli enti locali sub-regionali' in L. Ammannati *et al.*, 1985.

Turani, S., *1985–1995 Il secondo miracolo economico italiano. Istruzioni per l'uso*, Milan, Sperling & Kupfer, 1986.

Turone, S., *Storia del sindacato in Italia 1943–1980*, Bari, Laterza, 1981.

Unioncamere *Rapporto 1983 sullo stato delle economie locali. Il delta del localismo italiano*, vol. 1, Milan, Franco Angeli, 1983.

_____ *Rapporto 1984 sullo stato delle economie locali. Il localismo da periferia a connettivo del sistema*, vol. 1, Milan, Franco Angeli, 1984.

_____ *Rapporto 1985 sullo stato delle economie locali. I sistemi locali d'impresa tra selezione e maturazione*, vol. 1, Milan, Franco Angeli, 1985a.

_____ *Rapporto 1985 sullo stato delle economie locali. Reddito regionale e profili provinciali*, vol. 2, Milan, Franco Angeli, 1985b.

Urbani, P., 'Riforma degli enti locali, livelli intermedi di governo e aree metropolitane', *Regione e governo locale*, May–June 1983.

Valenza, P. (ed.), *Il compromesso storico*, Rome, Newton Compton Editore, 1975.

Vandelli, L., 'I modelli associativi nei progetti di riforma del governo locale', *Regione e governo locale*, March–April 1982.

Villone, M., 'L'associazionismo tra enti locali. Profili evolutivi' in FORMEZ, 1984.

Vinciguerra, M., *I partiti italiani dallo statuto albertino alla partitocrazia*, Bologna, Calderini, 1968.

Vitali, W., 'Consigli di quartiere: L'esperienza di Bologna', *Regione e governo locale*,

September–December 1983.

Votaw, D., *The Six-Legged Dog*, Berkeley, University of California Press, 1964.

Weber, M., *Italia: Paese europeo?*, Milan, Franco Angeli, 1986.

Wiskermann, E., *Italy Since 1945*, London, Macmillan, 1971.

Zacchia, C., 'Pianificazione territoriale e insediamenti industriali: esperienze regionali' in Fuà & Zacchia (eds), 1983.

Zanniboni, S., 'Relazione introduttiva' in Ellena (ed.), 1982.

Zariski, R., *Italy: The Politics of Uneven Development*, Hinsdale, IL, The Dryden Press, 1972.

Zucchelli, M., 'Il commercio estero dell'Emilia-Romagna: 1963–1976' in Formica & Totola (eds), 1980.

Index